JOHN

"THE TRANSITIONAL POPE"

JOHN

"THE TRANSITIONAL POPE"

by

ERNESTO BALDUCCI

Translated by

DOROTHY WHITE

"When on 28 October 1958 the Cardinals of the Holy Roman Church chose me to assume the supreme responsibility of ruling the universal flock of Jesus Christ, at seventy-seven years of age, everyone was convinced that I would be a provisional and transitional Pope. Yet here I am, already on the eve of the fourth year of my pontificate, with an immense programme of work in front of me to be carried out before the eyes of the whole world, which is watching and waiting. As for myself, I feel like St Martin, who 'neither feared to die, nor refused to live'."

—Extract from *The Journal* of
Pope John XXIII, Aug. 1961, p. 303.

McGRAW-HILL BOOK COMPANY
New York   Toronto   London

This is a translation of Papa Giovanni (*Vallecchi
Editore, Florence, 1964*)

© Vallecchi Editore, Florence, 1964

English translation © Burns & Oates Ltd, 1965

Library of Congress Catalog Card Number: 65-23217

03550

PRINTED IN GREAT BRITAIN. NIHIL OBSTAT: P. ADOLFO GARCIA-DURAN, SCH.P., CENSOR, P. GIORGIO
SHANTA, SCH.P., CENSOR. IMPRIMI POTEST: P. VINCENTIUS TOMEK, SCH.P., PRAEP. GEN., ROMAE, 19 MAII
1964. IMPRIMATUR: CAN. JOANNES BIANCHI, VIC. GEN., FLORENTIAE, 21 MAII 1964.

LETTER FROM
ARCHBISHOP ANGELO DELL'ACQUA

1964

Rev. Father Ernesto Balducci,

During a short period of rest at Nemi I have read your book on Pope John. On finishing it I feel impelled to say how deeply grateful I am to you. You have succeeded in presenting the figure of a great Pope who, with deeds and gestures which will remain memorable in history, has opened new ways for the apostolate. And you have done this in such a moving way as to arouse feelings of profound admiration and emotion, not only in the minds of those who were privileged to be his close assistants, but in the minds also of all who read your book—and this is a great joy for the heart of a priest.

With profound esteem, believe me devotedly yours in Christ,

✠ ANGELO DELL'ACQUA

"*On the morrow of his election Pope John may have seemed to be a 'transitional Pope'. And this he certainly was, but in an unexpected way which the expression, in its habitual meaning, does not suggest. When history has been set in its proper perspective men will undoubtedly be able to say that he opened a new era for the Church, and prepared the passage from the twentieth to the twenty-first century.*"

— CARDINAL SUENENS, in his commemorative address before the Council.

Contents

Preface

As I finish writing this book I feel as cheerful as a man who has finally fulfilled a vow. Perhaps something of this sort will never happen to me again, just as it will never again be possible for me to feel I have already written a book at the very moment when I begin to write it. I have merely interpreted in articulate terms the crowding intuitions which I had been storing in my mind during the last five years, always with the confused presentiment that one day or another I should have to bring into the light of day what I had been saying over to myself alone.

Even the least well-disposed reader will have to admit that the image of Pope John which emerges from these pages is sincerely drawn, traced on the emotional background against which it first appeared. It was so welcome and so unexpected, so simple and yet so mysterious when it first came before my eyes, which, like the eyes of all men, were long unaccustomed to the miracle of evangelical childhood.

No, for me Pope John has not been a pretext for talking about other things; he has not been, in short, to use a Dantesque term, a pope to use as a "screen". It is so easy to make use of him as a weapon in polemics, or as a convenient term of comparison, in moments of bad temper! And it is so easy to leave him behind and proceed to develop a theme entirely one's own, of which he would never have accepted the paternity, except out of the goodness of his heart, which could not bear to leave any man or any idea fatherless.

I have thought over his history in the same spirit, or at least with the same intention, with which he might have thought of the history of any one of us, gently and joyfully. In my case the gentleness has come not from me but from him, and if there is any joy in these pages of mine, it has not issued from my pen but has risen from my subject, springing up, as it were, between the lines.

In doing this, however, in refusing to consider Pope John against the usual perspectives, have I not perhaps been lacking in realism? Have I sufficiently filled my pages with facts, names, dates, in a word, with something more solid? And when, in the second part, I have traced the lines of the historic reformation initiated by Pope John, why have I dispensed with bright colours and intriguing allusions, in fact with all the more outstanding features of the picture, leaving on the white paper barely a pencilled outline?

I can answer this criticism only by reminding the reader once more of the origin of the book, which was written not after but during the extraordinary pontificate, and not with the intention of finally putting forward certain theses which I held, and still hold, dear. It was with the eager desire to record, while it was still being imparted, such unforeseeable Christian teaching, the meaning of which was, and is, that the future is created without violent deeds and that the future countenance of the Church is to be sought in the humble simplicity of daily life: true peace lies in obedience alone and, in obedience, succeeds in inspiring the most daring gestures, the most far-flung schemes. It is impossible to be faithful to this lesson unless we remain above all polemical questions.

In this deliberate fidelity to its self-imposed limits lies the first, if not indeed the only value of this book. The complex threads linking the interior life of Pope John with the wide historical movement which it initiated should in these pages reveal their essential unity and harmony of design. Even the quotations from the speeches and writings of Pope John have been chosen to bring out this design more clearly, without overloading it too much with its developments and adornments.

It may be that, after the publication of the immense wealth of manuscripts which he left after his death, the design traced in this book may be partly modified. But it is more likely that a man whose real language was everyday life, simple gestures and spontaneous speech, may have left little else to be revealed. During his death agony we believed we had arrived at a complete understanding. When it comes to expressing all that we have understood, that is a different matter; in fact it is impossible. When God sends a man like Pope John it is not, surely, so that we may write books about him, but so that it may be impossible to continue to live and think as if he had never come among us.

ROME, *11 April 1964. One year after the publication of "Pacem in terris".*

CHAPTER ONE

Ecumenical Death

I. THE LIGHT IN THE WINDOW

THE central point of perspective to which the lines of this book must refer is that moment which on our calendar corresponds to 3 June 1963, at seven forty-nine in the evening, but which for me will never be a moment of time past.

As I leant against one of the columns which form a circle round the obelisk in St Peter's Square, my eyes were fixed on the window which had suddenly been lit. The crowd held its breath. The Mass had hardly ended and the words of the liturgy, solemnly uttered in the great silence, had worked like a purifying leaven in the general emotion, raising it to the height of the moment which all awaited.[1] Even the transistors had ceased to annoy: they were like the throbbing of our own hearts. It was they perhaps which gave the news first and it spread in rapid whispers: He is dead. On my knees in the midst of a group of young people I felt a strange joy. Only a few hours before he had said to his grief-stricken secretary: "What is there to weep for? This is a moment of joy, a moment of glory!" Against the clear sky which only then began to darken, the shining rectangle of light was cut out like an opening into the world beyond, into the glory in which Pope John had already for some days been immersed, even before the links which bound him to his pain-racked body had been broken, and the smile with which for days he had consoled and sanctified our anguish had faded.

[1] Pope John's confessor, Mgr Alfredo Cavagna, who was by his side until he died, has remarked upon a strange coincidence: "St Peter's Square was becoming more and more crowded with people, silent and prayerful; Cardinal Traglia was celebrating Holy Mass: two sacrifices were united in a single offering, that of the altar and that of the dying man. At the last Gospel Cardinal Traglia said those words: *Fuit homo missus a Deo, cui nomen erat Joannes* (There was a man sent from God whose name was John) in which we seemed to see the whole life of the Pope reassumed. Just at that moment the man sent from God was breathing his last breath."

Long before, in 1934, he had said to the Bulgarians when he took leave of them: "No one knows the ways of the future. Wherever I may go in the world, if anyone . . . should pass before my door, at night, and in dire need, he will find a lamp lit in my window. Knock! Knock! I shall not ask you whether you are a Catholic or not." The ways of the future had indeed been hidden and his home was now—how could he have known this?— at the centre of the world. And we may well say that the whole world for many nights saw his window lit and all, Catholics or not, felt they were invited, with equal rights, to enter his home.

That is why, because of their dire need in this comfortless world, it was some people without faith who felt most desolate after his death. There were many of these in the Square, under the lighted window. They had come there to "knock". They had been accustomed to think of the Vatican as a sort of royal palace, remote from daily life, and instead they had seen it inhabited by a man dying a death just like that which they fear for themselves, and sustained by a hope just like that which they, from time to time, desire.

As for myself, ever since that moment, every time that my thoughts or expectations pass, as is natural with Christians, beyond the limits of earthly life, into that far mysterious world where all our hopes and fears gravitate, I feel myself freed, not only from the metaphysical effort entailed in passing from the seen to the unseen, but even from the obscurity of faith. I find myself again, as at that moment, staring at the lighted window, against the darkening Roman sky.

The development of our spiritual life is less subject than we think to the logical development of an idea. However coherent its efforts towards transcendental values may seem, its actual movement is determined by facts, in which it seeks some sign of itself, support or confirmation based on experience. There may even be some who think that Pope John's death was noble and worthy to be remembered with admiration, but no more. Once the emotions of the moment have subsided events must be reduced to their proper proportion. I can only say that, now that some time has gone by and so many other great events have come between me and that death, I still feel that it remains one of the turning-points of our present history, a point at which the line of time has crossed the line of eternity, and so been touched with fire.

In the same way this book, although it sets out to consider on broader and more tranquil lines the truth of an extraordinary life, can only find its starting-point in that moment. I still preserve in its entirety the treasure of truth which I then gathered in my soul: there are days when I ponder over it, and in doing so find once more, in the heartfelt impressions of that day, the same sense of gratitude.

I thank you, Pope John, not so much for your encyclicals, although we shall find in these new weapons for the bloodless battles of our lives, not so much for the Ecumenical Council, although it comes to satisfy the expectations of centuries and inaugurate a new era; I thank you above all for your glorious death, which has ennobled us all before God and consoled us for ever. While you were dying you found time to recall your child-hood, your friends, the humble folk who served you, and those who were bound to you by the bonds of the flesh, in a word, our common life, and you raised all this to the level of your own dignity: even the outcasts of the Roman suburbs felt that you were one of them, not because of your princely benevolence but be-cause you shared the poverty of their living and dying. You were the heart of the world, and you made us all feel the mystery of the eternal Light, even those who, when they are by themselves, can see nothing but darkness. You spoke in your own language, but everyone heard you in his own tongue. I too heard you in my own tongue and I shall spend the rest of my life repeating what I have understood, which is so hard, so very hard, to make others understand.

You made us live a more joyous Christianity, not because it was less exacting in its demands, but because it was set free from old age and made subject to an order which assigns the highest place to the joy of mutual love. Naturally you knew you were causing embarrassment to us all, but you did this only to wean us from wrong ways of thinking and doing that had been handed down for so long that we had not even noticed that they had seeped into our blood—in fact, in the account-book of our conscience we had entered them in the column of our virtues. From now on I do not know how we shall manage to get our accounts into order again unless someone comes along who can teach us how to transcribe neatly the hasty corrections you dictated. It will not take long for the politicians, diplomats and scholars to straighten out their ideas, and then we shall all be a little sadder, because a little "wiser". It was certainly in order to avoid this danger that the Holy Spirit made us the gift of your glorious death.

2. REVELATION OF THE CHURCH

For too many people the power of the Church is of the same nature as the power of earthly institutions: too many fail to understand that on the contrary the meaning of that power is the service which God, by humbling himself, rendered to man, and not so much to man in his efforts to dominate the earth as to man in his terrible necessity of having to leave it. If Michelangelo's dome and Bernini's colonnade, and a pope borne shoulder high and robed in kingly attire, deserve my love, it is only because everything in the Church serves to light and guard the lamp which was placed in my hand on the day of my baptism. The only miracle that can move people today is that which shines through the obscurity of daily life, like a bright window opened in a wall beyond which we thought there was nothing. I know that the Holy Spirit dwells in the Church, unites her members and continually infuses new life into them: the Church lives by her sacraments and the sacraments act through the Holy Spirit. But the world of today is not content with a Presence which cannot offer practical proofs and which seems of no avail for us in life or death. The Church lives by a truth which the Holy Spirit imparts to her, but this is apparent only to those who have faith. Those without faith find her remote from life, for ever sealed in her antiquity. It was so very necessary for us all that the Holy Spirit should act through his visible gifts of grace: and the miracle is coming to pass in many ways. Perhaps this miracle of the humble life and glorious death of Pope John has been one of the most effective.

Christianity is proved, not so much by the testimony of its splendid doctrines, as by the death of the children of God. In such a death every man may read and discern his own mystery, precisely because, when it is really Christian, it is not merely a heroic or a resigned death; it is a wholly human death, an out-pouring, even in the midst of the anguish of flesh and soul, of all the most profoundly hidden vital reserves, uncontaminated either by the artifice of indifference, the cry of rebellion, or the groan of despair, but directed with confident serenity towards a fullness which has already been possessed and enjoyed in the secret of faith. A living man may be false, without anyone being aware of it, but a dying man cannot conceal his falsehood. Even if he dies in an admirable way, like a hero, his death will always be, as it were, a death that is cheated, eluded, submitted to, not a death that has been lived through. To live through death one must have hope, and to have hope one must have faith, and to have faith one must have God's Holy Church.

Even if we never say so, we are all convinced that the only real problem is that of our death. If culture does not attract us, if progress does not convince us, if politics wearies us, it is because during the night death comes to mock us, and we do not know how to escape its presence except by filling our days with culture, progress and politics. This is why the Lord came, to save us from our death and from its cause, which is sin. This is why the Church accompanies us through this life, to achieve our salvation and to say to us, at the moment of death: Go in peace. This is why we have the sacraments, the priests, the bishops and the pope. The Church labours to pull down every screen which separates the mystery of God from the mystery of man. Glory belongs to the mystery of God, and death to the mystery of man. Pope John experienced death and glory as if they were one and the same mystery, and this was surely a special gift from God, in order that he might reveal to men the Holy Spirit, whose joyful herald he was throughout his life. Pope John turned his agony into a manifestation of the Holy Spirit. Not only did he not rebel at the hour of death, but he lived through it moment by moment as if he were taking possession of it, while it took possession of him; at the same time he revealed to us what lies *after* death. Most human, as always, even able to console with a smile those who tried to allay his sufferings, and yet so immersed in God that he was able to reflect his divine light for the strengthening of our faith and the overcoming of our incredulity.

3. REVELATION OF UNITY

In this way he succeeded in identifying his teaching office with the teaching of his life. In the former he was a great pontiff, and in the second a true Christian, that is, so profoundly and universally human that everyone, even the unbeliever, found his own self in him. But, above all, people saw in him the humble man, who had learnt to die not through speculative research but through the tradition of his family, the humble man who does not feel faith as a painful enigma, but sees it only in its obvious aspect, and speaks of the dead as if they were there, on the other side of the wall, waiting for him. Two years previously he had written to his brother Severo:[2] "I always keep by my bedside the photograph that gathers all our dead together, with their names inscribed on the marble: grandfather Angelo, '*barba*' Zaverio, our revered parents, our brother Giovanni, our sisters Teresa, Ancilla, Maria and Enrica. Oh what a fine chorus of souls to await us and pray for us! I think of them constantly. To remember them in prayer gives me courage and joy, in the confident hope of joining them all again in the everlasting glory of heaven."

And more than thirty years before he had noted in his diary: "The dead are on the other side of this life, and we are this side. But there is not much distance between them and us. The same faith in God, the same charity unite us. We must live as long as possible, but at the same time remain in holy intimacy with our dead. This spiritual communication makes us more serene and tranquil in all our affairs" (*Algisi*, p. 262).

This kind of simplicity seems necessarily allied to a primitive

[2] See the whole letter on page 107.

way of representing the life beyond the grave and of obstinately insisting on the permanence of ties of blood even in the heart of the greatest of all mysteries. In a pope we would have expected a very different solemnity, both in speaking about death and in facing it. But Pope John felt that there was always something artificial in solemnity, especially in moments which of their very nature place man in a direct relation with God. It was in these moments that he returned naturally to the language of his childhood, without forgoing the wisdom of the theologian, or the truly universal intention with which he, the Pope, was to gather to himself and transform the history of his own time: "I am suffering with pain but with love. . . . With death begins a new life . . . Jesus, Jesus . . .! that they may be one." Several times he said that he wished on his death-bed to be like a sacrificial victim offered "for the Church, for the Council, for peace". He did not, as it were, seek refuge in a "private" death; until the end he remained at the heart of the world, receiving and transmitting love. He died with the simplicity of an old peasant who has just stored much corn in his granaries and departs for the other world, satisfied with the work he has brought to a good end, but he died also with the awareness of a pope who has been responsible for the life of the world. He invested with papal dignity the death of the humble, and removed the deceptive veil of grandeur from the death of the great. And this was not because, as our reasoning mind teaches us, death levels all by putting an end to all, but because, as our faith teaches us, the dying man is about to go before God, and before God even a pope is only a creature, who opens his arms to his father's loving embrace.

In this way, without failing in any of his responsibilities, indeed reassuming them all in accordance with the will of God, Pope John revealed to men, even to those least well disposed, how it comes about that in the Church there is peace between the human and the divine, between life and death.

He had always spread a message of peace, but this was certainly not because he was unaware of the mystery of evil in which man is submerged, and of the mystery of divine justice. It was faith that led him beyond sin and beyond justice, to the flowering gardens of divine mercy. This also made him kind and gentle to sinners and the erring, and even kind towards the flesh and blood which sometimes deceive us, promising us a Paradise without God. He had enjoyed the fatherly love of God since he was a child, and as soon as his years and sacramental grace enabled him to do so he simply poured out the reflections of this love on all around him, concealing in secret the many trials he endured and the ingratitude with which he was surrounded. In the days of his agony it was really as if everyone of us saw his old father on his death-bed. Our grief was not filial merely by a figure of speech, it was filial by virtue of an instinct that he had aroused and blessed. "When it is all over," he said to his secretary as he lay dying, "go to Sotto il Monte to see my family; go and see your mother." With us all he had restored, or taken the place of, the presence of our parents, so much so that he had made earthly life seem to us much more beautiful just when he was about to leave it.

His death, then, was truly ecumenical, in the sense that it was a universal event, like all the great events that God sends to remind men of his merciful design for them. It was accompanied by the prayers of men of every religion: even atheists allowed themselves to be drawn, unresistingly, to the threshold of the mystery, and to become aware, to say the least, of the excessive temerity of their confident negations.

"He who is not against you is for you", said the Lord: in those days no one, except in shameful silence, was against the Vicar of Christ. After such an experience mankind has become more grown up, that is, more capable of appreciating the infinite importance of consent or denial. And Christians themselves have become more grown up, have shaken off their crude medieval adolescence, and are more conscious of the paths that lead God to the hearts of men.

On that evening of 3 June 1963, when, after having knelt in prayer on the pavement of St Peter's Square, I rose to my feet, I noticed that beside me three young men were praying fervently. One of them was a friend of mine. He saw me and introduced the other two. They were a pastor of the Seventh Day Adventists and a Waldensian pastor. "We have been coming here every evening, to pray", they told me. And they were as full of joy as I was. And I understood more fully that this death was the perfect seal set on a miraculous pontificate. In fact it was putting an end to the age of divisions and quarrels and, with an irresistible gesture, was ushering in the age of universal brotherhood.

"If I were to be Pope . . ."

Death comes to all, and yet I never think of it. Every step I take, every fleeting moment brings me nearer to death. I am full of noble dreams, of ideals of study, of work, of a life spent for Christ's glory, for the good of the Church and society. This is all very fine, but often there is pride there too. What if I were to die before I am ordained? Tomorrow, on the threshold of my priestly life?

This thought seems to make no sense. It really looks as if God has lavished upon me his most tender and motherly care; he has led me out of so many difficulties, and through countless acts of kindness he has brought me here to Rome. It must be for some particular purpose of his: there can be no other reason for my Master's infinite generosity. It is hard for me to think that even after all this he might still take my life away. And yet, for him, nothing could be easier! Does he need my help? Has he ever promised me a certain length of life? And who am I to claim to know his plans? After all, did he not treat St Aloysius, St Stanislaus and St John Berchmans in this way?

O Lord, do with me whatever you will; I accept even death with satisfaction and contentment, if that is your wish. After all, you are the centre, the synthesis, the final goal of all my ideals. But at least let me die in your holy love. The strength you have given me to praise you and to make you loved on earth I will use to love you and to praise you more ardently in heaven.

On the other hand, let the thought of death, which may be near at hand, serve to give me graver thoughts. Down with pride, ambition and vanity! With death so near, have I any time to give to these miseries?

"It is appointed for men once to die, and after that comes judgment!" Even if I were to be Pope, even if my name were to be invoked and revered by all and inscribed on marble monuments, I should still have to stand before the divine judge, and what should I be worth then? (*Journal*, 1902, p. 87.)

The man who taught him to die

The strength of mind and patience which Monsignor Radini Tedeschi continued to show were almost unbelievable. In order that his closest relations should not be too much upset by the sight of his sufferings, he tried in so many ways to control himself and to hide the spasms of pain that were tearing him apart when his sister or brother was near him, that one was moved to tears.

Later on he said to me again: "Our Holy Father (Pius X) has gone to heaven. But I hear his voice . . . he keeps on calling me. I am going to see him, you know, I am soon to follow him."

The night was a dreadful one: he could not close his eyes. It was an endless succession of bouts of pain, and at the same time a long series of most fervent acts of patience, resignation and abandonment to God. About half past three, after I had obeyed his order to try to get some rest, he called me back to him. As soon as I approached him and bent down to raise him a little, I felt his arms and head fall back upon my shoulder in a gesture of such exhaustion and abandonment that at first I was bewildered and surprised. Monsignore was sobbing like a child. . . . Then he calmed himself completely; pausing a little between one thought and another, he continued with his customary serenity: "Death! I am not reckless, you know, in the face of death; I feel I am a man: I fear it and it frightens me. But neither am I a coward: if the Lord really wants me to die, for his glory, and in expiation for my sins, for the good of the Church and of souls, I do not say to him merely: 'I am resigned to it, I accept it', but: 'I want it', you understand, 'I want it. . . .'"

He added with great humility and kindness other things which concerned me particularly, and the service I had given him for ten years: and the remembrance of those last words will be one of the sweetest comforts of my soul as long as my life shall last.

Let me here humbly confess that on no other occasion perhaps did I feel so strongly confirmed in the truth of all that the Christian faith teaches me . . . as I did by the bedside of this dying bishop. His calmness, peace and interior joy told me, told all of us . . . that it is quite true then that beyond the veil of this life there is Someone who awaits us, who counts our deeds one by one, and rewards us on the last day: it is true that the repose, the joy, the perfect glory of the soul are in him and in him alone, and that it is worth while to toil and spend oneself here below to see him come towards us, a kind judge and father, in our last hour. . . .

At a certain point he seemed to have lost all sense of hearing, and I fell silent: his pulse too, now very rapid, now slow and almost imperceptible, made us fear he had lost all sensibility. But instead, as soon as he became aware of my silence, he opened his eyes and with a final movement of his left hand clasped my right hand, murmuring in my ear: "Courage, courage, Don Angelo! that is all right, go on, I understand everything, you know!"

He closed his eyes again, and I went on . . . but now his lips were no longer moved by the gentle murmur of his words.

Nevertheless I still went on: "O my crucified Jesus, I offer you willingly . . . the sacrifice of my life . . . in expiation of my sins and those of my people . . . for the Church . . . for the new Pope whom you will send her, for my priests, for my seminary . . . for all my friends near and far . . . for my country. . . ." At this point he opened his eyes, fixed his profound gaze on something he saw far away, and in a clear strong voice added: "And for peace . . . for peace. . . ."

All present were shaken with emotion. Even when he was dying Monsignore was fully conscious of himself: he was still a bishop: a vast and splendid idea still illuminated his whole thought: his magnanimous and generous heart still throbbed for a great and holy cause. . . . (*Mons. G. M. Radini Tedeschi*, Don Angelo Roncalli, Ed. di storia e letteratura, Rome, 1963, pp. 159–75 *passim*)

Thoughts on Death

I must not disguise from myself the truth: I am definitely approaching old age. My mind resents this and almost rebels, for I still feel so young, eager, agile and alert. But one look in my mirror disillusions me. This is the season of maturity; I must do more and better, reflecting that perhaps the time still granted to me for living is brief, and that I am drawing near to the gates of eternity. This thought caused Hezekiah to turn to the wall and weep. I do not weep.

No, I do not weep, and I do not even desire to live my life over again, so as to do better. I entrust to the Lord's mercy whatever I have done, badly or less than well, and I look to the future, brief or long as it may be here below, because I want to make it holy and a source of holiness to others. (*Journal*, 1945, p. 264.)

As regards my life, the central thought of these days is of my death, which is perhaps near, and of my preparation for it. Now that I am in my sixty-seventh year, anything may happen. This morning, 12 December (1947), I celebrated Mass for "the grace of a good death". In the afternoon, while adoring the Blessed Sacrament, I recited the penitential psalms together with the Litany, and also the prayers for the departing soul.

I think this is a good devotional practice. I shall make frequent use of it. This rendering myself familiar with the thought of death will lessen and soften the shock when my hour comes. (*Journal*, 1947, p. 266.)

This 25 November (1948) I enter the sixty-eighth year of my age. Yesterday evening I made my confession to the Father Prior, Germain Barbier of Auxerre. My mind is at peace. From my small Benedictine bed I have made my preparation for a good death, reciting very slowly the eight prayers set by Bossuet for this exercise. I now consider that my life has come to its end. Whatever the Lord may send me, be it years or days, I shall receive as something extra. I must often repeat the words of St Paul, and live them: "For I have died, and my life is hid with Christ in God" (cf. Col. 3.3).

This state of mystical death now means, more decidedly than ever, absolute detachment from all earthly ties: from myself, my own pleasures, honours, successes, material and spiritual benefits, and complete indifference to and independence of all that is not the Lord's will concerning me. (*Journal*, 1948, p. 270.)

When one is nearly seventy, one cannot be sure of the future. "The years of our life are three score and ten, and even if we are strong enough to reach the age of eighty, yet these years are but toil and vanity; they are soon passed and we also pass away" (cf. Psalm 89. 10–11). So it is no use nursing any illusions: I must make myself familiar with the thought of the end, not with dismay which saps the will, but with confidence which preserves our enthusiasm for living, working and serving. Some time ago I resolved to bear constantly in mind this reverent expectation of death, this joy which ought to be my soul's last happiness when it departs from this life. I need not become wearisome to others by speaking frequently of this; but I must always think of it, because the consideration of death, the *judicium mortis*, when it has become a familiar thought, is good and useful for the mortification of vanity and for infusing into everything a sense of moderation and calm. As regards temporal matters, I will revise my will once more. I am poor, thank God, and I mean to die poor. (*Journal*, 1950, p. 276.)

In all things "consider the end". The end is drawing nearer as my days follow one another. I must be more concerned with the thought of imminent death, and with dying well, than with lulling myself with dreams of a longer life. But I must not be sad about this or talk too much about it. "The will of God is our peace" always, in life and, still more, in death.

The thought of what lies in store for me, honours, humiliations, opposition, etc., nothing of all this causes me any anxiety or preoccupation.

This year I hope to complete the publication of the *Atti della Visita Apostolica di San Carlo Borromeo a Bergamo*. This satisfies my ambition as a good Bergamasque, and I desire nothing else.

My only wish is that my life should end in a holy manner. I tremble at the thought of having to bear pain, responsibilities or difficulties beyond my poor capacity, but I trust in the Lord, without claiming any successes, or extraordinary or brilliant merit. (*Journal*, 1952, pp. 279–80.)

"Give me more light as evening falls." O Lord, we are now in the evening of our life. I am in my seventy-sixth year. Life is a great gift from our heavenly Father. Three-quarters of my contemporaries have passed over to the far shore. So I too must always be ready for the great moment. The thought of death does not alarm me. Now one of my five brothers also has gone before me, and he was the youngest but one, my beloved Giovanni. Ah, what a good life and what a fine death! My health is excellent and still robust, but I cannot count on it. I want to hold myself ready to reply *adsum* at any, even the most unexpected moment.

Old age, likewise a great gift of the Lord's, must be for me a source of tranquil inner joy, and a reason for trusting day by day in the Lord himself, to whom I am now turned as a child turns to his father's open arms.

My poor life, now such a long one, has unwound itself as easily as a ball of string, under the sign of simplicity and purity. It costs me nothing to acknowledge and repeat that I am nothing and worth precisely nothing.

The Lord caused me to be born of poor folk, and he has seen to all my needs. I have left it to him. As a young priest I was struck by the motto *Oboedientia et Pax* of Cesare Baronius, who used to say it as he bowed his head to kiss the foot of St Peter's statue—and I have left everything to God and have allowed myself to be led in perfect obedience to the plans of Providence. Truly, "the will of God is my peace". And my hope is all in the mercy of God, who wanted me to be his priest and minister. He has been too kind about my "countless sins, offences and negligences" and he still keeps me full of life and vigour.

I think the Lord Jesus has in store for me, before I die, for my complete mortification and purification and in order to admit me to his everlasting joy, some great suffering and affliction of body and spirit. Well, I accept everything and with all my heart, if it is for his glory and the good of my soul and for the souls of my dear spiritual children. I fear my weakness in bearing pain; I implore him to help me, for I have little faith in myself, but complete faith in the Lord Jesus. "The white-robed army of martyrs praise you." (*Journal*, 1957, pp. 291–2.)

The course of my life over these last two years—28 October 1958–59–60—shows a spontaneous and whole-hearted intensification of union with Christ, with the Church and with the heaven which awaits me.

I consider it a sign of great mercy shown me by the Lord Jesus that he continues to give me his peace, and even exterior signs of grace which, I am told, explain the imperturbable serenity that enables me to enjoy, in every hour of my day, a simplicity and meekness of soul that keep me ready to leave all at a moment's notice and depart for eternal life.

My failings and incapacities, and my "countless sins, offences and negligences" for which I offer my daily Mass, are a cause of constant interior mortification, which prevents me from indulging in any kind of self-glorification, but does not weaken my confidence and trust in God, whose caressing hand I feel upon me, sustaining and encouraging.

Nor do I ever feel tempted to vanity or complacency. "What little I know about myself is enough to make me feel ashamed." What a fine saying this is, which Manzoni put in the mouth of Cardinal Federico!

"In thee, O God, have I hoped; let me never be confounded."

At the beginning of my eightieth year it is all-important for me to humble myself and lose myself in the Lord, trusting that in his mercy he will open for me the gate to eternal life. Jesus, Mary, Joseph, may I breathe forth my soul in peace with you! (*Journal*, 1960, p. 301.)

His last words

[To the faithful assembled in St Peter's Square, 22 May 1963, at 10.40 a.m.]

I was expecting you at midday. But we have put our appointment forward a little. I must remind you that the rendezvous was to have been in St Peter's. But, as you know, it's always good to be at St Peter's, inside or outside. So we have brought midday forward, also because this is in memory of Easter. I wish you all a happy Feast of the Ascension! Let us hasten after our ascending Lord; as we cannot follow him yet but must remain on earth, let us nevertheless imitate the apostles, who were gathered together to invoke the Holy Spirit. You also have heard him invoked today. And you hear this every day, "in the name of the Father, of the Son and of the Holy Ghost!" Greetings, greetings!

Message to the pilgrimage of Polish working men at the shrine of Piekary, 26 May 1963, ten o'clock, a.m.

We shall spare ourselves no effort, as long as life remains, in our anxiety and care for you. Have faith in the Church's love for you, and entrust yourselves calmly to her, in the confident knowledge that her thoughts are thoughts of peace and not of harshness. . . . When with the eyes of our spirit we admire such a great multitude of strong and upright men, rich in faith, who guard their spiritual life intact as a most precious inheritance, we feel our heart moved, as if we were embracing you with infinite love.

To Cardinal Cicognani, Secretary of State, 28 May 1963, eight o'clock, a.m.

Because the whole world is praying for the sick Pope it is quite right that this prayer should be given a proper intention. If

God desires the sacrifice of the Pope's life, may this serve to invoke abundant favours for the Ecumenical Council, Holy Church, and mankind that longs for peace. If instead God wishes to prolong this pontifical service, may it be for the sanctification of the Pope's soul and the souls of all who with him work and suffer for the extension of the kingdom of our Lord, Christians of old and Christians of today and throughout the whole world.

To Cardinal Cicognani, 30 May 1963, nine o'clock, p.m.

Oh how grateful I am! The fact of being the object of so much delicate attention moves me, yet leaves me perfectly serene in my habitual simplicity, because I feel more than ever united with the vast number of people who suffer in hospitals or in their homes, and who are in trouble in various ways. This interest in the Pope, who humbly represents the Lord, will mean a new fervour of prayers, thoughts and peaceful intentions, the firm and clear conviction that in life all that matters is what is still the message of the Gospel, that is meekness, goodness and charity. I wish all to receive the token of my heartfelt gratitude, so that, as they wish to remain united with me, so they may draw from this unity a motive and impulse of brotherly, mutual love. . . . I bless and encourage them.

To Cardinal Cicognani, 31 May 1963, ten o'clock, a.m.

I am glad because they have told me that we go into the house of the Lord.

To his Collaborators, 31 May 1963, at 11.50 a.m.

I have loved the Church and the souls who have been entrusted to me. God grant that the Fathers of the Council may crown with success the great work they have begun. I thank my collaborators, especially the Cardinals, and I greet my beloved dioceses of Rome, Bulgaria, Greece, Turkey, France and Italy, all the countries in which I carried out my ecclesiastical duties. I offer all my sufferings "that they may be one", that all may be one with Christ.

Spiritual testament

Venice, 29 June 1954

On the point of presenting myself before the Lord, One and Three, who created me, redeemed me, chose me to be priest and Bishop and bestowed infinite graces upon me, I entrust my poor soul to his mercy. Humbly I beg his pardon for my sins and failings; I offer him what little good, even if imperfect and unworthy, I was able with his help to do for his glory and in the service of Holy Church and for the edification of my fellows, and I implore him finally to welcome me, like a kind and tender father, among his saints in the bliss of eternity.

I wish to profess once more my complete Christian and Catholic faith, belonging and submitting as I do to the Holy, apostolic and Roman Church, and my perfect devotion and obedience to its august Head, the supreme Pontiff, whom it was my great honour to represent for many years in the various regions of East and West, and who finally sent me here as Cardinal and Patriarch, and for whom I have always felt a sincere affection, apart from and above any dignity conferred upon me. The sense of my littleness and worthlessness has always kept me good company, making me humble and tranquil, and permitting me the joy of putting my best efforts into a continual exercise of obedience and love for souls and for the interests of the kingdom of Jesus, my Lord and my all. To him be all the glory: for me and for my own merits, only his mercy. "God's mercy is my only merit." "Lord, you know all things: you know that I love you!" This is enough for me.

I ask forgiveness from those whom I have unknowingly offended, and those whom I have not influenced for good. I feel that for my own part I have nothing to forgive anyone, because in all those who knew me and had dealings with me—even if they have offended or despised me or, no doubt justly, had little regard for me, or given me cause to suffer—I recognize only brothers and benefactors, to whom I am grateful and for whom I pray and will pray always.

Born poor, but of humble and respected folk, I am particularly happy to die poor, having distributed, according to the various needs and circumstances of my simple and modest life in the service of the poor and of the holy Church which has nurtured me, whatever came into my hands—and it was very little—during the years of my priesthood and episcopate. Appearances of wealth have frequently disguised thorns of frustrating poverty which prevented me from giving to others as generously as I would have wished. I thank God for this grace of poverty to which I vowed fidelity in my youth, poverty of spirit, as a priest of the Sacred Heart, and material poverty, which has strengthened me in my resolve never to ask for anything—positions, money or favours—never, either for myself or for my relations and friends.

To my beloved family according to the flesh, from whom moreover I have never received any material wealth, I can leave only a great and special blessing, begging them to preserve that fear of God which made them always so dear and beloved to me, and to be simple and modest without ever being ashamed of it: it is their true title of nobility. I have sometimes come to their aid, as a poor man to the poor, but without lifting them out of their respected and contented poverty. I pray and I will ever pray for their welfare, glad as I am to see in their new and vigorous shoots the constancy and faithfulness to the religious tradition of the parent stock which will always be their happiness. My most heartfelt wish is that not one of my relations and connections may be missing at the final joyful reunion.

About to leave, as I hope, on the heavenward path, I greet, thank and bless the infinite number of souls who made up, successively, my spiritual family in Bergamo, in Rome, in the East, in France, and in Venice, my fellow citizens, benefactors, colleagues, students, collaborators, friends and acquaintances, priests and lay folk, men and women of the Religious Orders, to all of whom, by the decree of Providence, I was the unworthy brother, father or shepherd.

The kindness shown my humble person by all those I met with along my way has made my life a peaceful one. Now, in the face of death, I remember all and everyone of those who have gone before me on the last stretch of the road, and those who will survive me and follow me. May they pray for me. I will do the same for them from purgatory or paradise where I hope to be received, not, I repeat, through my own merits but through the mercy of my Lord.

I remember them all and will pray for them all. But my

J.T.P.—3

Venetian children, the last the Lord has given me, for the final joy and consolation of my priestly life, shall here receive special mention as a sign of my admiration, gratitude and very special love. I embrace them all in the spirit, all, everyone, clergy and lay folk, without distinction, as without distinction I loved them all as belonging to the same family, the object of the same priestly love and care. "Holy Father, keep them in thy name, whom thou hast given me, and that they may be one, even as we are one" (John 17. 11).

In the hour of farewell or, better, of leave-taking, I repeat once more that what matters most in this life is: our blessed Jesus Christ, his holy Church, his Gospel, and in the Gospel above all else the *Our Father* according to the mind and heart of Jesus, and the truth and goodness of his Gospel, goodness which must be meek and kind, hardworking and patient, unconquerable and victorious.

My children, my brothers, I take leave of you. In the name of the Father, the Son and the Holy Ghost. In the name of Jesus our love; of Mary, his sweet Mother and ours; of St Joseph, my first and most beloved protector. In the name of St Peter, of St John the Baptist, and of St Mark; of St Lawrence Giustiniani and St Pius X. Amen.

ANG. GIUS. CARD. RONCALLI, PATRIARCH.

These pages written by me are valid as proof of my final dispositions in case of my sudden death.

ANG. GIUS. CARD. RONCALLI.

Venice, 17 September 1957.

And they are valid also as my spiritual testament, to be added to the testamentary provisions here enclosed, under the date of 30 April 1959.

JOANNES XXIII Pp.

From Rome, 6 December 1959.

Castel Gandolfo, 12 September 1961

Under the dear and trustworthy auspices of Mary, my heavenly Mother, to whose name the liturgy of this day is dedicated, and in the eightieth year of my age, I hereby set down and renew my will, annulling every other declaration concerning my wishes, made and written previously, on divers occasions.

I await the arrival of Sister Death and will welcome her simply and joyfully in whatever circumstances it will please the Lord to send her.

First of all I beg forgiveness from the Father of mercies for my "countless sins, offences and negligences", as I have said and repeated so many, many times when offering my daily sacrifice of the Mass.

For this first grace of forgiveness from Jesus for all my sins, and for his acceptance of my soul in his blessed and eternal paradise, I commend myself to the prayers of all who have known me and followed my whole life as priest, Bishop, and most humble and unworthy servant of the servants of the Lord.

It is with a joyful heart that I renew wholly and fervently the profession of my Catholic, Apostolic and Roman faith. Among the various forms and symbols in which the faith finds its expression I prefer the Creed of the Mass, said by priest and Pontiff, resounding and sublime, in union with the universal Church of every rite, every century, every land: from the *Credo in unum Deum patrem omnipotentem* to the *et vitam venturi saeculi*. (*Journal*, p. 345.)

CHAPTER TWO

A Pontificate that was a Special Gift from God

I. GOD'S DELIGHT IN MEN

POPE JOHN'S death was perfect also in the logical sense of the word because it was the perfect fulfilment of his wide ranging life. It came at the climax of an activity which, during those last months, had seemed entirely devoted to the carrying out of his own creative purposes—without any human considerations. Yet it was a death that interrupted nothing, suffocated no vital germ. Even the programmes which remained suspended seemed to have been brought to the right point so as to guarantee, in his successor, a continuity of direction. As in classical tragedies the epilogue resolves in rational unity the intuitive understanding that has been divided and dispersed in the plot of the story, so, in the days of his agony, the humble John proclaimed to the amazed world, in clear language, the secret of his long life.[1] In spite of all appearances he had always been a man alone in the presence of his God: with what cheerful modesty he had succeeded in concealing the sources of his wisdom!

The Lord God delights in the world, says Holy Scripture, "playing in the world" (Prov. 8. 31, *Douai*). When God plays in the world he needs men of faith who will understand his secret

[1] Cardinal Suenens, in his speech of 28 Oct. 1963 before the assembled Council, emphasized the way in which Pope John's death had perfected and proclaimed his life: "The death of the Saints, says Holy Scripture, is precious in God's sight. The death of Pope John XXIII was precious also in the sight of the whole world. He transformed it into a supreme proclamation of faith and hope; he almost turned it into the celebration of an Easter liturgy.

"John XXIII breathed his last, the day after the Feast of Pentecost, at the moment when in St Peter's Square a priest was saying the *Ite, missa est*. This dead man's work also was accomplished, the offering was complete, in a spirit of supreme fidelity to the Holy Spirit."

and guard it freely and disinterestedly until the hour strikes. The dial of human life may never record the right hour but, even so, God will still have played, and won. Men of faith, that is, men accustomed to sharing God's secrets, are aware of his triumph and bear the marks of this in their faces but, sunk in apparent failure, they are taken for fools. At times, however, even we are aware that the hour has struck; even unbelievers are obliged to take notice of the miracle by which God has won. With the pontificate of Pope John the hour did strike, and divine wisdom played, making use of a man created on purpose to confuse the wise.

He had succeeded in arriving at the threshold of old age giving the impression merely that he was little more than an honest man, of pleasing conversation, who kept a good table, and was somewhat conservative when confronted with the great problems of new knowledge which were disturbing the ecclesiastical world, a diplomat of no outstanding quality but one who could be counted on for total obedience: in short, one of those prelates who are able, without any diminution of ascetic values, to present an attractive combination of the jolly good nature of a peasant and the subtlety of a Curial official. He had had a successful career, not so much because of his extraordinary qualities but because in three or four different sets of circumstances, the Vatican had needed an obedient servant, able to keep his temper even in the most complicated situations. He became pope, as is generally admitted, as a man of compromise, that is, for the very same reason that had favoured his career. There was need of a "transitional pope" who, just because of his lack of a personal standpoint, would allow time for the divergent trends in the College of Cardinals to prepare a choice that was to be more carefully pondered and more unanimous, and who because of his advanced age, offered the possibility of such a choice being made within a brief period. It does not appear that he made humble protestations as soon as he was elected, or even that he suffered from painful perplexities. He was certainly not ignorant of the quite legitimate calculation which had favoured his election, but he did not feel at all hurt by this, just as he did not feel in any way bound by it. He began at once to play the Pope, easily and skilfully as if he had always been trained for this. Set free from the yoke of obedience, under which he had been willing to die without leaving any special memory of himself, he began to wield the supreme authority, and in doing so revealed, from the very first moment, the creative genius which had till then been humbly held in subjection.

He had begun to understand the needs of the Church when, almost as soon as he was ordained, he was appointed secretary to Mgr Radini Tedeschi, the Bishop of Bergamo, and received the confidences of that great misunderstood soul. His prolonged diplomatic training had forced him to live in direct contact with the world outside the Church and in this way to discover the nature of the obstacles which stand between thirsty man and the spring of his salvation. Accustomed, by character and training, to free his conscience from all that could impair faith in God or the discreet loyalty of a servant of the Church, he may have seemed to most observers merely a diligent and good-natured prelate. Instead, he had unconsciously been preparing, through the slow accumulation of experiences lived through in the freedom of his soul, a programme of daring innovations. The fact that this programme was not planned with the eagerness of one who aspires to rule, but wholly evolved in the silent depths of a soul already prepared for the summons of death, is a sure sign of its disinterestedness.

When Angelo Roncalli became John XXIII, a new man seemed born in him;[2] it was as if mediocrity had given birth to genius. In a certain sense this impression is right, the paradox is a real one. The "genius" of the pontiff responsible to God alone was already present in the "mediocrity" of the ecclesiastical functionary; it was, as it were, its essence distilled in secret; his freedom in action was the reverse side of his humility in obedience. It is the obedi-

[2] Etienne Borne (in *La Croix*, 7 June 1963) emphasizes the apparent discontinuity between the two Roncallis: "When Cardinal Roncalli became Pope a second man was born in him and the Pope rose to his supreme mission, leaving behind him the man who for so long had been a diplomat. His understanding became an inspired sense of the hidden hopes of man, his political prudence was transformed into a clear intuition of the needs of a whole epoch, and his easy good nature into a consuming fire of love. It was as if the most Catholic of all offices had the mysterious power of bestowing upon the man elevated to it the fullness of Christianity."

ent man who is victorious! In a few years he brought things to
pass for which many had lost their peace, even their peace of mind,
merely by dreaming about them, and the conclave which followed his death has not only not been able to consider his "transitional" pontificate as a parenthesis, but has remained spiritually
dominated by it. He himself, moreover, soon realized that he had
nothing "provisional" about him, except such as was due to the
presumable imminence of his death. On 10 August 1961 he noted
in his *Journal of a Soul* with subtle humour:

> When on 28 October 1958 the Cardinals of the Holy Roman
> Church chose me to assume the supreme responsibility of rul-
> ing the universal flock of Jesus Christ, at seventy-seven years of
> age, everyone was convinced that I would be a provisional
> and transitional pope. Yet here I am, already on the eve of the
> fourth year of my pontificate, with an immense programme
> of work in front of me to be carried out before the eyes of the
> whole world, which is watching and waiting. As for myself,
> I feel like St Martin, who "neither feared to die, nor refused
> to live".

Seldom before in history has there been so clearly demonstrated what Vico called the heterogenesis of the ends, the law
by which the event far exceeds the intentions of its artificers.
John's pontificate has been called a miracle even by men who use
this term very frugally, and without giving it a supernatural
significance, because of the charge of creative energy which
distinguished it.[3] Christians, on the other hand, and not only
Catholics, are able to use the term in its most legitimate sense. It
was in fact a "separated" bishop[4] who applied to Pope Roncalli

---

[3] See Walt Lippmann (in the *New York Herald Tribune*, 7 June 1963): "The pontificate
of Pope John has been a marvel, and all the more amazing when one considers how he
succeeded in arousing so much love in the midst of the bitter animosities of our time. It
is a modern miracle that anyone should have been able to overcome all the barriers of
class, caste, colour and race, and to touch the hearts of all peoples. Nothing similar had
ever happened before, at least not in our own times."

[4] The Patriarch of Istanbul, Athenagoras, to whom Paul VI, during their meeting on
5 Jan. 1964, expressed the gratitude of the whole Catholic Church, saying: "You have
desired this meeting since the time of our unforgettable predecessor John XXIII, for whom
you showed your esteem and sympathy, applying to him with amazing intuitive truth
the words of the Evangelist: 'There was a man sent from God whose name was John'
(*John* 1. 6). He also had longed for this meeting, as you well know; but his sudden demise
did not allow him to realize this heartfelt wish."

the Johannine text: "There was a man sent from God whose name was John." Our reason is bewildered when we examine, in synthesis and analysis, those five extraordinary years, and finds its own truth only when faith is called in to explain history.

2. THE INSTITUTION AND THE CHARISMATIC GIFT

Faith teaches us that the Church, in her entirety, is the expression, in history, of the Holy Spirit. Ever since Pentecost the Church has possessed, as her life-giving principle, the Spirit which proceeds from the Father and the Son. The visible aspects of the Church, those which we call "human", are also informed by the Spirit of God and adapted for a purpose which surpasses them: the salvation of the world, which God loved so much that he sent his only-begotten Son to it, and which his only-begotten Son loved so much as to send his Spirit there. The veneration with which the faithful surround the person of the pope, whoever he may be, is inspired by motives quite extraneous to those psychological depths from which the cult of personality springs: it is an expression of faith, and in this respect not dissimilar to the homage which is paid to the consecrated Bread and Wine. Even an Alexander VI, as pope, deserves reverence and obedience in the name of the Holy Spirit. In this sense also Pope John taught us lessons of extraordinary importance, divesting the papacy from the mythical trappings with which popular ingenuousness and outworn traditions had encumbered it. His meekness of manner when he sought contact with the people disappointed those who have a naturalistic notion of hieratical dignity, but consoled and edified those who are repelled by all that resembles a cult of individuals, and therefore detracts from the one Lord. Faith has as its one object the mystery of God, One and Three: I believe *in* God the Father Almighty and therefore I believe the Church; I believe *in* the Holy Spirit, Giver of Life, and therefore I believe the pope. This objective immersion of the Spirit of God—the true object of faith—in the visible organism of the Church is independent of the intellectual and moral qualities of the men in whom, in the course of history, this organism is expressed. Their power of order and jurisdiction, although exercised within the freedom of second rational causes, is the "conjoint instrument" of an indefectible First Cause, which is in fact the Spirit sent by Christ. The distinction and comparison which are made between one pope and another must never be pushed to the point of transforming enthusiasm or criticism into a distortion of the faith, which embraces all popes with the same devout homage.

But the Spirit of God has a second way of operating, never in contradiction with the former, in fact such as to render more evident to the eyes of men his unfailing presence in the Church and his unending work for our sanctification. If we may call the former way institutional, we may call the second, by a biblical term, charismatic. The charismatic gift is a free gift with which God endows this one or that among his faithful in order that this man may, in the bosom of the community, be a convincing witness of the divine mystery which, invisible but real, works to bring about God's kingdom. Properly speaking, the Church as a whole has possessed the "best gift", which is charity, since the day of Pentecost, and transmits it through her sacramental life. This primary form, however, may be called the normal form, the expression of the positive will of Christ, who willed the Church and, in the Church, the constant presence of the sources of grace. That which is quite freely given is normal in the present scheme of salvation. But there is also freely given that additional grace which God freely bestows, not so much for the benefit of a person as for the benefit of the whole Church and, through the Church, for that of the whole world. For example, in the Church of the thirteenth century the Spirit of God acted through Innocent III and through Francis of Assisi, that is both through the normal institution and through the special charismatic gift.

It almost seems as if the Church depends too confidently on its own institutional instruments and shows a methodical distrust of charismatics. The reason is that it is not easy to distinguish the true charisma from the false: the story of Christianity is full of false charismatics. There are, however, some distinctive signs, the chief of which is the true charismatic's acknowledgment of the Church. He does not set the creative liberty of his spirit in opposition to the legitimate rigidity of the ecclesiastical institution; his work aims at protecting the Church and freeing its true image from the distortions imposed by men. The true charismatic does not seek to cast upon God the responsibility for his own judgments and actions: with profound humility he welcomes the inspiration and acknowledges its authority but, with regard to his own decisions, he prefers to keep these within the sphere and responsibility of his personal wisdom. The true charismatic does not spread around himself anxiety or distress, but cheerfulness and consolation, because he is a real instrument of that Spirit who is called the Comforter.

Well then: in Pope John the Spirit of God was present both as the principle of the pontifical institution and as a free charismatic creation.[5] We may say that God loved the Church with a particular love through his humble servant John. There have been numerous and authoritative acknowledgments of this. The present Pope, Paul VI, then Archbishop of Milan, announced to his people the death of Pope John on 3 June 1963, and exclaimed, weeping: "We must remember this pontificate as a great phenomenon of interior Catholic rebirth, leading to a renewed capacity for dialogues that will bring about the salvation of mankind." The day before, during the long agony, he had with great precision enumerated the wonderful ways in which Pope John's charism had been shown:

> Blessed be this Pope who has given to us and to the world the image of pastoral kindness, and has presented, to whoever has the responsibility of governing the Church, the evangelical example of the "Good Shepherd". Blessed be this Pope who has shown us that goodness of heart is not weakness and irresolution, not equivocal "irenism", not the renunciation of the great rights of truth and the great duties of authority, but the primary virtue of Christ's representative in this world. Blessed be this Pope who has given us joy, in this

[5] François Mauriac (in *La Croix*, 7 June 1963): "This great Pope was humble. The Holy Spirit found no obstacle in him, and for this reason a few months of this pontificate sufficed to make a breach for grace, a breach that will last for centuries. Through this breach the Holy Spirit will pass, and there will be nothing to stop him."

world. Blessed be this Pope who has shown us once more that the Church's authority is not desire for power, is not conventional paternalism or remoteness from the community of the faithful. Blessed be this Pope who has enabled us to enjoy an hour of fatherly love and spiritual intimacy, and has taught us and the whole world that mankind needs nothing else so much as love.

In the following pages we shall be able to show clearly, in Pope John, all these signs of the authentic charism here enumerated by Cardinal Montini. We must first, however, trace in a few rapid strokes what we might call the fundamental lines of the miraculous design of his pontificate.

3. THE "CHARACTERISTIC LINES" OF HIS PONTIFICATE

Many people have been surprised to see that whereas no pope, during recent times, has had as much as Pope John a love of the past and a serene respect for existing institutions, ecclesiastical or otherwise, yet no pope has shaken them and renewed them from their foundations as he did. In his friendly relations with the Italian State, seen in his journey to Loreto and Assisi, that is into the territory of the ex-Papal States, he was guided by the idea, which others in other times had pursued with intellectual arrogance and immoderate zeal, of freeing men's minds from any survival of clerical or anti-clerical irritation, and of testifying that the rule of the Church is according to the spirit, not according to the flesh. He gave a gentle burial to the remains of centuries-old quarrels, without thereby humiliating the State, which indeed saw its own sphere recognized in its complete autonomy, and without disowning the behaviour of the Church in the past, but placing himself, with all his old affections, in the heart of the new age. Spiritual and temporal values found themselves set once more within an orderly hierarchy even before the theological and cultural doctrine of his *Pacem in terris*, and he achieved this by a series of actions almost always performed quite simply, with his customary cheerfulness. Seen through the transparent veil of his simple, frank dignity the tangle of events that stretches from Porta Pia to our own times is unravelled and assumes the shape of a providential design: the confusions of history are resolved into their essential clarity.

So it is with regard to the Church: to say he was a revolutionary would be far from the truth. What was lacking in the Catholic consciousness was the perception of the purely relative value of certain religious customs, certain juridical dispositions, and a certain cultural tradition. In a word, no distinction was being made between the essential and the contingent. He did not condemn the contingent aspects of ecclesiastical dispositions, nor did he belittle them; he merely subordinated them more strictly to their proper aim, which is to serve the essential truth and reveal it better. This was a method which was born not of cunning but of a wise knowledge of men and of the mutability of any institution which does not proceed directly from God.[6] He had not the slightest desire to destroy those conventions which had become outworn, but he felt free to judge them, sometimes humorously, for what they were, and therefore to keep them at a proper distance from those conventions which are founded on the Word of God.

It was clear to us all, for example, that the almost princely pomp with which he, as pope, was surrounded, made no impression on him at all, although he made no attempt to do away with it, just as one refrains from pulling down old plaster, already half detached from the bare walls, for fear of destroying some vestiges of old frescoes. Even if he had not said it in so many words, we would have understood that he had no desire to be the custodian of a luxurious museum: he wanted to be the servant of the Church which, as he had said in a speech at Istanbul in 1935, "had not yet finished being born". His special charism was the gift of making us realize the youthfulness of the Church, without indulging in "primitivism" or "progressivism", yet

---

[6] In the same way, for example, he showed the greatest respect for the Cardinalate; indeed, from the first day he showed that he considered himself, in the midst of the College of Cardinals, a brother among brothers: "I am your brother, Joseph!" Yet there is no doubt that he gave this ecclesiastical institution a new spirit, freeing it from outmoded forms and giving it clear instructions about its pastoral mission. With this intention in mind he insisted that all the Cardinals should be made bishops because the episcopacy is the divine source of all pastoral responsibility.

making us aware of the throb of life which beats beyond all the contingencies of time.

In a Church which seemed agitated by the two currents of the progressives and traditionalists, he surprised both, recalling them to considerations above and beyond their programmes, to a sphere where programmes no longer count. His dismay, occasionally apparent, was not at the thought of traditions being threatened by modern times: it was due to his conviction that Christianity had not yet understood all the requirements of the Gospel.

Mgr Guerry, Archbishop of Cambrai, tells us:

> On 3 May last year, in private conversation, the Pope confided to me his grief that so many men of good will in the world thought that the Church rejected and condemned them. Then, showing me the crucifix upon his table, he said with emotion: "But I must be like Christ. I open wide my arms to embrace them. I love them and I am their father. I am always ready to welcome them." Then, turning to me, he said: "Monsignore, all that the Gospel requires of us has not yet been understood."

This opening wide of arms to welcome all men is a requirement of the Gospel that a thousand recent traditions have prevented us from fully understanding. He opened his arms wider than our human prudence would have permitted.

When a pope speaks of his children he may give to this word different affectionate meanings. He may be thinking of the Catholics who are faithful to him, or of all baptized people, or of all men, without any distinction. In Pope John this last was the immediate and overriding meaning he gave to it, and he was so sincere that it was often the prodigal sons who understood him best, and some of the "elder brothers" who were scandalized, for it is these latter who, with their too strictly legal conception of Christian fidelity, have shown hardness of heart and a Pharisaic spirit with regard to him.

The most important of his documents, and that which opens a new era in the history of the Church, the Encyclical *Pacem in terris*, is even dedicated to "all men of good will" (*ad universos bonae voluntatis homines*). This dedication was quite new, at least in its form, and clearly illustrates the transition effected by the charism of Pope John: the transition, as Yves Congar has written, from a "Church concentrating upon itself" to a "Church for all men", to the dialogue with "others". Before Pope John we were inclined to imagine this transition as above all an opening towards the world (*ad extra*): it was right to be aware of the risks of this adventure. Pope John instead gave primary importance to the opening into her own depths (*ad intra*), to the return to her own supernatural sources. The Church becomes more modern only as she becomes more profoundly herself, and because of her own intrinsic youth shakes herself free from the historical contingencies which weigh her down and make her seem archaic.

In a lecture given on 5 October 1959, Mgr Loris Capovilla[7] recounted an episode which, occurring during the first year of Pope John's pontificate, sets in a clear light the purpose of his activity. He was walking with the Pope in the Vatican gardens when, admiring the spectacle of Michelangelo's dome lit by the sun, Pope John stood still. He was listening to the reading of some of his notes "for a document that will shortly appear", the Encyclical *Princeps Pastorum* of 28 November of that year.

> A brilliant sentence seemed to shine forth [said Mgr Capovilla], a passage of great wisdom from St John Chrysostom, one of the Fathers most loved by Pope John and most familiar to him: "Christ has left us on this earth so that we may become shining beacons and teachers who know how to instruct; so that we may perform our task as angels, that is as messengers to men; so that we may be adults among children, and spiritual men among the worldly, in order to win them over; so that we may be sown as seed, and bear abundant fruit. It would not even be necessary for us to expound our doctrine, if our life were in this way so radiant; it would not be necessary to have recourse to words if our deeds gave such testimony. There would be no pagans if we all behaved like real Christians." There were a few moments of silence. Then the Pope said: "This is the truth. Anyone who asks what are

[7] Loris Capovilla, *Giovanni XXIII*, Sette Letture, Libreria Editrice Vaticana, 1963, pp. 13–14.

the characteristic lines of my pontificate, may be answered with this or with other similar words. That is all there is to it."

Just three years afterwards these "characteristic lines" were to be solemnly proclaimed in the opening speech of the Council. "It was", wrote Cardinal Montini, "prophetic in both senses of the word, that is full of lyrical and religious fervour which still inspires our life today, and also full of prophetic vision of the future of the world."

Pope John's intuition will, by means of the Council, be bequeathed to the whole Church of the future. According to this intuition, the Church, abandoning functions and forms required in other epochs, must reassume her own essential character, revealed by the Gospel, and make herself present among men not as a treasury of culture, philosophy, technical skill, politics or material wealth, but as the peaceable and radiant witness of the kingdom of God. This is the Church's service to the world, this is the pope's service too. As far as the doctrine goes, this is no new intuition. The pope has always been called the "servant of the servants of God". But it was Pope John who restored this service to its pristine purity of expression, who freed it from princely encumbrances, and translated it into gestures, words and examples which fully satisfied the expectations of the world: this was his special gift, his charism. One must ponder particularly on his perfect understanding of the expectations of the modern world. It was such as no theologian and no scholar could have foreseen or planned. We are convinced that it was not only due to his own wisdom, even though this was deepened by his wide experience of peoples and men: it was the Spirit of the Lord. "I sometimes think I am an empty sack," he said once whimsically to a friend, "an empty sack that the Holy Spirit suddenly fills with strength." His reserve has certainly kept hidden from our eyes the miraculous aspect of those sudden interior illuminations, which he reflected on to us in a mild familiar light. However, he allowed us some glimpse of these, on several occasions, when he spoke of how the idea came to him of summoning an Ecumenical Council. "In the case of the summoning of the Ecumenical

Council we received an inspiration: in the humility of our soul we considered the spontaneity of this inspiration as an unforeseen and unexpected command" (*O.R.*, 29 April 1959).

The peaceful rhythm of his spiritual life absorbed the impulses of God, made them seem familiar, and turned into the substance of human feeling even the most daring contemplative experiences. With exemplary level-headedness he distrusted men who were always being inspired and always indulging in fanatical devotions: in this also he rendered us a loving service. He sat at our table, joined in our common speech, broke the daily bread of our sorrows and our joys, until at last we became aware that the Lord had spent an hour with us and had changed our hearts.

"My only real Cross"

I feel quite detached from everything, from all thoughts of advancement or anything else. I know I deserve nothing and I do not feel any impatience. It is true, however, that the difference between my way of seeing situations on the spot and certain ways of judging the same things in Rome hurts me considerably: it is my only real cross. I want to bear it humbly, with great willingness to please my principal Superiors, because this and nothing else is what I desire. I shall always speak the truth, but with mildness, keeping silence about what might seem a wrong or injury done to myself, ready to sacrifice myself or be sacrificed. The Lord sees everything and will deal justly with me. Above all, I wish to continue always to render good for evil, and in all things to endeavour to prefer the Gospel truth to the wiles of human politics.

I want to study Turkish with more care and perseverance. I am fond of the Turks, to whom the Lord has sent me: it is my duty to do what I can for them. I know that my way of dealing with them is right; above all, it is Catholic and apostolic. I must continue in this with faith, prudence and sincere zeal, at the cost of any sacrifice.

Jesus, Holy Church, the souls in my care, and the souls of these Turks too, no less than those of our unfortunate brethren the Orthodox: "O Lord, save thy people, and bless thy heritage." (*Journal*, 1936, p. 228.)

"I leave cunning to everyone else"

My own temperament and training help me to show friendliness to all and forbearance, with courtesy and patience. I will not give up this way of behaving. St Francis de Sales is my great teacher. Oh, if I could really be like him, in everything! In order not to disobey the Lord's great precept, I will be ready to endure even scorn and mockery. To be "meek and lowly of heart" is still the brightest glory of a Bishop and a papal representative. I leave to everyone else the superabundant cunning and so-called skill of the diplomat, and continue to be satisfied with my own bonhomie and simplicity of feeling, word and behaviour. In the end, all turns out for the good of those who are faithful to the teaching and example of the Lord.

J.T.P.—4

The longer I stay in France the more I admire this great country, and the more sincerely fond I grow of "this most noble Gallic people". I am, however, aware of a contrast, which sometimes gives me a twinge of conscience. I am delighted to praise these dear brave Catholics of France, but I feel it is my duty, one inherent in my mission, not to conceal, through a desire to be complimentary and not to give displeasure, a certain disquiet concerning the real state of this "elder daughter of the Church" and certain obvious failings of hers. I am concerned about the practice of religion, the unsolved question of the schools, the insufficient numbers of the clergy, and the spread of secularism and Communism. My plain duty in this matter may be reduced to a question of form and measure. But the Nuncio is unworthy to be considered the ear and eye of Holy Church if he simply praises and extols all that he sees, including even what is painful and wrong.

This means a continual watch over what I say. A gentle silence, without severity, kinds words full of mercy and forbearance, will do more than criticisms, even if made in confidence and for a good purpose. For the rest, "there is one who discerns and judges". (*Journal*, 1947, pp. 268–9.)

". . . *that he may be a saint and a maker of saints*"

One word as I am about to enter the Conclave. It is like a prayer that I shall utter, *through the voice of the Bishop*, to all that is most dear to my heart as a good Bergamasque. When I remember many dear and venerated images of Mary scattered throughout the diocese, and all our holy patron saints, and Bishops and illustrious and saintly priests, and all the men and women in the religious orders so distinguished by their virtue, my soul is comforted in the confident hope of a new Pentecost which will give Holy Church, under a new Head and with a reformed ecclesiastical organism, a new impulse towards the victory of truth, goodness and peace. It matters little whether the new Pope is Bergamasque or not. The prayers of all must ensure that he be a man to rule wisely and gently, that he may be a saint and a maker of saints. Excellency, you understand me. (Letter to the Bishop of Bergamo, 25 Oct. 1958; *Algisi*, pp. 286–7.)

"Vocabor Joannes"

When I hear your voice "I tremble and am full of fear". What I know of my worthlessness and insufficiency is enough to make me feel ashamed.

But seeing in the votes of my Brothers, the eminent Cardinals of our Holy Roman Church, the sign of God's will, I accept the choice they have made: I bow my head to drink from the bitter chalice, and I bow my shoulders to the yoke of the Cross.

On the Feast of Christ the King we have all sung: "The Lord is our judge: the Lord is our lawgiver: the Lord is our King: he will save us."

I have chosen the name John. This name is dear to me because it was my father's; it is dear because St John is the patron saint of the humble parish in which I was baptized; it is the solemn title of innumerable cathedrals scattered all over the world and, first of all, that of the most sacred Lateran Basilica, our own cathedral.

In the long series of Roman popes more have been called by this name than by any other. In fact there is a list of twenty-two Sovereign Pontiffs of undoubted legitimacy who bore the name John. Almost all of them had a brief pontificate. I have chosen to hide the humility of my own name behind this magnificent succession of Roman Pontiffs. St Mark the Evangelist too, the glory and protector of our beloved Venice, he whom St Peter, Prince of the Apostles and first Bishop of the Roman Church, loved as his own son, had John as his first name.

But I love the name of John, so particularly dear to us and to the whole Church, because it belonged to the two men who were closest to Christ our Lord, Divine Redeemer of the whole world and Founder of the Church.

John the Baptist, the forerunner of our Lord, was not the light itself but was a witness to the light; and he was truly an unconquerable witness to truth, justice and the liberty of preaching, in his baptism of penitent sinners and in his own blood poured out.

And the other John: the disciple and evangelist, beloved with a special love by Christ and his sweet Mother, who at the last supper rested on the Lord's bosom and learnt from Him that charity which made him a living apostolic flame, until extreme old age.

God grant that both Johns may make their voices heard throughout the universal Church through our very humble pastoral ministry which succeeds to that so well followed to its end by our much mourned predecessor of revered memory, Pius XII, and that of his glorious predecessors in the Church: may the clergy and all the people understand the meaning of our efforts to "make ready a perfect people for the Lord, to make straight his paths . . . so that the crooked may be made straight and the rough ways may be made smooth, and all flesh may see the salvation of God" (Luke 3. 4–6).

And may John the Evangelist, who, as he himself tells us, took Mary the Mother of Christ, who is our Mother too, to live with him, with her assistance further the same appeal, which concerns the life and joy of the Catholic and Apostolic Church, as well as the peace and prosperity of all peoples.

"My little children, love one another; love one another because this is the Lord's great commandment."

May God in his goodness grant, Venerable Brethren, that we, honoured with the same name as the first of this series of Supreme Pontiffs, may with the help of divine grace, obtain the same holiness of life that he had, and the same strength of soul, and even, if God so desires, the spilling of our blood. (Allocution of 28 Oct. 1958, immediately after his election.)

"*Every pontificate has its own distinctive character*"

In this memorable hour we seem to hear the voice of Peter, which reaches us across the centuries; we hear also with equal love the voices of the two Johns who were and are the closest to Christ, and whose dear and honourable name we have chosen to assume.

But in these days of great mystery and trepidation, as we listen to the voices that rise to our ears from this earth, we are comforted and encouraged by the general joy and exultation which have greeted our elevation to the supreme pontificate, while at the same time we feel anxious and perplexed at the thought of the variety of the huge tasks which weigh upon our shoulders. In various ways these tasks are assigned to us on every hand, everyone endeavouring to entrust to us some special mission, confined within limited horizons, suggested by his own personal habits, his own experience and his own conception of individual and collective life. In fact some expect the Pope to be a statesman, a diplomat, a scientist, a social organizer, or one who is willing to accept all the forms of progress shown in modern life, without any exception.

O venerable brothers and beloved children, all these people have strayed from the right path, because they have formed a conception of the Supreme Pontiff which is not fully in harmony with the true ideal.

The new Pope, after the vicissitudes of his life, is like the son of Jacob, who, meeting his brothers in distress, reveals to them the tenderness of his heart and bursting into tears says: "I am Joseph, your brother" (Gen. 45. 4).

The new Pope, let us repeat, first of all expresses in himself that shining image of the Good Shepherd, as he is described to us by the evangelist St John in the same words that were used by the Divine Saviour himself (cf. John 10. 1–21). He is the door of the sheepfold (John 10. 7). We wish to make this clear, that is, that we cherish as dearest to our heart our task of shepherd of the whole fold. The other human qualities—learning, intelligence, diplomatic tact and organizing skill, may serve as an adornment and completion of Papal rule, but can never be substitutes. . . . Every pontificate takes its own characteristic expression from the person who assumes it and represents it. It is true that all the faces of the popes who have succeeded each other in the course of the centuries are reflected, and must be reflected, in the face of Christ, the Divine Master who trod the ways of this world only to spread the good doctrine and light of a wonderful example.

Now the divine doctrine and its diffusion are reassumed in his own words: "Learn from me, for I am gentle and lowly in heart" (Matthew 11. 29). Therefore, great gentleness and humility.

Pious souls, fervent souls throughout the world, we implore you to pray constantly to the Lord for the Pope, with the intention of obtaining for him the exercise of perfection in gentleness and humility. We are very sure that many graces will be the reward of this exercise; and the continuation of the eminently spiritual work of the Father of all the faithful will be of immense service also to the whole social order of our own age on this earth. (Coronation speech, 4 Nov. 1958.)

"It seems but a day!"

A year has gone by since, through the vote of the venerable members of the Sacred College of Cardinals, the Lord's will was shown concerning our humble person. A year, and it seems but a day! The first sign of heavenly grace entering our soul is this continuation of simplicity, of spiritual childhood and confidence, which, uniting us more intimately to Jesus, whose Vicar on earth all call us, keeps our mind, heart, words and arms open to all who are brothers and children in Christ. . . .

The good wishes for the aims, prosperity and success of the pastoral work we have begun, which are expressed to us with so much kindness and affection, certainly touch our heart. But they do not distract us from the thought of the other world which awaits us, and from which there comes to our ears, as we trust in the Lord's mercy, the invitation to join the Church Triumphant, which is the constant hope of all souls who believe in Jesus, Saviour and glorious and immortal King, world without end.

Furthermore, you understand that although it is natural for us, like everyone else, to wish to abandon our priestly soul to the embrace of the Lord who awaits his faithful servants, nevertheless it is also good and right to preserve this gift of life, as long as it is granted to us, for the lofty responsibilities of the sacred office and pontifical ministry, placed on our shoulders and in our heart by divine providence.

So, venerable brothers and beloved children, when we consider the first experiences which the Lord during the last year has permitted us to enjoy in our contacts with the episcopate, the clergy, people of every nation and every sort, and also with all those who, under another name, still bear the sign of Christ on their brows, we must say that never before so vividly, as on this first day of our second year, have we been aware of the general design of the great mission of the Pontificate, as the guardian of Christ's testament. This is what we perceive as we contemplate once more the salient points of the prayer which Jesus on the mount taught his followers, almost as if he were tracing the shining paths of the apostolate of Holy Church. Remember these phrases, these petitions of the *Our Father*: seven in all, perfect and magnificent in comprehensiveness and meaning.

It is along this safe way that the Holy Church of Christ is sustained; it is in this vessel that the life and history of the world are borne along; it is in this continuation of light, strength and grace that we see perpetuated all that, even from a merely human point of view, is the extension of knowledge, progress and true Christian civilization.

These are indeed benefits of a temporal nature, but they prepare the eternal benefits which await us, and enable us to enjoy the foretaste of them here below. (General Audience of 28 Oct. 1959.)

CHAPTER THREE

Obedience and Peace

I. THE "RONCALLI MYSTERY"

"WE have understood nothing": with this confession Robert Rouquette,[1] immediately after the death of Pope John, expressed the amazement of most Frenchmen, priests or laymen, who had made the acquaintance of the Nuncio Roncalli without any presentiment of his greatness. And it was not only the French who were amazed.

However much we can and must attribute, as we have already done, to the miraculous action of the Holy Spirit, the interior life of Pope John seems to us so ruled by the law of peaceful continuity that we feel obliged to seek a more natural explanation of this apparent contrast. Rouquette himself puts one forward, when he writes that "*dans sa sagesse paysanne, il menait une politique d'équilibre, dont nous ne voyons qu'un côté*". The balance here referred to was between the instructions of the Holy See and the restless ferment of French Catholicism in the post-war period. The fact that the Vatican decision to end the experiment of the worker priests was announced from the Nunciature some months after Mgr Roncalli had vacated it may perhaps throw some light on the difficulties of retaining that balance. It is one of the duties and customs of the diplomat to conceal his personal convictions when it is a question of carrying out orders that do not admit of any modification and leave no room for private discretion in interpretation. Everything points to the conclusion that in those years the Apostolic Nuncio to the French Republic was burdened with an extremely onerous mission: if Mgr Roncalli entertained

---

[1] "*Nous n'avons rien compris alors . . .* " (R. Rouquette S.J., "Le mystère Roncalli" in *Etudes*, July–Aug. 1963, p. 11). Rouquette, an eye-witness, describes many episodes which justified the diffidence felt by most representative French Catholics with regard to the Nuncio: "*Nous avons cru qu'il penchait vers l'intégrisme.*"

his visitors turning over the pages of an album of pictures of his beloved Bergamo or in evasive conversations, we can believe that this was in the nature of a tactical expedient, even if also congenial to his temperament, in order not to be brought face to face with problems the solution of which had already been decided elsewhere. Rome had sent the Apostolic Delegate of Istanbul to Paris because she had already proved his absolute docility, allied to the resources, most useful in that moment in Paris, of a jovial and imperturbable character. In a diplomat of the Holy See obedience is not merely a virtue of the profession. Angelo Roncalli had a very clear idea of how total, irrevocable and independent of the actual forms of its exercise is the consecration that the priest makes of himself to God and his Church.

The diplomatic life of a prelate of the Holy See [he wrote on 11 October 1954] is like a great and continual Mass, with its canon which shrouds in secret mystery the substance of the sacrifice which is celebrated: but before and after the canon there is an intermingling of teaching, prayer and praise which are the joy of the soul, the delight of the priest's heart and the edification of the faithful, stirring their hearts.

Another Nuncio, a good friend of mine, who also passed away some time ago, wrote publicly saying the same thing, and observing that a diplomat of the Holy See, as such, is a book closed with seven seals, to be opened only in the presence of the Pope.[2]

In a man of this stamp, firmly convinced that the will of God is expressed through ecclesiastical institutions, whether these be of divine origin or the expression of a positive right, obedience entails also the refusal to make any private reservations, and the obligation to keep within his heart, if necessary, as a final sacrifice, any convictions or plans not in keeping with the commands of authority. For indeed the obedience of these men is adorned with a certain filial loyalty which is anxious to safeguard the dignity of their superiors at all times in the eyes of others, even when it would be quite within their rights to reveal to all that an unpopu-

[2] *Scritti e discorsi*, vol. I, p. 330. The pastoral value of ecclesiastical diplomacy was very clear in the mind and testimony of Mgr Roncalli. The writings published by Mgr Loris Capovilla in the volume *Souvenirs d'un Nonce* are ample proof of this.

lar attitude was due to obedience and not to their own personal convictions.

Those who had but a superficial acquaintance with him perhaps considered him little more than a good-natured man, always willing to do a service, but somewhat insensitive to the anxieties of thinking Christians.[3]

But on the contrary he had his secret: he was celebrating in silence the "canon" of his Mass. The treasure of light that was suddenly taken out from under the bushel and set on a stand so that it gave light to the house of men was already there in him, but held hidden either by the obligation of diplomatic obedience, or, more frequently, by the self-sacrifice which, as a servant of the Church, he had made and constantly renewed in the sight of God. It is only when we take into consideration this interior life with its strict self-control that it is possible to understand the "Roncalli mystery".

"This is the mystery of my life", he said himself to some pilgrims from Venice, on 15 March 1959. "Do not look for any other explanation. I have always borne in my mind the words of St Gregory Nazianzen: 'Non voluntas nostra sed voluntas Dei pax nostra': not our own will but the will of God is our peace."

Most probably there is not much else in the way of data, apart from what Pope John himself has indicated, that can explain this mystery. It is likely that, endowed with such a sound and healthy psychological organism, he was formed in such a way as to disappoint the specialists who will seek to reconstruct the spiritual drama from which emerged, for the good of the whole world, the gift of his consoling serenity. The notes of his diary, at least those which are known to us, were filtered through

---

[3] Don Giuseppe De Luca (*Giovanni XXIII in alcuni scritti di Don Giuseppe De Luca*, ed. Morcelliana, 1963, pp. 60–61) seems to be alluding to this widely held opinion which was already losing ground when he was writing, in 1961, the following passage of glib but delightful psychology: "At the risk of contradicting the general opinion, I must say once more that I am not one of those who consider him an easy man, affable, approachable, a jolly fellow, at home or in College. Quite the contrary. He knows very well what he wants, but he does not say it, or get anyone else to say it. And he gets what he wants. He smiles, he jests, but he keeps his secret. His prayer is as hidden as his soul, and although our dearest friend could not give us a more frank and cordial welcome, no one will ever be able to boast that he has taken his measure. The first idea, if he has to form an idea about anything, is his own; and he arises every morning, as unpredictable as the day that dawns."

a shy reserve which refused to dwell on suffering, preferring to banish it to the world of the things one does not talk about, in order to give as much space as possible, even in the privacy of his own room, to gratitude and joy. They may serve however, and this is a line of inquiry useful for our purpose, to define the manner and moment in which in the young Roncalli there evolved that particular style of sanctity which will for evermore be associated with his name.

2. THE "CONVERSION" OF ANGELO RONCALLI

Angelo Roncalli always wanted to be a saint: the notebooks of his seminary years, published in the *Journal of a Soul*, convince us that he wanted this even too ardently; that he had, one might say, an insistent, almost an angry desire for holiness, as is often the case with beginners. In the seminary of Bergamo, and later in that of Rome, his spiritual teachers were obliged to teach him, according to the principles of spirituality then prevalent in places of ecclesiastical training, a strict technique of sanctification, of which a great part consisted, poor boy! in the persevering and constant mortification of the eyes, tongue and palate, and at the end of which, as if at the end of a narrow avenue of cypresses, there awaited, with pale faces and eyes upturned to heaven, those model saints, Aloysius Gonzaga, John Berchmans and Stanislaus Kostka. Every young Catholic, especially every seminarist, has for the last three hundred years had to do violence to himself to attain the exact stature of one or other of these incorruptible youths. The young Bergamasque peasant lad, who until then must have had sharp eyes, a ready tongue and a healthy stomach, and above all an exuberantly affectionate heart, struggled to make himself mortified and recollected to the best of his ability. His notebooks record only his failures: "Oh, poor me! I am still at the same point as before!" "In fact, during meditation, in my visit to the Blessed Sacrament, and during Vespers, ah! those Vespers! there is always something missing." "How ashamed I feel!" It was in vain that he renewed every morning his resolve to imitate St Aloysius ever more closely, and exclaimed: "St Aloysius is the witness of my promise to observe all these rules and he will help me to keep it" (*Journal*, p. 26).

Although the young Roncalli's docility during his seminary training was whole-hearted, it certainly did not help him to discover, over and above disciplinary obedience, what was the will of God concerning him. His peace of mind was to date from that discovery: from that time on his understanding with God, without authorizing any exterior disobedience, was to open for him the way to the spiritual liberty which brings perfect peace and joy. That moment came, and judging from his *Journal*, it was at the beginning of 1903. Under the date of 16 January there is a page which we might call the page of his conversion:

> Practical experience has now convinced me of this: the concept of holiness which I had formed and applied to myself was mistaken. In every one of my actions, and in the little failings of which I was immediately aware, I used to call to mind the image of some saint whom I had set myself to imitate down to the smallest particular, as a painter makes an exact copy of a picture by Raphael. I used to say to myself: in this case St Aloysius would have done so and so, or: he would not do this or that. However, it turned out that I was never able to achieve what I had thought I could do and this worried me. The method was wrong. From the saints I must take the substance, not the accidents, of their virtues. I am not St Aloysius, nor must I seek holiness in his particular way, but according to the requirements of my own nature, my own character, and the different conditions of my life. I must not be the dry, bloodless reproduction of a model, however perfect. God desires us to follow the examples of the saints by absorbing the vital sap of their virtues and turning it into our own life-blood, adapting it to our own individual capacities and particular circumstances. If St Aloysius had been as I am, he would have become holy in a different way.

He was little more than twenty years old. He had just come back from his military service ("*post captivitatem Babylonis*", he writes) and his innocent and terrified eyes had seen many kinds of wickedness the very name of which he had not known before, but at the same time he had been in contact with the life of freedom, in which goodness succeeds in flowering and expanding without having to keep its eyes lowered to the ground. Perhaps that pause had enabled some green shoots to spring, buds for which the seminary sunlight had been too pallid. He returned with joy to the old discipline, but his heart had changed. He had discovered himself, his own natural humanity, and had understood that in "diversity" the will of God is made even more clear than in the techniques of asceticism, which are only valid in so far as they serve that will. Once he had clearly understood the harmony between the will of God and his own human spontaneity, the young Roncalli began to breathe freely and started on his own interior ascent, which was joyful and serene. Every now and then, at first, he was tempted to return to the old methods, but he corrected himself at once: "So, no slipping back into old ways and customs. Serenity and peace!" he notes, 2 February, after his "discovery".

Ten years later his *Journal* has already the free sure movement of his maturity and old age: "I will not try to save my soul by defacing an original painting, which has its own merits, in order to become an unsuccessful copy of someone else whose character is entirely different from mine", he wrote on 10 August 1914. A saint was already born, although we were not to know it for another half century.

Even his models of holiness, during those first months of 1903, changed. The place of St Aloysius was taken by St Francis de Sales:

What a magnificent figure of a man, priest and Bishop! If I were like him, I would not mind even if they were to make me Pope! I love to let my thoughts dwell on him, on his goodness and on his teaching. I have read his life so many times! His counsels are so acceptable to my heart. By the light of his example I feel more inclined towards humility, gentleness and calm. My life, so the Lord tells me, must be a perfect copy of that of St Francis de Sales if I wish it to bear good fruits. Nothing extraordinary in me or in my behaviour, except my way of doing ordinary things: "all ordinary things but done

in no ordinary way." A great, a burning love for Jesus Christ
and his Church: unalterable serenity of mind, wonderful
gentleness with my fellow men, that is all. (*Journal*, p. 110.)

And together with St Francis de Sales he revered that other
model of a Christian Humanist, Philip Neri, the saint to whom he
is most frequently compared, the Florentine who, living amidst
the luxurious conventionalism of sixteenth-century Rome,
succeeded so well in dissimulating the intimate world of his
griefs and disappointments that to many, even to St Charles
Borromeo, he seemed like a sort of ecclesiastical clown, a lover of
inopportune jests and foolish witticisms. Certainly the saintly
Florentine had a more extensive psychological range, more
capable of holding within the limits of normality a behaviour so
original as to seem crazy. Roncalli was, after all, not a wild lad
from the other bank of the Arno, but a boy from the Bergamasque
countryside, and therefore full of good sense. Nevertheless, he
also belonged to the spiritual family of those Christians who do
not know how to take themselves seriously: once they have taken
the step of total dedication to God they remain at peace within
themselves, in spite of all opposition; nor do they allow themselves
to be attracted or disturbed by ambitions, calumnies or human
judgments—they know so well that human measurements are
more deserving of laughter than of tears.

I wish I had the time and ability to write of this holy man
as I would like and as my heart would dictate. St Philip is one
of the saints most familiar to me and his name is linked with
so many dear and personal memories. I feel I have a special
love for him and I commend myself to him most trustfully,
O my good Father Philip, you understand me even if I do
not put my thoughts into words. Time is drawing on; where
is that faithful copy of you I was to have made of myself? Am
I a replica of your virtues? O teach me the true principles of
your mystical school for the education of the soul, so that I
may profit by them: humility and love. I need great concentration of mind, blessed Philip, pure and holy gaiety and
enthusiasm for great works. (*Journal*, p. 126.)

That this is not a forced comparison with the Founder of the Oratory is proved also by the fact that the motto "*Obedience and Peace*"[4] (which in 1925 Pope John was to choose as his episcopal emblem: "These words", he wrote then with the spirit of prophecy, "are in a way my own history and my life! Oh, may they be the glorification of my humble name through the centuries!") was adopted by the young Roncalli in 1907 when he was studying the life of Baronius, Philip Neri's beloved disciple. There was one particular episode concerning the great Cardinal which he himself narrated in an article[5] written just at that time, on the occasion of the third anniversary of his death.

In Rome, about the hour of Vespers, for many years a poor priest could be seen, crossing the Ponte S. Angelo every day, and walking with a grave and thoughtful expression towards the Vatican Basilica. The little beggar boys who were waiting around the doors of the church, Arrighi tells us, rejoiced as soon as they saw him in the far distance and used to say: "Here is the priest with the big shoes", alluding to the thick shoes he used to wear, "here he is!" The priest used to give those urchins, who fell on their knees around him, a penny each; then, reverently entering the Basilica he would walk straight to the bronze statue of St Peter and kiss the apostle's foot, always pronouncing these two words: *Oboedientia et Pax*, obedience and peace. It was Baronius.

The article concluded on a prophetic note: "May such greatness be ours too one day: through the way of obedience joyfully to win the glorious conquests of peace!"

For Baronius obedience was the virtue which preserved him in his faith, exposed to the hard trials of historical research. For

[4] Pope John was always very fond of this motto and frequently used it to illustrate various spiritual variations on the theme of obedience and peace. After his election as Pope, on 17 Nov. 1958, during an audience granted to the staff of the State Secretary's Office, he told them, as we read in the official account: "The heraldic consultants, when asked to make suggestions for the transformation of the ancient coat of arms of the Cardinal and Patriarch into a coat of arms for the Supreme Pontiff, reminded him of the ruling custom which admits of no motto on the Papal emblem. So the Holy Father consented to the omission of the words *Oboedientia et Pax*, which, however, he preserves with unshakable loyalty in his heart; naturally he has not ceased to obey the profound meaning of these words: it is an unusual motto."

[5] Angelo Roncalli: *Il Cardinale Cesare Baronio. Conferenza tenuta il 4 decembre 1907 nel seminario di Bergamo ricorrendo il terzo centenario della morte*, Rome, Edizioni di Storia e Letteratura, 1961, p. 35.

the youthful Roncalli obedience was total conformity to the discipline of the Church and, once he had become a bishop and diplomat, the firm decision not to pay any attention to his own point of view but to make himself the faithful executor of the Pope's slightest desires and, in general, of the desires of all set in authority over him. If he had been without strong views and a will of his own, if he had not had a great love for the Church and shared in her sufferings, such a mission would have offered him a peaceful way of life, and perhaps even a less varied and difficult career, such as it offers to many. But he was very much alive; even if he did not seem, and did not wish to seem, an intellectual, he was a man of vast and vital ideas; his *esprit de finesse* kept his mind alert to possible contradictions between the carrying out of rigid diplomatic programmes and the free movements of events. Placed by the will of his superiors on the frontiers of Catholicism, he had occasion to experience the incongruity of methods which, suitable for nations of a long Catholic tradition, are much less effective where the Church enjoys neither great prestige nor a large following. His good sense, therefore, often led him to elaborate projects which were afterwards crushed by overriding considerations of diplomacy; his zeal for souls led him to subordinate bureaucratic routine to his pastoral mission; his faith in man induced him to ignore the precautions of a more cunning approach, and his temperament led him to escape whenever possible from behind the velvet curtains of ecclesiastical offices into the roads and squares where living men and women move, the crowds among whom Jesus Christ himself moved, full of patience and mercy. It is only when we bear in mind that in a man of God obedience is not only a moral virtue but a specific principle of faith and, as such, has "reasons that reason cannot understand", only then, as we have seen, is the Roncalli mystery explained: the world of ideas and plans that he might have brought to fruition, if he had been a free agent, was sacrificed by him, so as to leave only the man of obedience alive. "That other self", he wrote on 25 November 1933 from Sofia, "which is always in me, although enchained, sometimes tries to arouse my compassion, and waves its shackles about, and wants to whisper or cry aloud. It must stay there in its prison, until death and beyond (*usque ad mortem et ultra*). I still bear aloft and unfalteringly my banner with its motto: *Obedience and Peace.*"

3. "PURE LOSS"

Until death then. And, in fact, he was already about to slip out of the hands of history, and later generations would have known nothing, or almost nothing, about him, when suddenly God took hold of him. Algisi gives us a letter he wrote to a friend, some years before his election to the papacy:

> We must live for each day as it comes. Nothing is ever lost, even if we feel, or look, as if we were wasting the years. In his *Elévations sur les Mystères* Bossuet has twenty-two chapters about the presentation of Jesus in the Temple. This is sweet and sublime doctrine. In his last meditation he says: "Simeon has sacrificed his love of life and sees it, as it were, poured out to God as a total loss" (*Simeon a immolé l'amour de la vie et la laisse pour ainsi dire s'exhaler à Dieu en pure perte*): what a mystery in this pouring out of life before God, as a total loss! And his life was not lost at all. The time he spent in waiting prepared him to present Christ the Saviour to the world. And now I will tell you that my own poor life continues to be poured out as you know: with my usual hairshirt, which is so dear to me, on my back (p. 289).

This extraordinary confidence is enough to lift the veil concealing the sources of a spirituality that has moved the world. "*S'exhaler en Dieu*" means giving up trying to find a human explanation for what is happening to us; it means letting ourselves be borne along, quite naturally and simply, by the breath of God. So this total loss can be described as the abandonment of all self-defence and all anxiety, and produces total human integrity. Whether as priest, bishop, diplomat, cardinal, pastor or pope, Angelo Roncalli never changed his style of living. The variety of his functions never interrupted the continuity of his way of being what he was. He was pope, without "playing pope". "I am a novice pope", he said to the faithful, in one of his first Audiences. But he was an excellent novice, because in fact he had nothing to learn: he had only to go on being what he was. The reason for this facility lay in his total abandonment to the simplicity of God's will, and in forgetfulness of self. It is said that one night when he could not sleep because of some great anxiety concerning the government of the Church, he suddenly said to himself: "But who is it who is governing the Church? Is it you, or is it the Holy Spirit? Well then, John, go to sleep!" And to the faithful gathered in the Lateran, in a very grave moment of his pontifical mission, he said very frankly: "Do not believe that the Pope passes sleepless nights. Oh no, the Pope sleeps very well." His certainty that the institutions of the Church are governed by the Holy Spirit was enough to give him a precise sense of the extent of his own responsibilities. Before he was made pope he found it easy to be obedient to others' commands, even when his own point of view was different: he knew that it was not for him to decide, but only to obey. Possibly, from time to time this docility was mistaken for "conformism" or narrow-mindedness: but he did not care for the judgment of men; it was enough for him to know that he had done what God through the Church had asked him to do. He made no attempt to avoid this yoke of the most willing and single-hearted obedience. Once he was made pope, with all power in his own hands, he began to act according to his own judgment, or better, according to his intuitive understanding of the will of God. It was thus that his originality became apparent, to the stupefaction of those who had judged him without taking into account the profound reasons for his obedience.

"The Lord knows in what way, and how much, this separation has cost me", he wrote in 1939 to a friend who had had to leave him. "Now all has been fulfilled according to the Lord's will. The alabaster vase has been broken (*fracto alabastro*): here is a first instance in which my motto has found its perfect application" (*Algisi*, p. 344).

4. THE WILL OF OTHERS

On several occasions, when comforting souls sorely tried by obedience, or confiding to someone the reason for his wonderful serenity, he referred to Book III of the *Imitation of Christ*, particularly to Chapter 23. André Baron[6] tells us that during an Audience he obtained in July 1962 Pope John confided to him that his whole life had been directed by that chapter, which had been brought to his notice by his spiritual director when he was still a seminarist. "I think", he said in conclusion, "that I have never sinned against any of the precepts taught in that chapter." The chapter is called: "About the four things that bring much peace to the soul." These are the four things:

"Seek, my son, to do another's will, rather than your own."

"Choose always to have less rather than more."

"Always seek the lowest place and to be inferior to everyone."

"Always desire and pray that the will of God may be wholly fulfilled in you."

"Behold, in this way a man enters the abode of peace and rest."

When he was in Turkey he received orders from Rome to go to Athens, to deal with some difficult matters which, in his opinion, would have been better left alone a little longer. The order was an implicit reproof. He commented on it: "We have not yet arrived at the departure of Padre Cristoforo for Rimini: but we are getting nearer. 'Good Monsignor Roncalli' is silent, smiles and goes" (*Algisi*, p. 176).

With this delightful expression, "good Monsignor Roncalli" he intended to record a widespread opinion, which would have been a source of bitterness to others, but which merely amused him. This opinion must have been held and fostered by certain ecclesiastical diplomats whom he, when already Nuncio in Paris, was to call "those of the other school". His smile was not that of a good-natured man who puts up with everything because he has no dignity: it was a wise smile, that of a man who looks into the far distance, in both senses of the word: far away in history, and far away in God. For example, when he was transferred from Bulgaria to Istanbul many considered this move was anything but a promotion: the way in which King Boris had deceived him about the baptism of his heir was on the lips of all. But he went when he was told, probably as cheerful as ever, silent and smiling. On that occasion he wrote:

[6] In *Humanitas*, double number dedicated to John XXIII, July–Aug. 1963, p. 687.

I am quite content. Many people, on both shores, European and Asian, are sorry for me and call me unfortunate. I do not know why. I give the obedience required of me, that is all. Certainly I am saddened to see the slow but fatal disappearance of many things which were the adornment of Catholicism and of nationalism in other ages. Perhaps there are sad days and painful situations in store for me. But I do not cease from looking upwards and far away. (*Algisi*, p. 125.)

Obedience did not spare him the ordeal of contradictions of thought, for he succeeded in avoiding the twofold danger inherent in obedience: one is the formalism of the Pharisee, which reduces everything to a mechanical docility to the rules of the institution, and the other is the mysticism which is content to resolve the contradictions between conscience and reality by taking refuge in the incomprehensible mystery of God, leaving the history of men a prey to the stupidity which seems to direct it. His scrupulous fidelity to the general and particular dispositions of the Church, which was always a sign of the innate nobility of the diplomat Roncalli, never caused any confusion in his mind between fidelity to the law and fidelity to God. The real guiding principle of his life was the will of God.

"I am becoming more and more dogmatic", he wrote in 1948, "about the effectiveness of this 'Thy will be done', which is indeed the *Obedience and Peace* of my episcopal motto. . . . I am convinced that this sacrament of our own will, absorbed into the sacrament of the will of God, is really the summit of our perfection, and the surest source of our interior joy and serenity" (*Algisi*, p. 354).

But this reliance of his on the divine will was not a way of escaping to the spiritual heights, where the problems of actual events cease from troubling. He did not give up thinking and looking far away, not only along the vertical line which led to God but along the horizontal line which ran through present time into the future, ran through the actual situation of the world . . . in which the "adornments of Catholicism" were bound to disappear . . . into a future situation: that which God, contrary to all expectation, was to entrust to his wisdom as supreme pontiff.

Souls who have had in their lives one purpose only, that of abandonment to the divine will, have recognized in this pope a Christian of their own race, of the race, for example, of a Teresa of Lisieux; men who are bringing about a renewal of the history of the world through the instruments of human wisdom have recognized in him a profound intuition of the real needs of human society and the capacity to use the simplest and most effective means to satisfy these. The men of the cloister and the men of politics will all have to ponder over him. We are at the beginning of an epoch in which the monastic ideal of abandonment in God tends towards recovering a more natural form of expression and a peaceful familiarity with God's creatures, while the political ideal tends to identify itself, unreservedly, with moral ideals. It becomes more and more clear that the contemplative order and the political order are really not so incompatible or contradictory as they were in the past. Peace is indivisible; it includes the tranquillity of the soul as well as peace between the continents. There has been no dearth in recent times, nor is there any dearth today, of politicians of lofty moral and religious fervour, and it is upon these that the modern world has depended, and without disappointment, for its own political hopes. Machiavellian complications have no meaning in our own times: even political science aims at the clearest simplifications.

"Look," said Pope John one evening to Jean Guitton, pointing to the cupola of the Observatory of Castel Gandolfo, "these learned astrologers, for the guidance of men, make use of very complicated instruments. But I do not know these. I am content, like Abraham, to go forward in the night, one step after another, by the light of the stars" (*O.R.*, 5 June 1963).

The genius for simplification guided him, step by step, towards successes, not only in the religious field but also in that of politics, and of such a nature as to surpass, for their durability, those achieved by men more expert in the art of government— and there are certainly many such men in our century.

... To have accepted with simplicity the honour and the burden of the pontificate, with the joy of being able to say that I did nothing to obtain it, absolutely nothing; indeed I was most careful and conscientious to avoid anything that might direct attention to myself. As the voting in Conclave wavered to and fro, I rejoiced when I saw the chances of my being elected diminishing and the likelihood of others, in my opinion truly most worthy and venerable persons, being chosen.

To have been able to accept as simple and capable of being immediately put into effect certain ideas which were not in the least complex in themselves, indeed perfectly simple, but far-reaching in their effects and full of responsibilities for the future. I was immediately successful in this, which goes to show that one must accept the good inspirations that come from the Lord, simply and confidently.

Without any forethought I put forward in one of my first talks with my Secretary of State on 20 January 1959 the idea of an Ecumenical Council, a Diocesan Synod and the revision of the Code of Canon Law, all this being quite contrary to any previous supposition or idea of my own on this subject.

I was the first to be surprised at my proposal, which was entirely my own idea.

And indeed, after this everything seemed to turn out so naturally in its immediate and continued development. (*Journal*, 1962, pp. 325–6.)

The "careful and conscientious way" in which, immersed in that sector of the ecclesiastical institution which of necessity demands impersonal obedience on the part of the executive, he sought to avoid being conspicuous and made no attempt at escape, had worked an extraordinary result. He was about to leave this world with the satisfaction of having put into practice the maxim of his beloved *Imitation of Christ*: "Love to be unknown and to be esteemed as nought." He knew that the cleverest diplomats considered him too talkative, too responsive to the impulses of the heart, too much inclined to cultivate friendships of doubtful theological value; intellectuals found him somewhat distrustful of the reforming power of theories; traditionalists noticed in him an excessive inclination to gather what was good and worthy, even if it grew in an enemy's field; progressives saw he was too much in love with the wholesome traditions of a devout and somewhat rustic form of Christianity, and too faithful to the claims of obedience; the Bishops did not see in him the conventional signs of episcopal solemnity. In fact, before he became pope and in a few months aroused the filial admiration of all, he had not managed to fit into any of the categories in which we measure and praise a man. He knew this and did not lose his peace of mind over it. Nor did he lose his peace of mind when, once made pope, he made no bones about it but went on just as before, with only this difference, that now it was no use trying to remain unobserved. His decisions now concerned the whole world. He ceased to obey men, but he was still at peace because he continued to obey God.

"What will become of me in the future?"

What will become of me in the future? Shall I be a good theologian or a famous jurist, or shall I have a country parish or be just a simple priest? What does all this matter to me? I must be prepared to be none of all these, or even more than all these, as God wills. "My God and my all." After all, it is easy for Jesus to scatter to the four winds my dream of cutting a brilliant figure in the eyes of the world.

I must get it into my head that, just because God loves me, there will be no plan for me in which ambition plays a part; so it is useless for me to rack my brains about it.

I am a slave; I cannot move without my master's consent. God knows my capacities, all that I can or cannot do for his glory, for the good of the Church and for the salvation of souls. So there is no need for me to give any advice to him, through his representatives here, my Superiors.

Is it not true that the saints, in their early years, appeared to set out on a road quite different from the one which their natural gifts and brilliant qualities had seemed to indicate? Yet they became saints, and such saints! Reformers of society, founders of famous Orders! They practised holy detachment: they were willing to listen to the voice of God who spoke to them as he speaks to me; they did not measure what they had to do by considering their pride, but cast themselves blindly into all that God wanted them to do. "Look," then, my boy, "look and make it according to the pattern," and this means everything. All my wanting to do and say is nothing but pride, there is no other word for it; if I go on in my own way I shall work and sweat over it . . . and in the end—what shall I be?—a wind-bag!

If I want to be really great, a great priest, I must be stripped of everything, like Jesus on his Cross; I must judge everything that happens in my life, and the decisions of my Superiors concerning me, in the light of faith. God forbid we should carry criticism into this field! "O blessed simplicity!" (*Journal*, 1904, pp. 154–5.)

"Let whoever will pass before me"

But my dominant thought, in my joy at having accomplished ten years as a priest, is this: I do not belong to myself, or to others;

I belong to my Lord, for life and death. The dignity of the priesthood, the ten years full of graces which he has heaped upon me, such a poor, humble creature—all this convinces me that I must crush the self and devote all my energies to nothing else but work for the kingdom of Jesus in the minds and hearts of men, as I do in my own simple way, even in obscurity; but from this time forth it must be done with a greater intensity of purpose, thoughts and deeds.

My own natural disposition, my experience and my present circumstances all indicate calm peaceful work for me, far removed from the field of battle, rather than controversial action, polemics and conflict. Ah well, if this is the case I will not try to save my soul by defacing an original painting, which has its own merits, in order to become an unsuccessful copy of someone else whose character is entirely different from mine. But this peaceful disposition does not mean pampering my self-love, seeking my own comfort, or mere acquiescence in thoughts, principles and attitudes. The habitual smile must know how to conceal the inner conflict with selfishness, which is sometimes tremendous, and, when need arises, show the victory of the soul over the temptations of the senses or of pride, so that my better side may always be shown to God and my neighbour.

I have now been a priest for ten years; what will my life be in the future? That remains hidden from me. It may be that but a short time remains before I am called to render my final account. O Lord Jesus, come to take me now. If I am to wait for some, perhaps many, years then I hope they will be years of intense labour, upborne by holy obedience, with a great purpose running through everything, but never a thought straying beyond the bounds of obedience. Preoccupations about the future, which arise from self-love, delay the work of God in us and hinder his purposes, without even furthering our material interests. I need to be very watchful about this, every day, because I foresee that with the passing of years, and perhaps in the near future, I shall have many struggles with my pride. Let whoever will pass before me and go on ahead; I stay here where Providence has placed me, with no anxieties, leaving the way clear for others. (*Journal*, 1914, pp. 183–4.)

"Honours and human wisdom"

It is now some months since I set up my own home and furnished it in a suitable manner. Nevertheless, perhaps now more than ever before, the Lord gives me to understand the beauty and the sweetness of the spirit of poverty. I feel I would be willing to give it all up here and now, and without regrets. I shall always try, as long as I live, to keep this feeling of detachment from all that is mine, even from what is dearest to me.

I pledge myself especially to seek perfect poverty of spirit in absolute detachment from myself, never feeling any anxiety about positions, career, distinctions or anything else. Am I not already too much honoured in the sublime simplicity of my priesthood and in the work I am doing now, not sought by me but entrusted to me by Providence, by the voice of my Superiors?

I dwell at length on this matter because it is fundamental for my welfare. I will never say or do anything, I will dismiss as a temptation any thought, which might in any way be directed to persuading my Superiors to give me positions or duties of greater distinction. Experience teaches me to beware of responsibilities. They are solemn enough in themselves if assumed under obedience, but terrifying for whoever has sought them for himself, pushing himself forward without being called upon. Honours and distinctions, even in the ecclesiastical world, are "vanity of vanities".

They assert the glory of a day; they are dangerous for whoever desires glory in eternity and paradise; even from the point of view of human wisdom they are worth very little. Anyone who has lived in the midst of these stupidities as I did in Rome, and in the first ten years of my priesthood, may well insist that they deserve no better name. Forward, forward, whoever wants to go ahead! I envy none of these fortunate souls. "It is good for me to be near God, and to place my hope in the Lord God." (*Journal*, 1919, p. 193.)

The Four Rules

During the 1904 vacation, the last I spent at the seminary, Father Francesco was in the country with us at Roccantica. It was his custom to gather us together once a week for a pleasant and useful discussion during which we considered, under his direction, for he was an expert in this subject, some particular moral question of his choice. Afterwards one of us would preach a short spiritual exhortation, and then he would conclude with a few words which were like the finest and most fragrant fruit of those gatherings. Once he asked me to preach the little sermon—this was before my inglorious trial at San Gioacchino!—substituting at short notice for someone who was unable to fulfil his engagement. I held out a little, perhaps rather too long; at last I gave in. Not having anything of my own ready to say, and thinking it would be rather pretentious on my part to improvise, I simply quoted from Book III, Chapter 23 of the *Imitation of Christ*: "About the four things that bring much peace to the soul", adding a few words of comment.

It is heavenly doctrine: who can forget it?

1. Seek, my son, to do another's will, rather than your own.
2. Choose always to have less rather than more.
3. Always seek the lowest place and to be inferior to everyone.
4. Always desire and pray that the will of God may be wholly fulfilled in you.

And since in those days I was delightfully absorbed in reading the life of St Francis, I found something to say about him too, ending with the story of Brother Leo on the mountain of La Verna, who, when the *Poverello* was raised in ecstasy, ran forward to clutch his feet and kiss them, weeping and crying: "My God, have mercy on me a sinner, and through the merits of this holy man grant me your grace."

I still see before my eyes Father Francesco's smile of pleasure at the subject and example chosen: "You see", he said to me, "how obedience has come to your rescue. Always obey, simply and good-temperedly: leave the rest to the Lord. It is he who speaks to our hearts."

Eighteen years later I think with great emotion of the truth of that doctrine expounded in the old book. To Father Francesco it must have been like a mirror reflecting the most substantial and characteristic part of his own spiritual teaching; I feel renewed in my heart the desire, ripened by experience, to live more intensely according to this doctrine, in order to enjoy even here below the sweetness of true peace. (*Journal*, Appendix IV, pp. 439–40.)

"Absolute and magnificent solitude"

A whole series of recent events has conferred on this retreat a special sense of loving abandonment to God, suffering and crucified, my Master and my King.

The trials, with which in recent months the Lord has tested my patience, have been many: anxieties concerning the arrangements for founding the Bulgarian seminary; the uncertainty which has now lasted for more than five years about the exact scope of my mission in this country; my frustrations and disappointments at not being able to do more, and my enforced restriction to the life of a complete hermit, in opposition to my longing for work directly ministering to souls; the inner discontent felt with what is left of my natural human inclinations, even if until now I have succeeded in holding this under control: all this makes it easier for me to enjoy this sense of trust and abandonment, which contains also the longing for a more perfect imitation of my divine Model.

All around me in this great house is solitude, absolute and magnificent solitude, amid the profusions of nature in flower; before my eyes the Danube; beyond the great river the rich Rumanian plain, which sometimes at night glows red with burning waste gas. The whole day long the silence is unbroken. In the evening the good Passionist Bishop, Mgr Theelen, comes to keep me company for supper.

My soul is absorbed all day in prayer and reflection. (*Journal*, 1930, p. 215.)

"You see what I have to do!"

Sofia, 15 January 1931

My dear Don C.,

Just two lines to tell you how deeply interested I am in your spiritual welfare, and to return your good wishes.

Your new position may at times tempt you to regret the greater good that perhaps you thought you were doing before, when you were in more frequent contact with souls. This is a temptation that must be repelled like all others. Thy kingdom come, Thy will be done: that is enough. It would be enough even if it happened that what the Lord asked of you personally were simply to say the Holy Mass and take a stroll every day round the walls to count the trees.

In this great organization in which we have been called to work, the Catholic Church, one job is as good as another, as long as one stays within sight of the Shepherd who knows all, and keeps a most careful account of all. I think this is characteristic of the Lord's servants, that they feel themselves called to do one thing and are instead obliged to do another.

This is rather what has happened to the friend now writing to you.

Could I not have been a good Canon of the Cathedral, helping the young seminarists to the best of my powers, teaching a little about religion, exercising patience with humble souls who are content with little? That might have been my life. Instead just look at what I have to do! I am invested with a dignity that I have done nothing to deserve, and special faculties which I cannot even exercise in the manner of a simple priest; very rarely the chance of delivering a spiritual homily; no opportunity of hearing confessions; occupied all day, now fortunately in a handsome Residence, with my typewriter or in wearisome conversations; in the midst of many difficulties and wounding experiences; among people who, although belonging to Jesus Christ and by right to the Catholic Church, are entirely lacking in the "sense of Christ", and still more in the "sense of the Church"; ever in contact with the so-called great ones of the earth but distressed by their mental incapacity to understand anything that is supernatural; carefully preparing events which ought to bring about such good results, and then obliged to observe the frailty of human hopes.

With all this, my dear Don C., we live in peace: because final success is always with those who with all their heart do the will of the Lord, take everything in good part, and with a good grace. (*Algisi*, pp. 337–8.)

Against "fervent sighs"

Readiness for self-sacrifice, such as the Lord wants from every one of us, and in the measure he requires, this must present a great lesson and warning for me. This is what loyal and sincere devotion means. Not just shedding consoling tears during prayer but preparing a ready will for God's service, whatever it may be. "My heart is ready, O God, my heart is ready", for much or for little, to do what God wants of me and understand what he does not want, which therefore must not be done. So frequently we are deceived about this. We take pleasure in fashioning for ourselves ways of serving the Lord which are in truth simply ways of expressing our own taste, our own ambition, our own caprice. "The pride of your heart has deceived you, you who dwell in the clefts of the rock" (Obadiah 3). You hardly know how to take, in God's service, one step outside your hole, in which, like a tarantula, you take refuge from the storms that rage, and yet you like to persuade yourself that you could fly like an eagle if you received a call from beyond the mountains and beyond the seas. In your piety you have unwittingly deceived yourself. Let the readiness of your will be seen in works done to carry out the will of the Lord, as this is made known to you day by day, and do not show this readiness merely by heaving fervent sighs. (*Journal*, 1940, p. 254.)

"Gentleness is the fullness of strength"

The fundamental principles of the spiritual life still hold firm, thanks be to God: to feel wholly detached from my own nothingness and to remind myself that, in the words of the Ambrosian Mass, I am the least of all, and a sinner. I must abandon myself completely to the will of the Lord and desire to live for nothing else but the apostolate and the faithful service of Holy Church. I must feel no concern about my future and be ready to sacrifice everything, even life itself—should the Lord think me worthy— for the glory of God and the accomplishment of my duty; I must have a great spiritual fervour, in keeping with the mind of the Church and the best tradition, without any exaggeration of external forms or methods, but constant zeal and mildness, with an eye for everything, always with great patience and gentleness, remembering what Cardinal Mercier quotes from Gratry: gentleness is the fullness of strength. And finally, I must always be familiar with the thought of death, which helps so much to make life carefree and joyful. (*Journal*, 1942, p. 259.)

Thoughts on peace

Rio di Pusteria, 9–13 July 1958

The Lord's peace implies perfect detachment from ourselves and the absolute abandonment of our own will as regards all that concerns the advantages and comforts of our life. When the soul achieves complete indifference with regard to persons, offices, and changes of place, position, and a more or less fortunate and happy career, that is true peace. The doctrine of the *Imitation of Christ*, Book III, Chap. 23: "Of the Four Things necessary to Peace", is precise about this: (1) to seek to do another's will rather than our own; (2) to choose to have less rather than more; (3) to choose the lowest place and be inferior to everyone; (4) always to desire and pray that God's will may be done, to such a point that, if this brings with it suffering and bitterness, these also may become a reason for joy. Remember: "Take, O Lord, all my liberty."

What doctrine and what warning there is in Christ's being "made obedient unto death"! And what solemn joy in the "because of which God exalted him" sung by St Paul and impressed upon the whole course of the history of the Church, and the history of those men who did honour to the Church in the ways of holiness and the apostolate, in all ages and in all parts of the world. Therefore seek the "Peace of Christ" which is obedience to Christ; which is the triumph of Christ in souls. Among the teachers of the primitive Church listen to St Ignatius: *Episcopum revereamini ut Christum Domini* (Revere the bishop as you would the Lord's Christ) and the other incisive expression: *nihil sit sine episcopo* (may nothing be done without the bishop). This is the discipline handed on for two thousand years; it is still so vital that nothing effective is achieved in the history of the Church and of Christian people, and nothing resists the corrosive action of time, that is not founded *supra hoc fundamentum apostolorum et prophetarum in Christo Jesu* (upon this foundation of the apostles and prophets, in Jesus Christ).

What is said about the "Peace of Christ" with regard to the work of grace in individual souls is true also of every association of human and Christian energies, directed towards the progress and peace of the public and social order.

Beware of misunderstandings: they arise, challenge each other and come to blows. We must be on our guard against them: if they cannot be avoided, at least let us not cultivate them, or allow them to be exaggerated in our imagination: let us try, unashamedly, to be the first to explain them away, to put things right once more, to disentangle them and to keep ourselves free from any feeling of resentment.

Even among cultured and spiritual people there may be a variety of opinions and views in matters open to discussion. This does no harm to charity and peace, as long as we preserve moderation of manner and harmony of minds. I will add moreover that the Lord makes use of these misunderstandings to bring about in other ways some great good. Thus Paul and Barnabas separated because of young John Mark. Thus there is some disagreement in certain letters and correspondence between St Jerome and St Augustine, as there was later on between St Peter Damian and Cardinal Hildebrand, who was to become Pope Gregory VII; all these souls were equally righteous and holy. With souls like these everything is set right by the Lord's grace. But this does not alter the fact that we must beware of misunderstandings and must try to clear them away. (*Scritti e Discorsi*, vol. IV, pp. 155-9.)

CHAPTER FOUR

Evangelical Realism

I. NATURAL HOLINESS

INTERIOR peace was not then a natural gift in Pope John. His peaceful way of approaching his fellow creatures, of treading this earth benignly, without any trace of disgust, without trampling on its flowers or fearing their luxuriance, was the mark of a balance of mind which was not easy and immediate but achieved after long efforts and which, in the end, also by reason of his age, had become so spontaneous as to seem as easy as breathing. The commemoration of him which Cardinal Suenens made before the Council, on 27 October 1963, reached its finest peak—emphasized by tremendous applause from "the whole Church" (the expression is exact!)—when he dwelt on this miraculous harmony. The passage deserves to be quoted in full:

> If one could reduce it all to a few words, I think one might say that John XXIII was a man singularly natural and supernatural at the same time. Nature and grace formed a single whole in a living unity full of charm and unforeseen variety.
>
> All sprang from the same source. He was entirely natural when supernatural, and was natural with such a supernatural spirit that it was impossible to detect the joining line. He breathed his faith, as he breathed physical and moral health, with open lungs. It has been written: "He lived in the presence of God with the simplicity of one who strolls along the streets of his native city."
>
> He was at home on this earth of ours; he interested himself in other people's affairs with a lively sympathy. He could pause by the wayside to exchange words with humble people, listen to a child, or console a sick man. He showed interest in the building of an airport, and prayed for the astronauts.

But he was also at home in the supernatural world, on familiar terms with angels and saints. He liked to share his favourites with others, and here also he had the courage of his affections. He surprised St Joseph by introducing him into the Canon of the Mass, and some saints of the Lombard Venetian region by raising them to the honours of the altar: for example, St Gregory Barbarigo and the Blessed Innocent of Berzo and Louis Palazzolo.

Such a happy combination of grace and nature explains this other harmony, so clearly seen in Pope John, between his life and his teaching. There was no dualism in him. After the example of the Lord, of whom St John says that "his life was light", the dead Pope was a light to men by the very fact of his existence. In him light and heat were inseparable, as they are in the sun which at the same time lightens and warms the earth.

The natural, immediate, always thoughtful kindness of John XXIII was like the ray of sunlight that scatters the mist, dissolves the ice, and penetrates everywhere before we are aware of it, as if it had a perfect right to do so. A ray of light that creates optimism as it passes by gives joy with its sudden appearance, and is undaunted by any obstacle.

So John XXIII appeared to this world: not like the tropical sun which blinds men with the brilliance of its splendour, but like the humble familiar sun of every day, which is up there, in its appointed place, always true to itself, even if sometimes momentarily veiled by a cloud, our own sun of which we take no notice because we are sure it is still there.

The mild radiance of Pope John, which will be an object lesson in Christian tradition, came to light us at the right moment, when the first young shoots of the Catholic renewal were finding it hard to open, to usher in the spring foretold by Pius XII. Pope John not only provided the warmth necessary to soften the wintry cold, but set in motion those laws that, in an organic and balanced way, direct every process of renewal in the Church, and first of all the laws that belong to the order of the mind.

In spite of the widespread rhetoric about the "kind-hearted pope", we may affirm that above all, Pope John restored prestige to the Christian intelligence, setting before all men's eyes its most traditional and most neglected characteristics. Parallel with the spiritual crisis of these recent centuries, the Catholic mind, shown in its historical manifestations, has suffered from a certain inhibition, from which Pope John seems all at once to have freed it. What is this inhibition?

2. THE CHRISTIAN MIND

Many have the impression that the intelligence of western peoples is now a worn out instrument, exhausted through excessive refinement and excessive use. On the one hand, its contracted habit of never accepting any concept without having first reduced it to the simple elements which compose it has deprived it of the power of synthetic intuitions, which grasp the idea in its essential principle, that which gives it unity and truth. On the other hand, its acquired habit of never in reasoning going beyond the positive data of experience, has left it content with descriptive processes, which never touch the final "reason" of the facts. Such a habit of thinking has done profound harm to the religious spirit, eating away the premises of "natural religion", upon which Christianity relied so much in the past and, in its reflex action, has done harm also to the Christian understanding.

The Christian intelligence, on the other hand, illumined as it is by the light of faith, more easily preserves its own natural integrity and, by means of the grace which comes to its aid, is enriched with a superior intuitive power, the specific object of which is the mystery of God, both as it transcends history and as it operates within history, transforming it by divine power. But the intelligence is a faculty which is necessarily affected by the historical condition of men: it has its own intimate historicity. In the present historical situation the Christian intelligence bears the marks of the crisis we have described above. In order to keep on a level with the prevailing intellectualism it has developed, in the field of theology, a fondness for systems, a taste for dialectic and theory. Bereft of much of its intuitive vigour, it has lost contact with the actuality of events, constraining itself to judge them according to metaphysical or moral attributes, without taking pains to understand their meaning as religious messages.

Almost forty years ago appeared a book by Julien Benda, which enjoyed a huge success. It was his *Trahison des Clercs*, and it denounced the world of scholarship, shut within its republic of abstractions, while men of action, with their violent hands and uneducated minds, laid hold of the history of men.

This disintegration had, to a certain extent, even entered the Catholic world. It is said that Pope John did not trust theologians; in fact an oft-quoted saying of his blames the theologians for many misfortunes that have befallen Christianity. This is probably a tendentious invention. It is more likely that Pope John was thoroughly convinced that, however respectable the role of theologians may be, it does not safeguard that particular function of the Christian intelligence which is the intuition of the signs of the times, the discovery, within the realm of events, of that divine intention which guides history and appeals to the faith of all believers. Christian intelligence is by its nature realistic; it has a biblical structure; the study of events, in order to discover the sacred nucleus, is its natural destiny.

With Pope John the revival of the Christian intelligence now seems to have begun. This revival does not seek to question anything handed down by tradition; it does not deny the indispensable value of systematic theology, or the usefulness of metaphysical and juridical learning; it is not, in a word, the revolt of irrationalism against rationalism! Nor is it the exaltation of simple faith, the "charcoal-burner's faith", against the faith of learned men. It is the reassertion of a right and a power inherent in faith. The faith which is repelled by religious concepts is sickly, but the faith which is satisfied with concepts is sickly too, in another way. A robust and integral faith tends to operate within its own sphere, which is the mystery of God, inasmuch as he is the maker of sacred history, as vast in its scope as the history of mankind. As it discovers the links which bind together, in one final purpose, the events narrated by sacred history properly so called (in which divine intervention is explicit and normal) and the events of our everyday life, faith traces the guiding lines of Christian behaviour; it pronounces a judgment which, if the will is courageous enough, is transformed into action.

Let us take as an example the event which was so much talked of in March 1963. The director of a Soviet newspaper was in Rome with his wife. They asked to see the Pope. This was a situation which could be judged from a political angle and resolved accordingly but which could also be judged in the light of faith, that is in the light of an intuition which discerned within this event a God-sent possibility which it would have been unwise to neglect. Pope John judged by the light of faith, and behaved according to his intuition, thus remaining, in every word he uttered, on the level of faith. What happened? Apparently nothing. Perhaps the husband and wife are still atheists: nothing substantial has changed between the Soviet world and the Catholic Church. And yet no one would dare to say that nothing happened. Men who were not Pharisees perceived in that action more clearly than in all the theological discourses that the Church was above politics. Throughout the world one small act produced more light and more benevolent awareness of Christianity than a hundred thousand Lenten discourses.

3. THE GOSPEL AND LIFE

The modernity of Pope John is seen essentially in this way he had of trusting, beyond the bounds of worldly prudence, in the power of the Gospel to illuminate the mystery of men, seen individually and collectively, and to trace a supreme rule of practical relations which can never be confused with any other rule, however good and legitimate that may be. He certainly had no intention of casting discredit on the rules of politics or economics, or of philosophical wisdom: indeed, he found no difficulty in perceiving and publicly defending their autonomy. It was only that as a Christian even more than as a pope, he reserved for himself the freedom to follow a higher law, the rule of faith (*regula fidei*), which belongs of right to the Church. His particular training and spontaneous fidelity to the simple forms of his childhood's devotions led him to prefer expressions of piety which were more in keeping with the impulses of the heart than open to the strict examination of the mind. But, if we consider the conscious motives to which he attributed his actions, the humblest as well as the most magnificent, and his very obvious preference for a robust and manly Christianity, nourished not so much on books of devotion as on the great traditional texts, if in short we know how to distinguish what was essential in him from what was humble compliance with his own and others' customs, we shall well understand the importance in his interior life of the Word of God, accepted as a rule of judgment and conduct. Here is a page from his *Journal* (13 August 1961, p. 308):

> The sublime work, holy and divine, which the Pope must do for the whole Church, and which the Bishops must do each in his own diocese, is to preach the Gospel and guide men to their eternal salvation, and all must take care not to let any other earthly business prevent or impede or disturb this primary task. The impediment may most easily arise from human judgments in the political sphere, which are diverse and contradictory according to the various ways of thinking and feeling. The Gospel is far above these opinions and parties, which agitate and disturb social life and all mankind. The Pope reads it and with his Bishops comments on it; and all, without trying to further any worldly interests, must inhabit that city of peace, undisturbed and blessed, whence descends the divine law which can rule in wisdom over the earthly city and the whole world.
>
> In fact, this is what wise men expect from the Church, this and nothing else.

The loving and precise way in which he quoted the Scriptures, especially in his solemn speeches, such as that on the opening of the Council, revealed a great power of discovering connections between Sacred History and the history of men.[1] Human history

---

[1] At the end of an Audience, 12 Feb. 1963, he urged the faithful who were present: "Let everyone who has been present at this Audience, on returning to his home, look to see whether he has a copy of the Holy Bible. If he has, let him frequently open those precious pages and feed his soul on them; if he has not, let him see to it without delay that the place of honour in his home shall be reserved for this Book above all others. In past ages we were somewhat reluctant to encourage familiarity with the Bible because, since some of our Christian brothers have cut themselves off from the Church and asserted that

had not in his eyes those contours that we have all learnt from pedantic textbooks, and which, for the most part, inspire us with great awe. He was not a man of learning in the modern sense of the word, which is probably an artificial and conventional sense. Between us and facts learning intervenes with its network of categories which, with their abstract logic, conceal a practical and pseudo-rational origin. There is one way of freeing oneself from this network of abstractions in order to make contact with reality: it is that of unprincipled Machiavellism which, exploiting "effectual reality", makes use of its dynamic in the pursuit of success. This is certainly not the realism of Pope John. When he freed himself from schemes of learning and abstract systematization he did so in the name of the reality of man who is not, as man, either a progressive or an illuminist, is neither liberal nor Marxist, is not, in short, an individual appendix to a system, not a "law case". For example, the true reality is the man who errs, not the error of a man; it is a historical movement, not an ideology which moves historically. Studious research had obliged Angelo Roncalli, for many years, to make most careful inquiries of a sociological order about the pastoral activity of St Charles Borromeo. The positive reconstruction of the life of social groups of the past is useful also because it calls into question the generalizations so beloved by professors. But it is above all the religious and moral necessity of direct discovery, behind the universal generalizations, of the individual drama of man himself, the positive and negative forces which in every time and place have agitated him. It is this intensely Christian genius for reality which led Pope John not to depend too much on the prudence of ideologists and to set out along those paths which so wonderfully led him into the midst of the tangle of forces which make our world today so great and so despairing, and led him to seek to modify it according to the mind of God.

The contemporaries of Christ also had their judicial categories which dispensed them from awareness of the individual man: "Samaritans", "Publicans", "Ethnics", and so on. Christ be-

by doing so they were remaining faithful to the Bible, and that they did not consider it necessary to have the Pope, the Church or the priesthood, we were almost afraid to run the risk of thinking and acting like them" (Account in *O.R.*, 13 Feb. 1963).

wildered them because, putting aside these concepts, he revealed behind these masks the face of man himself. Man, every man, in spite of his explicit intentions, is born sacred. Every series of events seen, as it were, against the pages of the Bible, is directed by a sacred law. One of Pope John's most fertile intuitions was that, in order really to make peace on this earth, we must accustom ourselves to seeing men as men, above and beyond those ideological classifications which seek to swallow us up in their conflicts. Ideological antitheses, when in control of the mechanism which rules our human contacts, become bloody wars.[2] In fact, at the source of modern wars are gigantic and diabolical abstractions: they have been ideological wars. Now, "the most profound longing of all mankind is peace: *pacem in terris!*" As long as we are reduced to placing between mankind's most profound longing and our own behaviour the filter of ideological discriminations, we shall not be men of peace. Pope John has given the world a lesson of true realism simply by banking on the goodness of mankind's longing for peace, and the all-powerfulness of God's purpose which works through history.

When his pontificate commenced, the thaw between the two "blocs", which with their obstinate opposition had seemed to paralyse the course of human history, had hardly begun. In this clash the Christians had let themselves be captivated by a crusading spirit, thus fostering that great error which Pope John was very careful to avoid: the mistaken notion that the West had the privilege of defending the Catholic faith, and the Catholics the advantage of having at their disposal in this struggle the strength, the wealth and the prestige of the West. Thus the Christian struggle was losing its religious character and running the risk of resembling a political, or even a military, battle. One should read most carefully this passage from a speech which Pope John delivered to the *Pontificia Unione Missionaria*:

---

[2] Angelo Roncalli as a young priest once had to comment on the lectures of a worthy and energetic Father who had been sent to the Seminary to confute the errors of the Modernists. Roncalli wrote that while he approved of the doctrine he did not like the method chosen: "I could not understand why, even if it was necessary to tell the truth and the whole truth, it had to be accompanied by the thunders and lightnings of Sinai, rather than by the calm and serenity of Jesus on the Mount and by the lakeside." See the whole passage farther on, page 287.

Yes, it is true that we are faced with the giant Goliath, and perhaps we are wasting too many words, which would instead be better used in prayer, and in good counsel for the sanctification of our own souls and those of our neighbours. We are faced with an enemy who looms enormous: but he is not strong, nor is he valiant, because his attacks are those of error, greed and violence. At times we are frightened, and we are dismayed at the thought of the future. And yet this giant will be forced to yield to the will, the grace, the mercy of God. Nor should we think that the victory of this Goliath would necessarily entail universal ruin and destruction, because, even in his own domains, there are still souls illumined by our own light, who remain faithful, and share with us the same Christian and apostolic ideal. The simplicity of the little David who confronts the giant is truly a figure of the Catholic Church; it represents the glorious band of our own champions, who go humbly and unitedly about their holy task, in the strength and joy of feeling themselves encouraged "in word, in deed and in prayers".

How magnificent and how true is this biblical image which Pope John has offered us of the presumptuous confidence of a certain world! He trusted to the grace and mercy of God. The giant has alternated words of defiance with words of reconciliation; but finally, surprised by the gentleness of the Church, a gentleness not of this world, he has not attempted to conceal his admiration. And, behind the giant, thus softened if not tamed, the bands of souls "illumined by our own light" have greeted us, after centuries of separation. During the rule of Goliath the seed of God had not died in that world, because God is stronger than any giant. Pope John, far from being a deluded idealist, has been proved a realist.

4. NATURAL INCLINATION AS WISDOM

It was without doubt his own intuitive genius, ripened by a long and varied experience of men and countries, which made it easier for him to acquire this supernatural wisdom. Even from the natural point of view he was truly a master of life. If comparisons from the world of culture were fitting in his case, one would say that he resembles Montaigne more than Pascal. His contact with the infinite was purely mystical: as for the rest, he preferred to make himself at home in the narrow space of a day, and accept, without the shudder of a Pascal, the limitations of daily life.

While he did not despise reading, he did not in this conform to the ideal of a learned priest: he read for edification, and so with the same disposition with which the soul turns to prayer or experiences life itself. Therefore he preferred to read the classics, the Fathers of the Church, and among these the great masters of the spiritual and pastoral life, such as St John Chrysostom or St Gregory the Great. And so in every moment he was true to himself, when choosing a book or choosing a companion, always obeying the same vital law which is, to use an expression of Bergson's, "not according to the understanding, but according to natural inclination". "If this natural inclination", continues the philosopher, "could explain its object and reflect upon itself, it would give us the key of vital operations." The object of the "natural inclination" of Pope John is not difficult for us to recognize as unity, understood as an objective principle which gradually gathers men together and then unites them with God.

Besides being a means of acquiring knowledge, the natural inclination of Pope John gave character to his whole being and was revealed in every gesture, in the way in which he gave his hand or looked, with shining eyes, at the beauty of nature. When in the most memorable of his improvisations, that evening of 11 October 1962, he spoke from the window of his apartment to the crowd gathered in St Peter's Square, he said, interrupting the robust and impetuous flow of his speech: "Even the moon has hastened out this evening . . ." and there was a throb of response in the crowd. That childlike candour which, on a truly historic day, rejoiced in the moon coming out to join in the festivity, was the clear sign of his unfaltering fidelity to primary impressions, of his capacity to remain untouched by the awesomeness of great occasions. Saddened, as we are, by forms of literary realism which reject form and style in the name of primitive immediacy—which culture has done much to suffocate in conventionalism and rhetoric—we found in him a much more substantial realism, so much the more difficult to attain because it was perfectly in keeping with universal objectivity.

5. THE SENSE OF PROPORTION

In the Catholic world there has developed, here and there, a religious realism of the existential type which has not yet freed itself from the spirit of anti-bourgeois protest or the ill-concealed fondness for irrationalism. In comparison with this the realism of Pope John was perfectly healthy: it never lost the sense of proportion. We shall see how his inclination to laughter and his quick-wittedness sprang from his Manzonian awareness of disproportions. It is even possible that in France he was sometimes disappointed by the proneness to excess of which, for at least the last thirty years, the Catholicism of the descendants of Pascal has given evidence. We also, before discovering him, had believed that he shared the same sort of psychological make-up that we know so well in Italy: the mentality that is slow to rouse to enthusiasms, because of fatigue or because of centuries old experience of disappointments, and above all very distrustful of doctrinaire dogmatism. One never suspected that his Italic temperament concealed such creative genius. Could the champions of reform have asked for more? And yet, with what a sense of proportion, with what a carefully graded series of initiatives he started the movement of reform! Throughout his life, and especially in his last years, he was always averse to argument, however holy it might be, and never, on the many occasions when he suffered from men's incomprehension, or worse, from their scorn, did he permit himself, as many pious souls have done, the somewhat declamatory attitudes of heroism. He did not even approve of an attitude of "cowering humility", which is to say that exasperated desire for self-abasement which causes generous souls, especially ecclesiastics, to scorn all pomp and exteriority. For example, he wrote on 31 March 1948 to a newly appointed Monsignore:

> It is true that, as our years increase, these personal honours fade before the higher dignity of the service which a well spent

priestly life renders to the Lord's Church. The splendour of souls (*splendor animarum*) is superior to the honour of office (*honor vestium*). Yet these are things which may easily be reconciled, and to know how to receive them and use them with simplicity and grace, without excessive show of humility as without conceit, gives pleasure to all and edifies our brethren and the people of Christ. (*Algisi*, p. 360.)

He was far from sharing the anxiety of those who find no other way of bringing the Church up to date than that of finding fault with the robes of the Monsignori. The "leap forward" which he was to ask the Church to make was to come about in a much more profound and organic way, that is on the level of the most essential values. As for the rest, he probably did not even trouble to make up his mind about the pomp of the prelates. He found an easy way of putting robes of silk and gold in their right perspective, when, for example, he pulled his handkerchief out of his pocket at the climax of a most solemn ceremony. His good taste always taught him to preserve the due distance between form and substance, between really important things and the trifles which to our impassioned gaze appear enormous. His was no quixotic soul, tormented by grandiose dreams. He had not much sympathy with heroes: he distrusted their obstinacy in always forging ahead when it would be more useful to go round.[3]

It is probable that the impression of his mediocrity was largely due to this repugnance of his for daring gestures or noisy assertiveness, and to his inability to appear, even when he had the right to do so, in the role of a victim who humbly, but visibly, bears his halo. He showed good taste even in the way he bore his crosses. When he was transferred from Sofia to Istanbul in 1934 he wrote to Mgr Bernareggi:

Tomorrow I shall leave for Istanbul, and I shall inaugurate my new ministry on the Feast of the Epiphany. As it is pour-

[3] Writing to a friend on 29 Jan. 1921—notice the date—he sang the praises of a Bergamasque priest, particularly emphasizing his imperturbable serenity and aloofness from all polemics, and added: "Our forebears in times of opposition, the last echo of which resounded even in my own ears, took as their motto: '*Frangar, non flectar*' (to be broken, not bent). But I prefer the opposite: '*Flectar, non frangar*' (to be bent, not broken), especially when it is a question of practical method; and I think in this I am in line with the whole tradition of the Church" (*Algisi*, p. 336).

ing hard in that land, I shall have to creep along close to the
wall, and as best I can. I wish to go slowly. Who can say that
by so doing I may not go far, in spite of the problems and
difficulties that await me. It is enough if I can get in, as I hope
to be able to.

Excellency, to everyone his own cross: and every cross has
its particular shape. Mine is indeed in true twentieth-century
style. Your prayers help me to bear it with honour and with
a certain good grace that is not displeasing to anyone, not
even to our Creator. (*Algisi*, p. 116.)

This meek man, who "creeps along close to the wall" and as
best he can, will arrive at St Peter's throne without becoming
changed. The world was astounded to see in a setting of such
grandeur, which until then had imposed its style even on simple
and saintly men, an old peasant who continued to amble along
flat-footed, like his father and grandfather before him, as if he
were walking over ploughed fields, waving his hands as if he
were casting seed. In vain they insisted on carrying him seated in
the *sedia gestatoria*: everyone understood that he was a man who
liked to walk on his own feet, who was in fact a man among
men, and entered the human situation not by the perpendicular
way of mercy but walking on the same plane as the ordinary man,
the horizontal plane of fellow feeling.

The glory of Pope John's death agony was singular just for
this reason, because it was the epilogue of a true sermon, full of
truth which was more human than metaphysical, an epilogue
without any external grandeur and therefore open for all to share.

Death cannot get the better of him [Alfonso Gatto wrote
during those days[4]], we feel that he lives, he speaks to us and
shows us, step by step, the long and weary way towards the
knowledge, the embrace of love.

He has spoken within man, within man's home, within the
fear and hope of man. He has brightened our lives with the
frank look of the parish priest who bears in his heart the God
of all, the God of the harvests and the wilderness, water and
thirst. . . .

[4] In *Testimonianze*, a monthly spiritual review. Double number (55–56) dedicated
to John XXIII, June–July 1963, pp. 448 *et seq*.

He has made us see in the creature the Creator, in the action the reason for action, in perfection the necessity of imitation, in imperfection the longing to do better, even the spur of optimism. This is his freedom, a fatherly gesture of deliverance which restores to man his freedom of choice!

After epochs during which authority had its own language, as different from the common language as its function was different, ages in which truth remained faithful to its own old formulae, as holy as they were unworldly, in which even the priesthood relied on a repetition of pre-established gestures and on the function of mercy, just then when the meeting between Christianity and the world seemed to depend not indeed on a modification of Christianity but on a change of heart on the part of the world, at that very moment, by virtue of one man, Christianity, without any change in itself, has taken the initiative of going out to meet the world at the right moment, and has proclaimed its truth not from the heights but from "within man, within man's home".

"What the Lord has done for me"

I love to think of how Jesus founded his Church! Instead of summoning the wise and the learned from the academies, the syna-
gogues and the schools, he cast his loving eyes on twelve poor
fishermen, rough, ignorant men. He admitted them to his school,
shared with them his most secret thoughts, made them the object
of his most loving care and entrusted to them the great mission
of transforming mankind.

In the fullness of time Jesus has been pleased to call me also to
extend his kingdom and to have some share in the work of the
apostles. He took me, a country lad, from my home, and with the
affection of a loving mother he has given me all I needed. I had
nothing to eat and he provided food for me, I had nothing to
wear and he clothed me, I had no books to study and he provided
those also. At times I forgot him and he always gently recalled me.
If my affection for him cooled, he warmed me in his breast, at the
flame with which his Heart is always burning. His enemies and
the enemies of his Church surrounded me, set snares for me,
dragged me out into the midst of the world, into the mire and
filth, and yet he has preserved me from all ill, he has not allowed
the sea to swallow me up. To inspire my soul with stronger impulses of faith and charity he has led me to this place, which is so
full of his blessings, where I may live under the protection of his
Vicar, beside the fountain of Catholic truth and the tomb of his
apostles, where the very sods are stained with the blood of
his martyrs and the air is balmy with the odour of sanctity of
his confessors, and he still cares for me without respite, day and
night, more than a mother cares for her child. Yet after all this,
in return for so much tenderness, he asks me anxiously one thing
only: My son, do you love me? Lord, Lord, how can I answer
you? See my tears, my throbbing heart, my trembling lips, and
the pen that slips from my fingers. . . . What can I say? "Lord,
you know that I love you."

Oh, if I could love you as Peter loved you, with the fervour of
Paul and all the martyrs! My love must be joined to humility, a
low opinion of myself and scorn for the things of this world—
and then make of me what you will: an apostle, a martyr, O Lord.
(*Journal*, 1902, pp. 90–91.)

"Simplifying everything more and more"

No temptation of honours in the world or in the Church can now affect me. I am still covered with confusion when I think of what the Holy Father has done for me, sending me to Paris. Whether I shall receive further promotion in the hierarchy or not is a matter of complete indifference to me. This gives me great peace of mind and makes it easier for me to do what I must do here, at all costs and at any risk. It will be wise for me to prepare myself for some great mortification or humiliation which will be the sign of my predestination. May heaven grant it may mark the beginning of real holiness in me, as was the case with those elect souls who, in the last years of their lives, received the touch of grace which made them truly holy. The thought of martyrdom frightens me. I distrust my resistance to physical pain. And yet, if I could bear Jesus the witness of my blood, oh what grace and what glory in heaven for me!

I am fairly pleased with my devotional practices which bring me near to God. After having skimmed through the doctrine of various authors, I am now quite content with the Missal, the Breviary, the Bible, *The Imitation* and Bossuet's *Méditations sur l'Evangile*. The holy liturgy and Sacred Scripture give me very rich pasture for my soul. So I am simplifying everything more and more and find it is better so. But I want to give more faithful and devout attention to the holy Eucharist, which I am blessed in being allowed to keep under my own roof, with direct access from my apartment. I shall take more pains about my visit to the Blessed Sacrament, making it more varied and attractive, with reverent and devout exercises such as the recital of the penitential psalms, the Way of the Cross, and the Office for the Dead. Are not all these contained in devotion to the holy Eucharist?

I have filled my room with books which I love to read: all serious books dealing with the requirements of Catholic life. But these books are a source of distraction which often creates a disproportion between the time I must give primarily to my current affairs, to preparing reports to the Holy See and similar matters, and the time that in actual fact I spend in reading. Here a great effort is needed and I shall set about it with all my might. What is the use of all this anxiety to read and to know, if it is detrimental to my immediate responsibilities as Apostolic Nuncio? (*Journal*, 1947, p. 267.)

The method of simplification

The more mature I grow in years and experience the more I recognize that the surest way to make myself holy and to succeed in the service of the Holy See lies in the constant effort to reduce everything, principles, aims, position, business, to the utmost simplicity and tranquillity; I must always take care to strip my vines of all useless foliage and spreading tendrils, and concentrate on what is truth, justice and charity, above all charity. Any other way of behaving is nothing but affectation and self-assertion; it soon shows itself in its true colours and becomes a hindrance and a mockery.

Oh, the simplicity of the Gospel, of the *Imitation of Christ*, of the *Little Flowers of St Francis* and of the most exquisite passages in St Gregory, in his *Moralia*: "The simplicity of the just man is derided", and the words that follow! I enjoy these pages more and more and return to them with joy. All the wiseacres of the world, and all the cunning minds, including those in Vatican diplomacy, cut such a poor figure in the light of the simplicity and grace shed by this great and fundamental doctrine of Jesus and his saints! This is the surest wisdom, that confounds the learning of this world and, with courtesy and true nobility, is consistent, equally well and even better, with the loftiest achievements in the sphere of science, even of secular and social science, in accordance with the requirements of time, place and circumstance. "This is the height of philosophy, to be simple with prudence", as was said by St John Chrysostom, my great patron saint of the East.

Lord Jesus, preserve in me the love and practice of this simplicity which, by keeping me humble, makes me more like you and draws and saves the souls of men. (*Journal*, 1948, pp. 270–1.)

"I keep true to my principle"

Last night I said Matins by myself; this morning in chapel I said the Hours with the *Miserere* four times and today's liturgy, uniting myself in spirit as I followed in my Missal, as if I were attending the ceremony in some great church, or as if I were still presiding over it in Sofia, or in the Cathedral of the Holy Spirit at Istanbul.

My present: here I am then, still alive, in my sixty-ninth year, prostrate over the crucifix, kissing the face of Christ and his sacred wounds, kissing his heart, laid bare in his pierced side; here I am showing my love and grief. How could I not feel grateful to Jesus, finding myself still young and robust of body, spirit and heart? "Know thyself": this keeps me humble and without pretensions. Some people feel admiration and affection for my humble person; but thanks be to God, I still blush for myself, my insufficiencies and my unworthiness in this important position where the Holy Father has placed me, and still keeps me, out of the kindness of his heart. For some time past I have cultivated simplicity, which comes very easily to me, cheerfully defying all those clever people who, looking for the qualities required in a diplomat of the Holy See, prefer the outer covering to the sound ripe fruit beneath. And I keep true to my principle which seems to me to have a place of honour in the Sermon on the Mount: blessed are the poor, the meek, the peacemakers, the merciful, those who hunger and thirst for righteousness, the pure in heart, the suffering and the persecuted. My present, then, is spent in faithful service to Christ, who was obedient and was crucified, words I repeat so often at this season: "Christ was made obedient." So I must be meek and humble like him, glowing with divine charity, ready for sacrifice or for death, for him or for his Church.

This journey in North Africa has brought home to me more vividly the problem of the conversion of the peoples without the faith. The whole life and purpose of the Church, of the priesthood, of true and good diplomacy is there: "Give me souls; take all the rest." (*Journal*, 1950, pp. 275–6.)

"I introduce myself"

I wish to speak to you with the utmost frankness of heart and speech.

You have eagerly awaited me; things have been written and said about me which far surpass my deserts. Now I humbly introduce myself.

Like every other man who lives on this earth, I come from a family and from a clearly defined starting point: with the grace of good bodily health, with enough common sense to enable me to understand things quickly and clearly, with a loving disposition towards men which keeps me faithful to the teaching of the Gospel, respectful of my own rights as of those of others, and incapable of doing ill to anyone; indeed it encourages me to do good to all.

I am of humble birth and I was trained to a contented and blessed poverty, which makes few demands and fosters the growth of the most noble and lofty virtues, a good preparation for the higher altitudes of life.

Providence took me from my native village and made me travel along the roads of this world in the East and in the West, bringing me into touch with people of different religions and ideologies, at grips with social problems which are acute and menacing, and meanwhile preserved my serenity, a balanced judgment and a spirit of enquiry. I was always engaged, naturally with fidelity to the principles of Catholic belief and moral teaching, more with what unites men than with what divides them and provokes conflicts.

At the end of my long experience I am returning here to Venice, the land and sea familiar to my ancestors for more than four centuries, even more familiar to my own studies and my personal predilections. No, I have not the courage to apply to myself what Francis Petrarch, a lover of Venice, said of himself; nor have I tales to relate, like those told by Marco Polo when he returned to his own people. But it is true that strong ties bind me to Venice. I come from Bergamo, the native city of Bartolomeo Colleoni, once part of the territory of St Mark; behind my hill is Somasco, where is the hermitage of St Jerome Emiliani.

These notes give you the modest physiognomy of the man before you.

Certainly, the position that has been entrusted to me in Venice is a great one, and far in excess of my deserts. But above all I wish to commend to your benevolence the man who wishes simply to be your brother, friendly, approachable and understanding. I intend to follow the same course which has served me well till now, and which has perhaps brought about my return to Venice, to live among a noble people particularly sensitive to the impulses of the heart, to simplicity of behaviour, of speech, of works, to that respectful and cheerful sincerity of dealings which is characteristic, even if within limited proportions, of the man who has deserved the title of a man of proven honesty, of an honest man without a stain who is worthy of confident respect.

This is the man, this is the new citizen whom Venice has today been pleased to welcome with such festive rejoicings. (*Scritti e Discorsi*, vol. I, pp. 16 *et seq.*)

"Expressing the good inspiration"

The various initiatives of a pastoral character which mark this first stage of my papal apostolate have all come to me as pure, tranquil, loving, I might even say silent inspirations, from the Lord, speaking to the heart of his poor servant who, through no merit of his own save that very simple merit of mere acquiescence and obedience, without discussion, has been able to contribute to the honour of Jesus and the edification of souls.

My first contacts with high and low; the charitable visits here and there; the meekness and humility shown in the approaches made to clarify ideas and give warm-hearted encouragement; my Lenten visits to new parishes; the unexpectedly successful outcome of the Diocesan Synod, the closer links between the papacy and the whole Christian world, achieved by the repeated creation of new Cardinals and Bishops from every nation and of every race and colour, and now this vast activity, of unforeseen and most imposing magnitude, for the General Council—all this confirms the wisdom of the principle of waiting on God and expressing with faith, modesty and confident enthusiasm the good inspirations of the grace of Jesus, who rules the world and guides it according to the supreme purposes of the creation, redemption, and final and eternal glorification of souls and peoples. (*Journal*, 1961, p. 314.)

CHAPTER FIVE

Loyalty to his Land

I. THE CHILDLIKE POPE

POPE JOHN'S realism springs, as we have seen, from the extraordinary harmony between the inclinations of his intelligence inspired by faith and the natural inclinations proper to his temperament. Without such a lively faith he would perhaps have been nothing more than a man of great practical sense, capable in the long run of outwitting men of clever, cunning and complicated diplomacy. And without his temperamental gifts he would not have had such a grasp on reality, such power of life-giving influence.

Although harmony between nature and grace may be assumed to be the goal of all Christian asceticism, it is by no means true that this harmony is generally achieved by the saints. In our conventional image of sanctity there must nearly always be some sign of harshness, some trace of interior struggle, some shade of melancholy not entirely dispelled by the sunlight of faith. When, through some charismatic gift, complete harmony is realized, the impression sanctity then gives is that of a childhood which has remained intact in spite of the passing of years and the gravity of our earthly tasks. Then it is that we break into laughter, in our soul, because we have discovered that it is easy to live, and that in the depth of all wisdom there is the law of delight, the law that presided over the work of creation, as Scripture tells us when it speaks of Wisdom, which played like a delighted child in the sight of the Almighty Father Creator, "rejoicing before him always"!

This sort of gentle laughter, which is both human and Christian, is what I have heard or seen on my own and others' lips whenever I have had occasion to speak of Pope John, before

learned and ignorant alike, among Christians as well as unbelievers. If we speak of Christian joy, we are now obliged to think of
him, and we rejoice in understanding, and making others understand, that this is not something secret and different from the
joy of every day, but a joy that sings in the same way that our
blood sings, has the same good smell as a well-laden table, and
knows how to enjoy living without even bothering to distinguish
this earthly life from the other which is eternal. In his still un-
published diary of 1958, written in a large engagement book,
we read, on the page which records the day of his election as
pope, of the preoccupations which, during the night, had somewhat disturbed his sleep, as the votes cast for him in the ballots of
the conclave steadily increased. And then, after having noted, in
two words only, that he had been made pope, his thoughts turn
at once to his father and mother, and he wonders whether they
could ever have imagined their "little Angelo" becoming Pope.
Here lies the secret of his admirable enjoyment of this life. He
remained still a child, even with all the wealth of wisdom of his
eighty years. He was never a "serious" man. He was serious
enough before God, and all who knew him agree that when he
bent his head absorbed in prayer, his face became solemn and
grave, almost as if he had sunk into a sound sleep, free from
thought. But when he observed human affairs he kept them at a
proper distance, that is, he continued to delight in seeing them
move about like paper boats on water, big and little boats.

"My affairs", he wrote when he was in Paris, "go satisfactorily,
thanks be to God. I keep calm and watch them carefully: one by
one I see them fall into their right and proper place. I bless the
Lord for the way in which he enables me not to complicate
simple things, but rather to simplify the most complex" (_Algisi_,
p. 357).

We are accustomed to believe that, with the increase of
authority, certain rights to light-heartedness and courageous
confidence must diminish. We shall shortly be speaking of his
mirth as an expression of his realism. Certainly the burden of
authority did not destroy the child in him; indeed it set it in a
clearer light, all the more so because of the paradoxical contrast

in which both these, authority and childhood, lived in him without ever destroying each other.

I confess that at first Pope John's habit of seizing every occasion to indulge in personal reminiscence caused me some embarrassment. Gradually, however, this aspect of his pastoral style seemed to me to be perfectly in keeping with the other aspects, and so became perfectly plausible. The biblical structure of his intelligence, on which we have already insisted, led him to discover and recount the workings of God in his own life through his doings and encounters. Those who deny all logical development that does not take place within the limits of time can make no sense of the events of their childhood, because these are anterior to their deliberate choice, and independent of that liberty without which man is not truly man. But for the Christian these events are the visible traces of an invisible love. Our earthly childhood is not simply and solely a beginning: in the totality of its occurrences, in the circle of its flesh and blood affections, in the first movements of the heart that learns to venture outside itself towards the small, firm horizon of domestic traditions, a Christian spirit discerns a divine plan, which bears the sure signs of a design from which he will no longer be able to stray with impunity.[1]

2. HUMBLE FOLK

Infancy is the *principium individuationis* of Sacred History: it is Sacred History assuming an individual form, by means of which it is possible to realize the universal plan of salvation. Moreover, when the transmission of flesh and blood was, as it was for Angelo Roncalli, the transmission also of faith, then the names of mother, father and all other dear ones are like the names of Abraham and Sarah, names sacred in the true sense of the word, names, that is, which give a resonance and expression to the wonderful design by which God, from generation to generation, has prepared our

---

[1] Mgr Loris Capovilla tells us (*Giovanni XXIII*, p. 27): "He himself told me late that night (it was 28 Oct. 1958) and once more on the day of his coronation, when he had been borne for the first time in the *sedia gestatoria*, what had been the most beautiful, most serene and most lasting impression of this whole transformation: 'I was thinking of my home at Sotto il Monte, of my father and my mother'."

joy: "What our parents have told us" (*quod patres nostri narraverunt nobis*).

> Having been brought up in the poverty and humility of Sotto il Monte, I have always done my best not to draw away from these. What graces the Lord has bestowed on me: holy parish priests, exemplary parents, a strong Christian tradition, a contented and tranquil poverty!
>
> Born poor, but of humble and respected folk, I am particularly happy to die poor, having distributed, according to the various needs and circumstances of my simple and modest life in the service of the poor and of the holy Church which has nourished me, whatever came into my hands—and it was very little—during the years of my priesthood and episcopate. Appearances of wealth have frequently disguised thorns of frustrating poverty which prevented me from giving to others as generously as I would have wished." (*Journal*, Spiritual Testament, p. 343.)

He always felt a religious reverence for his "humble folk"; he always respected their state of honoured poverty, even when, without failing in the Gospel spirit, he might have made their circumstances more easy. But this was never, either for him or for his brothers, a source of sacrifice or scandal. Fidelity to their origins was an obvious thing for them; it was a natural homage to pay to something that is of worth in itself and by itself, and which, even considered by earthly standards, can be offered no better alternative. The temptation of nepotism never touched him, and this not only because he was anxious to honour the Church with a totally disinterested service, but also because, we must believe, he considered the simple life as a treasure to be guarded, in his family and in his own private way of living, even when high office obliged him to give up outward appearances of simplicity.

Madame Adzhubei noticed that his hands were those of a peasant, but this was true not only of his hands but also of his tastes, manners and even his way of looking at people, with those flashes of good-humoured shrewdness which country people acquire and keep, nobody knows how. The letter to his brother

Severo, written in the Vatican on 3 December 1961, is a master-piece in every sense of the word, but above all a masterpiece of wholesome and robust simplicity. From beginning to end it seems to be accompanied by a smile of good-natured shrewdness, which is barely concealed, and heightened by the contrast, of which the writer was well aware, between the pontifical pomp and the brotherly camaraderie of two peasants who, in spite of their widely differing destinies, had preserved the same inherited wisdom.

Now all that is over, it may be said that the Pope's brothers have been an honour to him: they struck no attitudes, they re-mained fixed in their ancient style, without allowing themselves to be flustered by the "wing of history" brushing them as it swept by. They came to take their leave of him when he lay dying, and then returned to their accustomed toil, leaving the world shaken by unprecedented emotion. It is easier to understand now why Pope John was so grateful to his family, his native village, his Christian countryside! He was right to recognize God's providence in the solidity and wide extension of the roots which bound him to his land: "when the root is healthy the tree grows vigorously even among stones!"

Many of us say that sociological Christianity, that is the Christianity of large compact masses, is about to come to an end, and that, when all is said and done, this end should not dismay us, because religion becomes so much more alive and productive of good when it is entrusted to the free choice of the personal conscience. And perhaps the future will prove us right. But, when we think of Pope John, we cannot deny the power for good which derives from a Christian habit of life observed by a whole com-munity, upheld by ancient traditions of ingenuous but living devotions. On his death-bed Pope John was still reciting prayers he had learnt in his childhood, and still pondering the truths of religion according to the ways and the images dear to his own people. His spirituality retained, as it were, its local colour, and although he was not unfriendly to movements of theological reform, and indeed made himself, with the Council, the initiator of a modification of theological formulae "so as to bring them into line with modern literary language", he did not himself suffer from intellectual unrest: he remained faithful to the saints of his childhood, even to those who, in the hierarchy of the universal Church, have been assigned but a modest place.

3. "I LOVE LIFE"

From such a man, who had lived the history of the Church for half a century in a position of great responsibility and wide-ranging vision, we might have expected greater attention to the problems of Catholic culture. From the time of the first modernists—Bonaiuti was a school-fellow of his—to that of the chief representatives of the New Theology, he had been in direct contact with the most dramatic developments of the Catholic intelligence during the twentieth century.[2] Yet, the nature of his Christianity never assimilated the theses and concepts by means of which a numerous band of theologians and pastors attempted, with diverse results, to renew the Church. His modernity was part and parcel of his human integrity: remaining true to himself, to his native region and his own experiences, he reached, along most original and therefore surprising ways, the hearts and minds of the men of today. His fondness for conversation, for travelling, for informal and exploratory walks, with him took the place of the reading and doctrinal polemics beloved of intellectuals. One might say that his long life did nothing but interpret and develop, with thoughtful understanding, the miracle of his early childhood, in which, by virtue of his peasant blood and peasant wisdom, the

[2] During his stay in France he showed no thorough understanding of the movement for theological and pastoral reform which was particularly active in those years. Robert Rouquette, as we have seen (see p. 42), gives firsthand and circumstantial testimony to the "integralist" attitude of the Nuncio Roncalli. Cardinal Suhard *"le craignait; il sortait sombre et inquiet de ses entrevues avec le Nonce"* (loc. cit., p. 11). As for Teilhard de Chardin, "it was he who said to me one day the famous words which were repeated all over Paris: 'This Teilhard . . . could he not have contented himself with his teaching of the catechism and the social doctrine of the Church, instead of raising all these questions?'" On the other hand, his biographer Leone Algisi (pp. 232–55) describes him as an Apostolic Nuncio much more open to the new problems of science, and relates, among other episodes, that of a "young Bergamasque priest, a student of ethnology at the Sorbonne, who one day found himself entrusted with the reading of the university lecture notes of Père Teilhard de Chardin" (p. 38) and adds that, to set the Nuncio's mind at rest concerning the great scientist it was enough for him to know that among his defenders was Cardinal Saliège. But most probably, as we have already said, the story of Mgr Roncalli in Paris will be retold on the basis of more exact and reliable documents.

treasures of grace and nature were fused into one. The hands which first caressed him were hardened with toil; the songs which ever afterwards resounded in his ears were songs of the people; his first discoveries of the world around him were made exploring the paths of his own countryside.

In Paris he was warned by Pius XII not to indulge in walks that were unbecoming to the dignity of an Apostolic Nuncio;[3] in Rome, after a slight hesitation, he broke out of his Vatican prison, taking advantage of every pretext to issue forth from the Leonine walls. (Some people called him "John outside the Walls"!) We read in his letter to Severo: "Our Giuseppe is right when he says to his brother the Pope: 'You are a prisoner *de luxe* here; you cannot do all you would'."

It is not irreverent to suspect that his pastoral sorties corresponded also to a physical and psychological need to escape from the somewhat artificial immobility of the Apostolic palaces. An eyewitness relates that during his journey to Loreto and Assisi he remained at the window of the train, looking at the sunlit slopes of the hills with the eyes of one who has found again a treasure he had lost.

Barely a month before he died, on 4 May, he was speaking to Don Gnocchi's crippled children and in a moment of emotion broke through his habitual reserve and lifted the veil that covered his secret:

"They tell us that when we become old and very old we go back to being like children. How wonderful to become a child! If we do not do so, if we do not possess this simplicity, it is more difficult for us to enter the kingdom of heaven."

Teilhard de Chardin relates that when he was five years old he took a stone in his hands and cried out with passion: "Sacred matter!"; without any diminution of his priestly asceticism he understood that in that almost blasphemous cry was already fore-

---

[3] Père Rouquette assures us that Pius XII "*le surveillait de près et allait jusqu'à lui interdire formellement de faire des promenades à pied dans les rues*" (*loc. cit.*, p. 11). This information is confirmed by *Algisi* (p. 255): "It was reported from Rome that the Holy Father desired the Nuncio's constant presence in his official residence. This was true. Pius XII knew everything that was going on and preferred to see all proceeding as it had done in the Nunciature of Berlin in his own day, when his only relaxation had been a long drive outside the city on Saturday afternoons."

told his great human and Christian vocation. I believe that the moral and religious figure of Pope John was already complete when he was ten years old. In him everything was already in its right place: loyalty to his God and tender and cheerful loyalty to his own land had but one flesh and blood, and but one voice.

"Since I left home, at the age of ten," he wrote to his parents on 26 November 1930, "I have read many books and learnt many things which you could not have taught me. But those few things which I learnt from you at home are still the most precious and important, and sustain, enliven and enrich the many others that I learnt later on, in so very many years of learning and teaching" (*Algisi*, p. 326).

It is not hard to understand which were the few but precious things which he learnt in childhood, and to which he remained more faithful than to the books he read. First of all, I believe, he had learnt a chaste reverence for the reality of the flesh, for its fecundity, and even for its instincts. The purity of Pope John was, it was generally agreed, extraordinary, but it was not that purity which old men owe to nature itself. It was the purity of childhood which remained unaltered and uninterrupted until old age. There was nothing in that candour of the embarrassment or fear which virginal men generally feel when brought face to face with the rites which prepare, preserve and glorify the fecundity of the flesh. In fact, even in his involuntary gestures, he showed a joyful sharing in the holiness of mother nature, a benevolent and respectful appreciation of that animal life which is the physical part of every motherhood and fatherhood. His secretary[4] tells us that one spring morning in the first light of dawn, Pope John, having recited the Angelus, went to look out of his window. Below lay St Peter's Square, solitary in the pale sunlight. One barely heard the soft murmur of the fountain. Two young folk (a married or engaged couple? who can tell?), holding each other's hand affectionately, were walking towards the façade of St Peter's. Pope John smiled and raised his hand to bless them. That spontaneous gesture revealed all his love of life ("Pray for your Pope," he said in an Audience, "because, let me say it quite

---

[4] Mgr Capovilla, *op. cit.*, p. 137.

frankly, I hope to live a long time yet. I love life!") and his human and Christian reverence for the man and woman who love each other, simply, without artifice or romanticism, as nature wills and as God wills, in short, as he had seen love with his child's eyes in the Roncalli home. At the conclusion of his letter to Severo he remembers, as a final message, "all the brides who have come to rejoice the Roncalli family and those who have left us to increase the happiness of new families, of different names but similar ways of thinking. Oh, the children, the children, what a wealth of children and what a blessing!"

4. SIMPLICITY WHICH WAS MODERNITY

We cannot deny that for centuries Catholicism has been accused of a fault which may not lightly be denied: the suspicion that all her attempts to make herself modern have been insincere, because of the diffidence she feels towards life, towards all that, in this world, grows and ripens in perfect joy. André Gide's accusations are unjust, but they represent a much wider and more ancient protest: that of Humanism against Catholic medievalism. The Church and the world probably need, not so much intellectuals capable of absorbing modern knowledge in the spirit of faith, as men who live their faith within the sense of life itself, in the same furrow in which their humanity lives and sings with joy.

The essential modernity of Pope John, which the world has grasped with immediate intuition, lay in the total sincerity with which he was able to accept the triumph of life, that of the child as well as that of the astronaut. I would not dare to say that he was modern in the common sense of the word: indeed, he was old-fashioned, in his language as in his psychology. He became modern because he was a man without reserves, and one who did not wish to impose many conditions on the world to make it worthy of the peace of God: the only condition was integrity, the fidelity of nature to itself, in short, life which, when it does not seek to deny its own profound impulses, is always in keeping with the moral law. His Christianity was not bred of distastes and fears, nor was it subject to frustration complexes.

The radical objection which the modern world has for some time raised against Catholicism is, as we said, this: In the Christian vision can the whole of life, can beauty, love and the conquest of space still find legitimacy and blessing? It is true that Christianity, in its preaching, makes much of the inevitability of death, pain and sin. It is understandable that, whenever our existence is flung against these rocks, religious feeling comes to the surface in a man's mind. But why should religion base its triumphs on human defeats? Why does it not succeed in being, not only a reason for serenity in death, but a reason also for the enjoyment of life?

The answers to these questions have been given long ago. But this time the answer came in living flesh and blood, not in a remote convent or in some humble Christian family, but actually in the Vatican, at the summit of the institutional Church. And it was an answer without artificiality or cunning, mild and defence-less, as living as a fruit on the tree, born of the earth, beneath the same rain and the same sun that ripen our common existence. All scholarly discourses about the antithesis between Christianity and Humanism will now have to be revised: even their appearance of truth has been dimmed, with the coming of Pope John, whose power of demonstration has perhaps been, in this respect, more effective and more universal than that elaborated, with the same intention, by Teilhard de Chardin.

"O sacred and blessed memories of my childhood! How precious they are to me in this sunset hour of my life, for they confirm the fundamental points of my search for holiness . . ." (*Journal*, 1961, p. 307).

We believe then that the fundamental quality in the holiness of Pope John may be seen in his fidelity to childhood, under-stood as the harmony between the supernatural and the natural, between the kingdom of heaven and the kingdom of this world. The perfect fusion between the two worlds remains, for most of us, a creation of the memory, which endows our early years with symbolic meaning. When we leave our childhood behind we must painstakingly rebuild for ourselves a less ingenuous Paradise and a world without the charm of a fairy-tale. Our "devotions" change also, acquiring theological seriousness and severity, our way of walking on this earth becomes more manly and more wary, because we are now aware of the extent to which the affairs of this world are abandoned to the malice of grown men. Pope John never really left his childhood behind; he brought to the throne of Peter the candour of his early years: he still prayed in the same way, and observed the work of Providence with a child's clear eyes. How he managed to do this, among people who were so different from him, in the midst of the wiles of diplomacy and the scorn of unbelievers is indeed a mystery!

We see, for example, how, on the eve of his death Pope John's paradise was still peopled with the saints of his childhood. "The devotions I learnt as a boy, at home, by the side of "*barba*" (great-uncle) Zaverio: Jesus in the Blessed Sacrament and the Sacred Heart, the Precious Blood, holy Mary, St Joseph, the three saints called Francis: Francis of Assisi, Francis Xavier and Francis de Sales, St Charles Borromeo, St Gregory Barbarigo, my Guardian Angel, the Holy Souls. . . ." (*Diario*, 20 May 1963).

There is no doubt that he was very much at home with the saints and without a shade of infidelity. He was always distrustful of "devotionalism" and had words of fatherly warning for a pilgrimage composed of devotees of St Anthony. But as for himself, in the world of his own private piety, he felt no need to become more up-to-date by abandoning the ingenuous piety of his old folk.[5]

As pope he was still very fond of statues of the Madonna, and took pleasure in remembering two of these during the last days of his life (*Journal*, 15 Aug. 1961, p. 314.)

On the feast of the Assumption I think with tender affection of Sotto il Monte, where I loved so much to venerate Mary represented in her two statues: the very devout robed

[5] His piety was simple but without sentimentality and without unwary mysticism, as his confessor Mgr Cavagna has told us. It was concentrated on his three great devotions: "the Name, the Sacred Heart, and the Precious Blood of Jesus". His first experience of the manifold cares of the Pastor of the Universal Church, he told the parish priests of the Archdiocese of Bologna on 21 June 1960, had given him the impression that some devout and pious souls were anxious to promote particular devotions, new titles of veneration and worship inspired by local considerations, and these devotions gave him the feeling that they "left too free a field to the imagination and not enough for spiritual concentration". For this reason he was fond of asking everyone to bear in mind all that is most simple and natural in the practice of Holy Church.

statue by Sansi at Brusicco, the church of my baptism, and the other fine and powerful statue by the sculptor Manzoni in the new parish church. This was a gift from the beloved parish priest Father Carlo Marinelli, one of the priests best known to me and most helpful in my ecclesiastical training, and very dear to my grateful heart.

This natural piety did not estrange him from the life around him; as for understanding the will of God, he expected to learn this not so much from statues as from what happened around him.

His way of speaking of the providence which guides the life of men showed not the slightest sign of conceit or presumption. He had learnt as a child that providence is at work in the stall as well as in the house, in sad as well as joyful events. From that time onwards he had always watched for its signs in the same way. When he was praying he could not detach himself from the thought of the world; instead of launching into the rarefied air of contemplation, he allowed himself, while still absorbed in God, to wander over the geographical map with the eyes of his spirit, as if he were turning over pages of his Missal:

> . . . Every now and then, while I am reciting the Rosary, I insert other intentions by the side of those you know already. Thus I retrace the path of my life. And I pray for my Bergamo, for my dear brothers in Bulgaria (oh, those ten years!), for the Turks and the Greeks. I see once more the eight years I spent with the French, who were fond of me, and whom I loved and still love so much. I see Venice once more, my own Venice, always near to my lips and my heart. And then I am here again, near to St Peter's and the Lateran. During the first years of this pontifical service I did not realize all that it means to be Bishop of Rome and therefore Pastor of the Universal Church. Then, as one week followed another, I came to understand it all. And I have felt quite at home, as if I had done nothing else but this my whole life long.

And if he dwells on the ways by which he was led to such great responsibility it is because, in the end, he perceives how fatherly and yet how strange and unexpected were the means used by God. His method of life was to keep in step with life itself: to hold firmly to the present, to accept what it offers: sorrows, friendships, new acquaintances and new separations, as if these were all forms of God's will working in our lives. We are woven into the web of history, and it is useless to wish to perceive the whole breadth of it: we must not lose the threads that pass through our hearts, that gather up and transmit our heart throbs. God will see to the rest. God comes into our lives through those events which seem fortuitous to us, but which, if we could but see them in the plan which secretly binds them together and makes them one unity, would seem to us what they really are: so many separate points of an uninterrupted and providential line. Hence the "spiritual positivism" of Pope John. Hence that way he had of scanning the horizon, sniffing the air, and casting the seed according to the mysterious intuition he had inherited from his own people. He did not care for prophesying: the future is all contained within the present, within this minute occasion not foreseen in any programme.

> Not to try to predict the future, indeed not to count on any future at all: that is my rule of conduct, inspired by that spirit of tranquillity and constancy from which the faithful and my collaborators must receive light and encouragement from the Pope, the head priest. . . .
> It is enough to take thought for the present: it is not necessary to be curious and anxious about the shape of things to come. The Vicar of Christ knows what Christ wants from him and does not have to come before him to offer him advice or to insist on his own plans. The Pope's basic rule of conduct must be always to content himself with his present state and have no concern for the future; this he must accept from the Lord as it comes, but without counting on it or making any human provision for it, even taking care not to speak of it confidently and casually to anyone. (*Journal*, 14 Aug. 1961, p. 313.)

This also is fidelity to the earth, to its free movement which, if we lacked Christian understanding, would seem to us fortuitous and sometimes absurd. "To live for the day" is also the motto of the worldly-minded. But, for the worldly-minded, the day brings to the mortal heart only its own mortality, the empty chain of its hours. But the man who is attentive to the message of the present, who knows that "chance" is the earthly face of Providence, knows that the day is the messenger of God; it is like a page of the Book of Life, brought to us by the wind, which we welcome like a love letter.

"Every day, like every month, is the Lord's hour: so they are all equally beautiful" (*Diario*, 12 Jan. 1939).

Few have known this as did the child of Battista and Marianna Roncalli.

"Like those good old Bergamasque priests"

I want to guard my faith carefully, like a sacred treasure. Most of all I want to be true to that spirit of faith which is gradually being whittled away before the so-called requirements of criticism, in the atmosphere and light of modern times. If the Lord should grant me a long life and the opportunity of being a useful priest in his Church, I want it to be said of me, and I shall be prouder of this than of any other title, that I was a priest of lively simple faith, solidly behind the Pope and for the Pope, always, even in matters not yet officially defined, in every detail of seeing and feeling. I want to be like those good old Bergamasque priests of old, of blessed memory, who neither saw nor desired to see further than could be seen by the Pope, the Bishops, common sense and the mind of the Church.

It will always be my principle, in all spheres of religious knowledge and in all theological or biblical questions, to find out first of all the traditional teaching of the Church, and on this basis to judge the findings of contemporary scholarship. I do not despise criticism at all, and I shall be most careful not to think ill of critics or treat them with disrespect. On the contrary, I love it. I shall be glad to keep up with the most recent findings, I shall study the new systems of thought and their continual evolution and their trends; criticism for me is light, is truth, and there is only one truth, which is sacred. But I shall always try to introduce into these discussions, in which too often ill-considered enthusiasms and deceitful appearances have too much to say, a great moderation, harmony, balance and serenity of judgment, allied to a prudent and cautious broad-mindedness. On very doubtful points I shall prefer to keep silent like one who does not know, rather than hazard propositions which might differ in the slightest degree from the right judgment of the Church. I will not be surprised at anything, even if certain conclusions, while preserving intact the sacred deposit of faith, turn out to be rather unexpected. Surprise is the daughter of ignorance. On the contrary, I shall rejoice to see God doing all this in order to make the pure treasure of his revelation more crystal clear and free from dross.

In general, it will be my rule to listen to everything and

everyone, to think and study much, to be very slow to judge, neither to talk too much nor to try to attract attention, and not to deviate by one jot or tittle from the mind of the Church. As Cicero said: "Time destroys the inventions of public opinion; truth remains and grows even stronger, and lives and lasts for ever."

Meanwhile I shall simply do my best to observe everything, appreciate everything and sympathize with everyone, and try not to probe too deeply into anything, especially into those matters from which my own piety and the feeling of the people may draw much spiritual advantage. Here in Rome, especially, I must take into account everything, however insignificant or even not fully confirmed by facts or sound reasons, in order to nourish my faith, never allowing it to grow stale, and in order to enrich it with a vigorous and whole-hearted determination and also with indescribable tenderness and appealing simplicity. This also is where the great counsel of Jesus must be followed: "Unless you turn and become like children, you will never enter the kingdom of heaven." (*Journal*, Dec. 1903, pp. 144–5.)

The thought of his mother

Istanbul, 6 March 1939

My very dear Signor M.,

My heartfelt thanks for your sympathy in my grief, for your letter of comfort and for your presence at the funeral at Sotto il Monte. Certainly I am delighted to confirm your membership of my family which, although humble, has characteristic treasures of good sense and of grace that leave me full of shame and admiration. Here is the last instance of this. My poor mother had told me that she did not want to die in my house though it was a fine house with every comfort. She said she preferred to go to her rest in the Lord in her family's rustic home, and to be taken thence for the last time to the church and then to the cemetery. It seemed to her that was most fitting for her condition as a humble woman of the people. And so her children did as she requested. She died at Camaitino surrounded by all the attentions and assistance that her far-away son could lavish upon her, and by the love of all her other most beloved sons and daughters. But on the eve of the solemn funeral the sad procession of her closest relatives accompanied her to her old home for the *Angelus*, and here her body passed its last night above ground: and so the next day it departed thence for the last blessing and the last dwelling.

As for my own sacrifice in not having been present myself to close those kind eyes which had opened mine to the light of nature and grace, I wish to unite this sacrifice with that which she herself had sustained, my dear friend, in never having known the caresses of her own mother. Her blessed mother's death in the act of giving life to her was the mystery of grace which presided over her whole life: it gave, and even now continues to give, its fruits, and one day she herself will understand it fully.

In the meantime I recover all my confident courage and I would like to share it with you. My sacrifice in having to stay far away, just at the last and most sacred moment, had already received its early reward in the fact that for fifteen years my dear mother was able to live with her son the Bishop and enjoy his company, during his holidays, and this meant a whole month every year. This was a blessing she much appreciated. At the end of the holidays she used to console herself, saying: "I am sorry he has to go away; but it is only right. After all, what should we do with a Bishop here in the country during the winter? And then, if he did not go away, we should think there was something wrong."

But enough, dear Signor M. While I remember and write this, my eyes fill once more with tears, but in the thought of her, of her simplicity and goodness, and her motherly protection from heaven, I find new inspiration and strength for my work. (*Algisi*, pp. 328-9.)

A Bergamasque in Paris

So I took everything calmly: one step after another, one public appearance after another: visits, words, silences, and patience, tranquil expectation and above all the continual diffusion of a spirit that is mild and serene and even a little amused at what is taking place before my eyes and is certainly worthy of admiration.

Three months have now passed since I left Istanbul, and began a new and unexpected life here; and now I feel as much at home

as if I had lived here for years. Even the experience of twenty years
in Eastern Europe, I do not know how, has made me more agile
and alert to keep myself free from the intrigues of the West. I
know what may happen to me and I hold myself ready for anything. Every time I leave my house I see monuments and records
of the mutability of men's fortunes in this variegated metropolis,
which certainly offers immense scope for every form of human
and priestly activity. The Lord's grace helps me always to remember my village and the fields where my own people work
with simplicity and faith, looking to the sun which is the splendour of God.

There are times when, with Don Abbondio, one could mourn
the fact that we are destined to end our lives in times of such sadness. But anyone who knows anything about history knows that
there is nothing new under the sun. . . . Today one can still hear
the Hosanna of the Feast of Psalms here, but who knows what
surprises the future may hold.

My relations with the members of the government are excellent. As for the political parties, we keep our distance. The
Nuncio is not tied to anyone's chariot: he is busy with his own
affairs and nothing else, putting into practice the advice: "Try all
things, hold on to what is good", which is a way of showing
respect for everyone. . . . I must say, moreover, that as my stay
here lengthens I am pleased to note that the French, although not
free from certain human failings, are an intelligent and distinguished race: even their excesses always preserve a refinement
which one must acknowledge. Certainly, the consideration shown
to this good Bergamasque, whom the Pope has sent them, who
has no pretensions of any kind, would cause me frequent embarrassment if I were not aware that even this would not be
worth while. So we live from day to day, trusting in God in
days of calm and for those days of trial which are bound to
come.

So much has been said, all leading nowhere. However, in
spite of the fear of the name of God—a little-ill will and a little
human respect—something has already been achieved, which is
after all of the essence of civilization.

My own affairs are going well, thanks be to God. I keep quite
calm about them, and watch them carefully. One after the other,
I see them fall into their right and fitting place.

I bless the Lord for the help he gives me in not complicating simple things, and trying rather to simplify the most complex. At least, that is what they say here, and I smile and let them say. I do not in fact find it easy to understand the mystery of official life here: great attention is paid to the lay aspect of existing civil institutions, combined with a respectful and even cordial friendliness shown to the Nuncio in all sections of this strange and crowded human agglomeration of the French capital. Sometimes I am reminded—may the Lord forgive me—of the miracle of St. Januarius at Naples. When the saint's head is set on the high altar in front of the phial of hard, dried blood, the latter begins to liquify. Perhaps in my case it has something to do with my determined effort not to forget my native village amid all these splendours, and with all the rest that comes to me by the mercy of God. (*Algisi*, pp. 202–3, 209–10.)

The geography of the Breviary

My dear Honourable La Pira,

I have received with much pleasure the letter you wrote to me on the Feast of the Nativity of Our Lady, and I found therein a ray of that light that shines in the heart of every man of good will, who trusts in God and shows mercy to his fellows.

I will confide to you that, since the Lord led me along ways of the world that brought me into touch with men and peoples of inspiration and civilization different from those of the Christian world (which are our great gift from God), I have distributed the daily "Hours" of the Breviary, so as to embrace in my priestly prayers, public and official, the East and the West, assigning part to the people of Greece, Turkey, and the "most noble Gallic race".

This will be enough to show you, my dear Professor La Pira, that our minds understand each other, and that I approve of your truly apostolic initiative.

In this way I am near to you, and I greet you. Affectionately and with my blessing,

Angelo Card. Roncalli

September 1958

"From Rome and back to Rome again; how can I thank you?"

Turning my thoughts in on myself and on the varied events of my humble life, I must admit that hitherto the Lord has spared me those tribulations which make the service of truth, justice and charity hard and distasteful for so many souls. I have lived through my childhood and youth without feeling the effects of poverty, with no anxieties about my family, my studies or situations of danger, such as my military service, for example, at the age of twenty, and again during the Great War, from 1915 to 1921.

Humble and unpretentious as I know myself to be, I was always warmly welcomed wherever I went, from the seminaries of Bergamo and Rome through the ten years of my life as a priest with my Bishop in my native city, and from 1921 until now, 1961, that is from Rome and back to Rome again, to the Vatican. O God, how can I thank you for the kindness always shown to me wherever I went in your name, always in simple obedience, not to do my own will but yours? "What shall I render to the Lord for all the things that he has rendered to me?" I know that my answer, to myself and to the Lord, is always the same: "I will take the chalice of salvation, and I will call upon the name of the Lord."

As I have already indicated in these pages, if and when the "great tribulation befalls me", I must accept it willingly; and if it delays its coming a little longer, I must continue to nourish myself with the Blood of Jesus, with the addition of all those great and little tribulations which the good Lord may send me. The short Psalm 130 has always made, and still makes, a great impression on me: "O Lord, my heart is not lifted up, my eyes are not raised too high; I do not occupy myself with things too great and too marvellous for me. But I have calmed and quieted my soul, like a child quieted at its mother's breast." Oh, how I love these words! But even if they were to lose their comfort for me towards the end of my life, Lord Jesus, you will strengthen me in my suffering. Your Blood, your Blood, which I shall continue to drink from your chalice, that is, from your Heart, shall be for me a pledge of eternal salvation and happiness. "For this slight momentary affliction is preparing for us an eternal weight of glory, beyond all comparison" (2 Cor. 4. 17). (*Journal*, 1961, pp. 312–13.)

The Pope's song

> *Quanto è soave al cuore*
> *il nome tuo, Maria.*
> *Ogni dolcezza mia*
> *da quel tuo nome vien.*
> *Che bella idea di amore*
> *da quel tuo nome appresi,*
> *che bei desiri accesi*
> *mi vien destando in sen.*

(How sweet is your name to my heart, Mary! Every joy I have is linked with your name, from which I learnt the beauty of love. You arouse such noble desires in my heart.)

These lines are the beginning of the first poem I learnt as a child, and I learnt it from the Second Reader then in use in the village school. I did my first year's schooling in the old village schoolhouse at Camaitino, the first house on the right-hand corner of the so-called Piazza, as you come from the Guardina. Opposite was the shop (*bütiga*) of Rosa Bonanomi and her sister Marianna, who was an invalid. That must have been in 1886 or 1887. The next year, with the completion of the new municipal buildings, the new school was opened at Bercio, and for two years I was among the first to attend it. (*Journal*, 1962, p. 324.)

Spiritual testament "to the Roncalli family"

Vatican, 3 December 1961

My dear brother Severo,

Today is the feast of your great patron saint, who bore your own real Christian name, which is Francesco Zaverio, the same as that of our dear great-uncle, our "*barba*", and now, happily, the name of our nephew Zaverio.

I think it is now three years since I last used a typewriter. I used to enjoy typing so much and if today I have decided to begin again, using a machine that is new and all my own, it is in order to tell you that I know I am growing old—how can I help knowing it with all the fuss that has been made about my eightieth birthday?—but I am still fit, and I continue on my way, still in good health, even if some slight disturbance makes me aware that to be eighty is not the same as being sixty, or fifty. For the present at least I can continue in the service of the Lord and Holy Church.

This letter which I was determined to write to you, my dear Severo, contains a message for all, for Alfredo, Giuseppino, Assunta, our sister-in-law Caterina, your own dear Maria, Virginio and Angelo Ghisleni, and all the members of our large family, and I want it to be to all of them a message from my loving heart, still warm and youthful. Busied as I am, as you all know, in such an important office, with the eyes of the whole world upon me, I cannot forget the members of my dear family, to whom my thoughts turn day by day.

It is pleasant for me to know that, as you cannot keep in personal correspondence with me as you did before, you may confide everything to Mgr Capovilla, who is very fond of you all, and speak to him just as you would to me.

Please bear in mind that this is one of the very few letters that I have written to any of my family during these first three years of my pontificate, and do your best to understand why it is that I cannot do any more, even for people of my own blood. But this self-denial too, that I impose upon myself with regard to my contacts with you all, does you and me more honour, and gains more respect and sympathy, than you can believe or imagine.

Now the great manifestations of reverence and affection for the Pope, on the occasion of his eightieth birthday, are at an end and I am glad because, rather than receive the praises and good wishes of men, I prefer to enjoy the mercy of God, who has chosen me for so great a task and who, I trust, will uphold me until the end of my life.

My own personal serenity, which makes such an impression upon people, derives from this: the obedience in which I have always lived, so that I do not desire or beg to live longer, even a day beyond that hour in which the Angel of Death will come to call me and take me, as I trust, to paradise.

This does not prevent me from thanking the Lord for having deigned to choose from Brusico and Colombera the man who was called to be the direct successor of the popes of twenty centuries and to assume the title of Vicar of Jesus Christ on earth.

Because of this choice the name Roncalli has become known, loved and respected all over the world. You are very wise to keep yourselves very humble, as I too try to do, and not let yourselves be influenced by the insinuations and tittle-tattle of the world. All the world wants is to make money, enjoy life, and impose its own will at all costs, even with violence, if this should unhappily seem necessary.

My eighty years of life completed tell me, as they tell you, dear Severo, and all the members of our family, that what is most important is always to keep ourselves well prepared for a sudden departure, because this is what matters most: to make sure of eternal life, trusting in the goodness of the Lord who sees all and makes provision for all.

I wish to express these sentiments to you, my beloved Severo, so that you may pass them on to our closest relatives at Colombera, Gerole, Bonate and Medolago, and wherever else they may be—I do not know the exact whereabouts of them all. I leave it to your discretion to do this. I think Enrica could help you, and Don Battista too.

Go on loving one another, all you Roncallis, with the new families growing up among you, and try to understand that I cannot write to all separately. Our Giuseppino was right when he said to his brother the Pope: "Here you are a prisoner de luxe: you cannot do all you would like to do."

I like to remember the names of those among you who have most to bear: dear Maria, your good wife, bless her, and the good Rita who with her sufferings has earned paradise for herself and for you two, who have cared for her so lovingly, and our sister-in-law Caterina who always makes me think of her Giovanni and ours, who looks down at us from heaven—and all our Roncalli relations and nearest connections, like those who have "emigrated" to Milan.

I am well aware that you have to bear certain mortifications from people who like to talk nonsense. To have a pope in the family, a pope regarded with respect by the whole world, who yet permits his relations to go on living so modestly, in the same social condition as before! But many know that the Pope, the son of humble but respected parents, never forgets anyone; he has, and shows, a great affection for his nearest kin; moreover, his own condition is the same as that of most of his recent predecessors; and a pope does not honour himself by enriching his relations but only by affectionately coming to their aid, according to their needs and the conditions of each one.

This is and will be one of the finest and most admired merits of Pope John and his Roncallis.

At my death I shall not lack the praise which did so much honour to the saintly Pius X: "He was born poor and died poor."

As I have now completed my eighty years, naturally all the others will be coming along after me. Be of good heart! We are in good company. I always keep by my bedside the photograph that gathers all our dead together, with their names inscribed on the marble: grandfather Angelo, "*barba*" Zaverio, our revered parents, our brother Giovanni, our sisters Teresa, Ancilla, Maria and Enrica. Oh, what a fine chorus of souls to await us and pray for us! I think of them constantly. To remember them in prayer gives me courage and joy, in the confident hope of joining them all again in the everlasting glory of heaven.

I bless you all, remembering with you all the brides who have come to rejoice the Roncalli family and those who have left us to increase the happiness of new families, of different names but similar ways of thinking. Oh, the children, the children, what a wealth of children and what a blessing! (*Journal*, pp. 334–7.)

CHAPTER SIX

Holy Folly

I. INEXTINGUISHABLE MIRTH

"WITHOUT a little holy folly the Church will not enlarge her tabernacles": this is a phrase which, according to *Algisi* (p. 245), Mgr Roncalli often repeated. He was quite convinced that the strict guardians of protocol and the suspicious Cartesians among the theologians did not approve of his way of expressing himself, or of his behaviour, which did not conform to diplomatic conventions. It was perhaps providential that almost his whole career took place in the frontier zones of the Church, among the Orthodox of Bulgaria, the Mussulmans of Turkey and the *libertins* of Paris, that is to say, in places more or less removed from canonical supervision and therefore exposed to the stimulating effect of the world that is alien to the Church, an effect which greatly fosters the growth of the imagination. Thus, without compromising himself, he had the opportunity to give free expression to his sense of humour, of which he made a screen and an instrument for the holy mirth of his soul.

Ever since his youth he had had good opportunities to indulge his native good humour, and particularly during his long and filial association with Mgr Radini Tadeschi.

"He has been the pole star of my priesthood", he wrote of him. "He was naturally more inclined to point out merits than to exaggerate defects. He treated everyone with the greatest respect. His conversation was delightful, enlivened with unexpected witticisms. He was no despot. He wished all the various energies around him to make their own contributions and accept their own responsibilities. He was discreet. There seemed to be in his soul an inextinguishable mirth."[1]

[1] Quoted by H. Fesquet, *I fioretti di Papa Giovanni*, Borla, 1963, p. 147. (English trans., *The Wit and Wisdom of Good Pope John*, London, 1965.)

The Catholic Church needed this inextinguishable mirth. "Blessed be this Pope who has made us enjoy the world!" exclaimed the then Cardinal Montini, as soon as he heard of the death of Pope John. And some days later he explained at greater length: "Every one of us has felt the charm of this man and has understood that the affection which surrounded him was sincere; it was no fashionable enthusiasm, nor was it inspired by superficial motives. It was a secret which revealed itself to us, a mystery which absorbed us; it was perhaps a perfectly simple combination of two qualities, truth and charity, which shone with its magic power before our amazed and delighted eyes."

The combination of truth and charity is not rare among the Pastors of the Catholic Church; what is more rare is its irradiation, because generally it is not so well and so prudently expressed, and still more because it lacks those appealing accompaniments which had a "magic power" in Pope John. Through him we have felt ourselves freed from centuries-old complexes and, above all, from a sort of inherited melancholy which, even when it assumed the conventional forms of sacred solemnity, was still merely melancholy. For centuries the Church has lived on a war footing. She has not lacked truly great popes, equal to their tragic times. The first half of this century was spent between one war and another, which left in the air an odour of gunpowder and putrefaction, and in our hearts a hard watchfulness. Our truths still went about armed: of course there was a heart in them, but their armour prevented us from hearing their heartbeats. It was even too clear, for us, that God needs men and all that men can do in his honour and defence, so clear as to make us forget that it is we who need God. We had seen the face of man disfigured by the wickedness of war: we had been taught that it is errors which cause wars. Therefore we were all determined to fight for the truth. But how? Everyone in his own way, the theologians with theology, the governments with legislation, the citizens with political programmes. We had grown solemn and suspicious, as is only to be expected when supreme values are at stake. Our idea of prudence was extremely rational: for example, to shake hands with an enemy was not a wise thing to do, because it suggested, to the pusillanimous at least, that the errors of our enemies were of no importance, and this is contrary to right reason. To cry aloud that we wanted peace at all costs was not wise because someone might fear that our openly declared and active will for peace would play into the hands of our enemies' armed belligerence. We seemed to have lost the sense of the distance between God and man, between his plans and ours, his ways and ours. Every now and then we read or heard about many saints who had loved to indulge in witticisms, and had laughed whole-heartedly at the ridiculous solemnity of human greatness. But these were like flowers of long ago, which had remained as if by chance in the clefts of our imposing bastions. Military seriousness was our common duty, and without taking into account any diversity of opinions.

Those who begged the Church to open out more towards the world begged this with impatience and irritation, with the mentality of conspirators. The progressive wing was dismayed by the fear, secretly diffused, of denunciation and persecutions. This fear fostered a psychology of passive resistance, like that of a secret society, which was even shown in the language used, full of esoteric overtones and enigmatic expressions. Today we have the clear impression that the progressives were unaware of the relativity of methods and the equivocal nature of modernism. Pope John had no great fondness for the progressives, perhaps because of their incapacity to see the funny side of their own ideas and programmes. Paraphrasing Pascal, we might say that one cannot be a modernist without laughing at modernism. Too many progressive ideologies smack of this incapacity for laughter: they accept as absolutes mere fragments of history and attribute the authority of principles to what are mere inductive generalizations. But the traditionalists too lost their sense of proportion. In them also fear of anything new extinguished Christian cheerfulness of heart, and they too attributed a mystical significance to purely human events, and saw the advance of the powers of darkness even when there was no question of anything more than a certain sociological reform of Catholicism.

When Angelo Roncalli became Pastor of the Church, there was a moment of general perplexity: which side would he take?

Then we seemed to understand: neither side. He placed himself on a higher plane, freeing both parties from their exasperated state, and using to good effect his own cheerful serenity.

> The man who has faith [he told the Sacred College on 17 March 1963] does not tremble; he does not rush into decisions, he does not alarm his fellows. . . . The spiritual serenity of this humble servant of the Lord draws continual inspiration from this; it does not derive from ignorance of men or of history, nor does it close its eyes to reality. It is a serenity which comes from God, the wise director of all human vicissitudes, whether the extraordinary occurrence of the Ecumenical Council or the ordinary onerous task of governing the universal Church.

If faith fails, the source of true serenity fails too, and there creeps in the "concealed pride" of those defenders of the Church who, fearing her defeat as if she had been forsaken by God, begin to make use of every means, sowing seeds of panic and presumption. Or there appears the anxiety of the innovators who, in spite of their boasted knowledge, are ignorant of the true signs of the times and full of defiant zeal, as if the Divine Redeemer needed their assistance.

> No matter how much events seem to be working against the good of the Church I must preserve a perfect tranquillity, which however will not dispense me from grieving and from imploring that "thy will be done on earth, as it is in Heaven".
> I must beware of the audacity of those who, with unseeing minds led astray by secret pride, presume to do good without having been called to do so by God speaking through his Church, as if the divine Redeemer had any need of their worthless co-operation, or indeed of any man's. (*Journal*, 13 Aug. 1961, p. 310.)

All true reform of the Church is born of faith, which is disposed to remove mountains, walk upon the waters, or cast wide its nets in spite of all disappointments.

Pope John removed mountains simply because he had faith: by faith he overcame, if not the physical laws of nature, at least the laws of history, obtaining the greatest success by the humblest means. His unalterable cheerfulness sprang from an inner furnace, in which his sound inheritance of flesh and blood was fused with his serene faith in God.

2. THE WISDOM OF CHEERFULNESS

Among the gifts of nature is also that of a sense of humour. This springs from the intuitive sense of the relation between an ideal proportion and its actual distortions, and is therefore the hilarious triumph of reason over the ridiculous solemnity of human affairs. On the natural plane it is a liberating energy, especially when it flows through the midst of our serious affairs, our proud records, and the juridical principles to which we cling because of our fear of life. Its purpose is not to destroy values, but to reduce them to their just proportions. If this sense of humour is possessed by a truly humble man, then it acquires also a quality of refinement which makes it no less penetrating but less pungent, more gentle. Pope John's light-heartedness was a natural gift, used and ennobled by charity.

For the jubilee of his priestly ordination he chose for the motto of his illustrated souvenir the words from Scripture: "Lord, teach us to count our days, so as to obtain the wisdom of the heart." He who has learnt always to bear in mind the brevity of life has already a reason for a wise sense of humour. Even in the midst of the greatest honours, Pope John seemed to remain obstinately apart from them, like any ordinary man; he looked on ceremonial pomp from outside it, so much so that, when death came, it found him like any other man, stripped of papal grandeur.

"The sense of my worthlessness and nothingness has always been good company for me, keeping me humble and serene." He wrote this in 1925, the year of his episcopal consecration. He always found it quite natural that few should hold him in any consideration.

"I do not deserve the Holy Father's consideration," he wrote from Istanbul when he heard rumours that he was destined to the high honour of the Archbishopric of Milan or Turin. And he meant what he said. Ambition inspired him not so much with moral repugnance as with amused compassion; he felt it was ridiculous, although during his long career he had come up against every kind and degree of it. As he gradually found himself higher and higher on the hierarchical ladder he could not make out why anyone had ever thought of him, and although he disliked that cowering humility that conceals pride behind its demure protestations, he never failed to make others aware of his sense of unworthiness, and to seize the chance for a quiet smile at himself and the vicissitudes of humanity.

How can we forget the verse of Merlin Cocai which he dared to quote in a letter written to Mgr Bernareggi on 23 March 1945, shortly after his appointment to the Nunciature of Paris?

> Feeling myself suddenly, like Habbakuk, seized and transported from Istanbul to Paris has been for me too like a sort of enchantment. Although for my own interior discipline I remembered the verse, I believe by Merlin Cocai: *ubi deficiunt equi trottant aselli* (where there are no horses you have to use donkeys), yet I could not deny to myself that the leap was great, and all the more so because it would have seemed to me quite impossible, and I should certainly not have had the courage either to conceive it myself, or desire it. My amazement grew when at the Vatican, where I called for a few hours, I heard in the Secretary's office that my nomination came from higher up; the Pope spontaneously informed me, perhaps for my encouragement: "It was I, Monsignor, who thought of you; it was I who decided, and no one else." (*Algisi*, pp. 194–5.)

When he became the Vicar of Christ ("Oh, I am not worthy of this name, I the humble child of Battista and Marianna Roncalli!") his amazement was extreme, but did not cause him any embarrassment. He continued to smile, as if amused at the trick God had played on the wise men; he was ready as ever to see the funny side of things, and jested about his new vestments, worthy of an "Eastern satrap", and when he was borne on his *sedia gestatoria* remembered his mother and imagined her exhorting her son with a characteristic gesture not to take himself too seriously. He cracked jokes about his brothers who, even if he had made them princes, as someone suggested he should do, would always have remained the peasants they so clearly showed themselves to be. In short, even then he could not bring himself to play the serious grown-up. The amazement became general and the whole world heard about it. Even those who, at first, could not disguise their disquiet when faced with this pope who did something original every day, at last perceived the humble candour from which this unalterable cheerfulness drew its inspiration. But the humble candour was also something more: it was a profound wisdom of the heart which, still smiling, found the true proportions within the tangles of artificiality, and quietly, without any fuss, restored to the character of the papacy the sublime humility of its essence.

3. FREEDOM FROM FORMALITY

As one day followed another, within the depths of our bewilderment there was taking place the unforeseen thaw of traditional rigidities, which were more alien to the spirit of the Gospel than we had realized. Anti-formalistic attitudes had indeed, in recent times, gradually become more frequent in the Church. In those attitudes there was this element of truth, the need once more to grasp the essence of things, that essence which remains quite unknown to those who forsake the natural rhythm of life to lull themselves with schemes or formulae and canons; but there was also, and this was unhealthy, the polemical spirit, which condemns old forms out of hand without having anything to put in their place, except new forms less tested and proved by tradition. Pope John was not an anti-formalist; imbued as he was by the spirit of legality—which is, even when it does not seem to be so—the defence of life as a supreme value, he knew how, with this end in view, to hold himself detached from laws without transgressing them. He said, for example, of Canon Law: "It is an imposing mountain, but one can always find a little tunnel which allows us to pass underneath it."[2] He got the better of formalism,

[2] Roger Aubert, "Jean XXIII, un 'pape de transition' qui marquera dans l'histoire" in *La Revue Nouvelle*, July-Aug. 1963, p. 19. The article deserves to be read in its entirety, also because the judgment of a great historian of the Church such as Aubert is more surely free from partisanship.

by defeating the spirit in which it is rooted, that is spiritual lassitude, which in its attachment to the letter of the law prepares and conceals a "colourless and wearisome old age". More than anything else he feared the old age of the soul, which freezes the inventive powers of the spirit, inducing it to cling to the false solidity of formulae: formalism is often a sign of despair.

It seems to me of the greatest importance, in this connection, to consider the acute diagnosis of formalism made by Pope John in a congress held at Mendola in 1956, while he was still a Cardinal, and repeated word for word in his speech of 19 February 1963 to the members of the *Convegno di Orientamento Pastorale*:

> The life of a priest in our own times is quite different from what it was in the past, and is exposed to new and seductive temptations: the attraction of positions and offices, and the tendency to a certain acquiescent serenity, with little zeal and little fervour for souls. And so it happens that instead of praying together, to the common edification of the faithful, instead of singing with joy in the light of day, it is easy to be overcome with fatigue; it is easy to find words only to mourn for ourselves and to indulge in complaints about others that are neither charitable nor pious. Oh, what a penance it is to have to live with some of our brethren, who are always talking about what is merely the exterior form of priestly activity and barely conceals an eager anxiety and ambition, not always veiled or modest, for promotions, for higher or more distinguished office: a habit of turning everything into a minor key, thus hastening the preparation of a colourless and wearisome old age. (*Scritti e discorsi*, vol. IV, p. 98.)

His own old age instead was so full of colour and so exhilarating that we almost seemed through him to have rediscovered our own youth. Since his death many forms of Catholic life are still left standing merely because of the charitable respect with which he treated them, but they are evidently destined to fall, since he took away from them, without arguing about it, all justification. Now it is possible for popes to plan reforms of the Curia and abolition of the Court of Nobles; they may go as pilgrims all over the world, they may go into private houses, into hospitals, into the suburbs, without arousing any astonishment. The prison of set forms has been broken open—and this not merely in the highest spheres of the Church—and it is worth repeating that it has been broken open without a blow having been struck, through the extraordinary youthfulness of spirit which, for five years, shook and crumbled resistance, from *inside*. Now it is easy to find the patience to bear what only yesterday seemed unbearable. Once the loophole has been found, bit by bit, "giving time its chance", as he was wont to say, the barrier of the ancient forms will fall, and will be reconstructed with new proportions and functions.

We found ourselves [Carlo Betocchi wrote with poetical acumen[3]] escaping from the formulae into which our faith so often fits itself. These formulae, we must admit, sometimes come to us from our pastors who, perhaps even without being aware of it and in good faith, behave with us and speak to us above all else as teachers. This means that so often ours is a faith which we feel we live, certainly, but only as something which it is almost impossible to realize, so that in our desperation we are reduced to the selfish longing finally to leave everything far behind in order to realize it completely in compassionate death. Instead, with Pope John faith once more became surprising and full of lively affections, like the faith of those pilgrims of Emmaus who sat down once more at the table with Jesus, three days after his death, content to find their faith again, alive and true.

It was not an easy thing for everyone to accept, from the very beginning of his pontificate, such total confidence in the grace of God and the vital energies of man. It seemed as if the inevitable result would be confusion, or worse: it was like disqualifying the obedient sons who, bound by their loyalty to orders previously received, could hardly be expected to understand such an uninhibited flow of youthful vigour. "This is the doubt that occurs to me," wrote one of these, a layman in a prominent position, a

[3] In *Il Popolo*, 12 June 1963.

few days after Pope John's death,[4] "is there no loving recompense
due to the obedient sons, as well as the special love and affectionate
understanding that is shown to the disobedient or restless children?
And when these obedient sons are asked to make sacrifices, to
share, to accept, to promise and to renounce in the name of objec-
tives and judgments defined as necessary, which are later on
abandoned or modified, would it not also be an act of charity to
understand the anguish and the dramatic alternatives set before
these obedient children?"

4. THE WISDOM OF THE HEART

Future events were not slow to prove the error of the "obedient son", stay-at-home and industrious, who murmured against
the Father who had killed the fatted calf and ordered dancing and
music for the prodigal son. If the testimony of the whole world
were not enough proof that the Father's folly was holy and the
anxieties of some sons selfish, it would be enough to point out
the approval given to Pope John by his successor and by the whole
Council, amid general rejoicing. It was right for us then to be
festive for five whole years. Before this our virtues had become
stale and wearisome, our zeal for the truth had divided us, the
good spied upon the good, the weak flattered the powerful, the
faithful sons had forgotten that the unfaithful children had been
too long away from home. Then this Father came along, and
taught us to love one another without scolding anyone, and taught
us this simply by offering each one of us the gift of his fatherly
love, which was whole and unreserved.

We had been thinking that reserve and solitude were necessary
to preserve dignity, and he had taught us that, as for dignity,
goodness alone is sufficient, and that the real joy of good men is in
being on equal terms with other men.

His was a goodness which we had almost forgotten, accustomed as we are to distinguishing between moral goodness,
which is one thing, and goodness of heart, which is another. But
no: goodness, when it is real and whole-hearted, makes the heart

4 Giovanni Gozzer in *Humanitas*, July–Aug. 1963, pp. 748–9.

reasonable and the reason warm-hearted, and even changes character. Born a peasant, he found himself directing the destiny of men, but showed no sign of satisfied ambition: the constant thought of the majesty of God led him to laugh at human greatness, not only false greatness but even true greatness, for this also is spoilt whenever it forgets to compare itself with the only really serious thing, which is God.

Goodness which is solemn has something unconvincing about it: perhaps it takes itself too seriously. There was no solemnity about his goodness; it reminded us all of the goodness of our grandfather, our father or our mother, that is of the goodness which dwells at the sources of our life and guards its beauty. For this reason everyone found his own self in him, and this was especially true of those who were not used to feeling themselves loved by the Church, with a love so warm as to be fatherly and motherly in the human sense of the words. Some attributed his cheerful goodness to his jovial temperament or, worse, to an ingenuousness incapable of grasping the complicated unfolding of men's story. Instead, he saw so shrewdly into hearts and their foolishness that, without the fire of faith, he would have been tempted to sterile scepticism, that sterile scepticism which he certainly knew so well!

He never fought against an enemy, but he won almost all of them over through his imperturbable faith in the all-powerfulness of love. He conquered evil with good, and when he did not succeed in this, at least everyone could perceive where evil is born and nurtured: in the hard heart which makes use even of truth to dispense us from charity. Pope John's good-heartedness never imperilled one jot of truth, although it accepted all the risks of charity. And, by so doing, he reawakened in the heart of every man, if not always faith, at least good will. All men, even those well bolstered with philosophies, understood that Pope John's appeal to good will was not a ruse to achieve other ends but sprang from a sincere faith in man, not in a man's truth or his capacity, but faith in that primary impulse of our being which is the desire for peace and brotherhood. It is right to distrust a flabby kindness of heart, which seems to live and prosper outside the intelligence or even in spite of it. But real goodness is intelligence itself, integrated in the full context of human energies; it is the *mens cordis*, the intelligence of the heart.

When we speak of the originality of this pope we shall be obliged to note that his originality was not expressed in that form and style by means of which we have for centuries been accustomed to measure a man's intelligence. He made his most brilliant decisions as if they were normal provisions, disguising their effective grandeur with a homely smile and joyful language. We may be sure that he was far-sighted; he measured our world in complete freedom from the conventional prejudices which seem to us to dominate the great men today who give us so much trouble and inspire us with such fear. We speak of little things with grand words; he spoke of grand things with humble words, and with the gestures of an old man in love with the past he traced the guiding lines of our future.

Now we have understood why that progressive spirit with which we were infected robbed us, and others too, of our peace: not because it was alive to the need for progress but because it was trying to open the ways of the future without having the key. Compared with him we all felt rather old and clumsy; those same things which we had conceived with pride in our hearts he brought to pass with simplicity and superabundant courage.

5. AGAINST SEPARATE THEOLOGIES

The truth was that the progressives, as we have seen, attempted to bring about reforms depending too much on human wisdom, seduced by modernism or trusting to the miraculous formulae of a new theology. Pope John was distrustful of theologians, old and young, not because he did not esteem theology, but because he knew only too well how easily the polemical spirit enters the theologian's way of reasoning, and never gets out once it has got in.

"It is the theologians who have got us into this difficulty," he said one day to an Anglican "Observer", "now it is for the ordinary Christians, like you and me, to get out of it."[5]

[5] *Church Times*, 7 June 1963.

He left to theologians the preparations of the schemata for the Council, taking care, as he had done for his great Encyclicals, that not too much use should be made of anathemas. A priest in high position, Robert Rouquette tells us, found him one day armed with a ruler, saying: "In this scheme there are thirty centimetres of condemnations!"[6]

Rouquette himself has given a precise explanation of this distrust:

> He was not an intellectual, although he has left us a precious mass of edited material; he was not a theologian and had no great fondness for theologians; he was not a bold spirit: I could quote many remarks of his made to me when he was in Paris; he was disconcerted by the contemporary exegesis which was totally dissimilar to what he had known in his far away youth; he was not a revolutionary by temperament: "One must give time its chance," he liked to repeat. But since he was totally without pride on behalf of himself or, which is more difficult, on behalf of the Church, very simply, tranquilly and I dare to say, naïvely, without worrying about the dismay he was causing to those who were lingering on the old ways, he followed the original ways of the most evangelical Christianity, that is the most traditional.[7]

One of the writers most interested in Pope John's judgments, Yves Congar, who at certain moments did not disguise his disappointment as a theologian, has recognized that in the Pope's almost instinctive decisions lay concealed an intuitive power of great theological significance:

> John XXIII acted less on the doctrinal plane than through initiatives which were suggested to him by instinct or by inspiration, and always in a certain style to which great importance must be attributed. This style, in fact, is a very different thing from the outward form, so characteristic and attractive, of some decisions and attitudes which might easily have been expressed in another way; the style was an integral part of these decisions, which were of such considerable consequence for the Church. The opening towards the world and towards "the others" was shown by practical gestures, and by the

[6] R. Rouquette, *art. cit.*, p. 16.   [7] In *Le Monde*, 5 June 1963.

power of this style of his that was at the same time pastoral, most human and sublimely evangelical, rather than by his speeches.

We were all amazed, we had not expected all this; but because until then no one had paid any attention to Mgr Roncalli. If, however, we read or re-read this or that speech of the Nuncio in Paris or the Patriarch of Venice, we shall find there already prepared, in their spiritual content, the great decisions of his pontificate.[8]

His whole pontificate, from the first day to the last, had this instinctive movement, from when he announced, amidst the general amazement, *"Vocabor Johannes"* (I shall take the name John)—and what wealth of purpose in this choice!—till when, on his death-bed, he suffered, though with the dignity of a pope, like any ordinary man: what a wealth of meaning in this smiling humiliation so cheerfully accepted! He accepted the pontificate and continued to follow the inspiration of his conscience, holding in little esteem a misunderstood spirit of traditionalism.

The idea of the Council, the greatest and bravest idea in the history of the Church for many centuries, came to him in a very simple way and he announced it, almost amused at the thought of the surprise it would cause, as if it were a thing of little importance, in ordinary language and his own natural manner. This indeed needed a "holy folly"!

This same holy folly was apparent in the style of his pontificate during which, as Cardinal Feltin wrote, "the spontaneity and daring of prophetic gesture were allied to the serene certainty of well pondered decisions. It seemed every time as if the Pope were assuming a personal initiative, but in reality he was responding to a profound inspiration, of which the Church and the world were well aware. That is why there was an immediate response to his actions, in all men."[9]

[8] In *Informations catholiques internationales*, 15 June 1963.
[9] *Cit.* in *Testimonianze*, no. *cit.*, p. 399.

"Pure refined joy"

The pure, refined joy which must always fill my heart finds its most sincere expressions in the humblest actions. I must take care then: it is not enough to bear vexations with patience of a sort, so that others may not notice anything; I must always feel within myself an indescribable gentleness and sweetness that will bring a smile to my lips, and an even brighter smile when I am trying hard not to lose my temper and feeling rather grim. In short, I must show a cheerful, smiling patience, not too solemn or there is no merit in it. "Jesus, meek and lowly of heart, make my heart like yours."

My obligation to aim at sanctification at all costs must be ever present in my mind, but it must be a serene and tranquil preoccupation, not wearisome and overmastering. I must remember it at every moment, from when I first open my eyes to the morning light till I close them in sleep at night. So, no slipping back into old ways and customs. Serenity and peace, but perseverance and determination. A total distrust and poor opinion of myself, accompanied by uninterrupted and loving union with God. This is my task, this is my labour. O good Jesus, help me. Mary, show that you are my Mother. (*Journal*, 1 Feb. 1903, p. 111.)

"Mortification and joy"

While reading that beautiful book by Father Faber, *The Blessed Sacrament*, I came across a thought which he develops very skilfully and which made a great impression on me. Among the flowers for the altar, that is, among the good results of a sincere devotion to the Blessed Sacrament, spiritual joy has the first place; this joy is a most important element of the spiritual life, the atmosphere of heroic virtues; it is courage, instinct, genius and indescribable grace. Joy is to be thought of as the true source of that liberty of mind which alone is able to unite the apparently incompatible qualities of the spiritual life, giving a freer rein to natural expressions of love, while remaining inseparably attached to mortification. In our joy we must be careful to keep our spirit mortified, and practise mortification in order to increase our joy.

I must therefore remain always and invariably happy, while

never for one moment desisting from self-denial. It is self-love which stunts the growth of the spirit and saddens us; self-denial restores life, serenity and peace.

The saints are always gay and monks and nuns so cheerful because, like St Paul, they chastise their bodies and subdue them, without mercy and with great discretion. He who denies himself is happy with a purely heavenly joy. (*Journal*, Dec. 1903, p. 143.)

"I smile and pass on"

There is no lack of rumour around me, murmurs that "greater things are in store". I am not so foolish as to listen to this flattery, which is, yes, I admit it, for me too a temptation. I try very hard to ignore these rumours which speak of deceit and spite. I treat them as a joke: I smile and pass on. For the little, or nothing, that I am worth to Holy Church, I have already my purple mantle, my blushes of shame at finding myself in this position of honour and responsibility when I know I am worth so little. Oh, what a comfort it is to me to feel free from these longings for changes and promotions! I consider this freedom a great gift of God. May the Lord preserve me always in this state of mind!

This year the Lord has tested me by taking some very dear persons away from me: my sweet, revered mother, and Mgr Morlani, my first benefactor; Father Pietro Forno, my close collaborator in the *Atti della Visita Apostolica di San Carlo*; Father Ignazio Valsecchi who was curate at Sotto il Monte during those years when I was at the seminary at Bergamo before going to Rome, 1895–1900; all are gone. And other acquaintances and very dear friends, especially my Rector, Mgr Spolverini. The face of this world is changing for me now. "The appearance of this world is altered." This thought must encourage me to become familiar with the world beyond, thinking that soon I may be there myself. My beloved dead, I remember you and love you always. Pray for me.

I have made my annual confession to Father Châd and I am at peace. To prepare myself well I celebrated Holy Mass and assisted at another Mass, and then got on to my knees, penitent and ashamed. "I am alarmed at the thought of my sins and I blush before you; . . . do not condemn me."

My confessor tells me that the Lord is content with my service. Really content? Oh, if this were true! I am only partly content. It is long since the "election" of my state was made; even as regards the details of my life and activity everything is made clear and well-defined by undertaking to "spend and be spent for souls". I do not actually neglect my episcopal duties, but alas! how badly I do them! Above all I am tormented by the disproportion between what I do and what remains for me to do, what I would do but do not succeed in doing. The fault must be partly my own. My letters are too lengthy because I am afraid of sounding cold or unfriendly if I say less and because I think I can serve the interests of charity and Holy Church better by saying more.

I must try to find the way of discretion which lies between, and if there still remains something to torment me, I shall have to put up with it. (*Journal*, Nov. 1939, pp. 232–3.)

"*The love of truth: perpetual childhood*"

The love of truth. On the day of my episcopal consecration the Church gave me a particular mandate concerning it: "Let him choose humility and truth and never forsake them for any flattery or threats. Let him not consider light to be darkness, or darkness light; let him not call evil good, or good evil. Let him learn from wise men and fools, so that he may profit from all." I thank the Lord for having given me a natural inclination to tell the truth, always and in all circumstances and before everyone, in a pleasant manner and with courtesy, to be sure, but calmly and fearlessly. Certain small fibs of my childhood have left in my heart a horror of deceit and falsehood. Now, especially as I am growing old, I want to be particularly careful about this: to love the truth, God helping me! I have repeated this many times, swearing it on the Gospel.

The revelation of the uncertain and hidden things of divine wisdom comes by itself. The love of truth means perpetual childhood, fresh and joyful. And the Lord reveals his most sublime mysteries to children and conceals them from the learned and the so-called wise men of this world. (*Journal*, Nov. 1940, pp. 244–5.)

"*Holiness smiling amidst trials*"

"To my hearing thou shalt give joy and gladness; and the bones that have been humbled shall rejoice."

When we hear that we are forgiven: "The Lord has put away your sin", we are full of joy and gladness. We have felt this so often when after the absolution we rise from kneeling before our confessor, especially when we are in retreat or on some other more solemn occasions in our life. The joy is in our understanding, the gladness in our heart. This twofold sensation is expressed also in the renewed physical vigour and energy of our bodies: "The bones that have been humbled will rejoice." There are some most moving references to this in the Bible: Isaiah tells us: "Your heart shall thrill and rejoice" (Isaiah 60. 5), and we read in Proverbs: "a glad heart makes a cheerful countenance" (Prov. 15. 13).

The mystery of spiritual joy, which is a characteristic of saintly souls, is seen here in all its beauty and charm. The Lord leaves us uncertain about our eternal salvation, but gives us signs which suffice to calm our souls and make us joyful.

"It is the Spirit himself bearing witness with our spirit that we are children of God" (Romans 8. 16). I ask you: is this a small thing, to feel we are God's children? This confidence, which is often in our hearts without our being able to account for it, is the inexhaustible source of our joy, the most solid foundation of true piety, which consists in desiring everything that is full and loving service to the Lord. The essential is that this desire of ours should be prompt and effective. That it should be a source of enjoyment also, that is, of tender affection, sweetness, delight and joy—this is also important, but accidental and secondary. The realization of Our Lord's goodness to us, and of our worthlessness, makes us happy and sad at the same time. But the sadness is lessened as it becomes an encouragement for our apostolate in the service of all that is sublime and noble, to make Jesus known, loved and served, and to take away the sins of the world.

The thought of holiness, smiling amidst trials and crosses, is always with me. Interior calm, founded on the words and promises of Christ, produces the imperturbable serenity which may be seen in face, words and behaviour, the expression of all-conquering charity. We feel a renewal of energies, physical as well as spiritual: sweetness to the soul and health to the body (Prov. 16. 24). To live in peace with the Lord, to hear that we are forgiven, and in our turn to forgive others, gives the soul that feast of "marrow and fat" of which the psalmist sang, and brings the *Magnificat* constantly to our lips. (*Journal*, Nov. 1940, pp. 246–7.)

"*The perfect answer*"

"Make me love thy Cross." I must frequently repeat this invocation! Until now I have suffered too little. My own happy nature, which is a great gift from God, has kept me immune from those afflictions which accompany daring and generous spirits who hurl themselves like living flames into their zealous labour for souls. But it is only to be expected that, before the end of my humble life, the Lord will send me trials of a particularly painful nature. Well, I am ready: provided that the Lord, who sends me these, will also grant me the strength to bear them with calm, dignity and sweetness. I read in the life of the last Mistress of Novices, Mother Maria Alfonsa, of these Sisters of Sion whose pleasant hospitality I enjoy, that the spirit of this Institute consists in *abnégation souriante*. Oh, this motto is just right for me! I desire always to be ready for the interior sacrifice, which must be borne with humility, in a spirit of penitence and with a contrite heart—"a contrite heart in ashes" as is said of all the most famous characters of the Old Testament, and as we read of the most beloved saints of the New. It is enough to think of St Francis of Assisi, whose prayer was always the same: "O Jesus, have mercy on me, a sinner." To help me to acquire this contrite spirit I will be most careful and fervent in celebrating Holy Mass, which transports me to the garden of Gethsemane, to the most secret sanctuary of Christ's sufferings. I shall find the necessary trials also in the series of daily pinpricks for which I have to find a perfect answer through compliance, patience, resignation and justice, dignity and peace. (*Journal*, Nov. 1940, p. 255.)

CHAPTER SEVEN

The Public Fountain

I. AUTHORITY AS SERVICE

THE most remarkable of the simplifications brought about by Pope John is undoubtedly that which, in a few years and without any apparent rupture, has modified some traditional forms in which authority was exercised within the Church.

It has never been denied in Christian tradition that the ecclesiastic authority has for its aim the growth of charity, and that its exercise must as far as possible model itself on the example of our only Lord and Master, and that the pope must be the "servant of the servants of God". But in fact the progressive accentuation, within the Church, of her institutional aspects, in perfect correspondence with the development of the theology of the ecclesiastical powers which culminated in the First Vatican Council, had produced, within the canonical regulations, and above all in the practice of Catholicism, a logical development not very dissimilar to that which presides over the exercise of the civil authority. This, intended as it is for public service, aims not at persuasion but at effective power, and cannot concern itself with the reaction of the private conscience, which is instead the decisive factor in the pastoral relation. In fact civil society, during these last centuries, has reformed itself, conforming more to the ideal of the legally constituted State, founded upon the principles of the sovereignty of the people, of the equality of all citizens before the law, and of the separation of powers. On the contrary, the ecclesiastical society has, within very much the same period, been giving a theological definition and juridical character to its own monarchical structure, based on the divine origin of its jurisdiction. It was almost inevitable that, in its legitimate purpose of resisting the attractions, through analogy, of the new democratic régimes, it should have made sacred and intangible the habit and mentality of an authoritarian nature, which is not really evangelic in origin at all but rather feudal and seventeenth century. Since the pope is not only the successor of St Peter but also the sovereign of an independent State he may be considered at the same time as the heir to a service of love and the owner of temporal rights. So it came to pass that around the same pontifical fulcrum there revolved the order of priests, destined to spread the love of God throughout the world, and the organization of a Court, invested with temporal functions not dissimilar to those seen in the courts of princes. "But", as Paul VI said on 14 January 1964, "history is moving. The Pope, even if he finds in the sovereignty of the Vatican City State the shield and sign of his independence of any worldly authority, cannot and must not wield any other power but that of the keys of the spiritual kingdom."

With these words Paul VI put an end to the "secular collaboration" of the Roman nobility and freed the Church "from some old regal robes left on her queenly shoulders", to re-clothe her "in a more simple style, more in keeping with modern taste". And not only, as it is easy to prove, in keeping with modern taste, but with the original idea inspiring the authority of the Church, which is the idea of fatherly service, of the *diaconia*, service of the poor and needy.

Those who have any intimate knowledge and familiarity with prelates know well that, behind their exterior pomp and hieratical solemnity, throb fatherly hearts and a sincere and disinterested longing to serve. Certainly the popes who have followed each other in recent times had no liking for pomp! They felt and expressed the primary importance of pastoral service above all their other characteristic functions. Nevertheless, they had to bear with a long inheritance of customs, not only external but also psychological and mental, and practical difficulties in the way of making their personal fatherly intentions prevail over the complications of a system which was so vast, and in its nature so holy. There was also perhaps the cautious prudence which feared that, once certain traditional rules of government had been abandoned, the spirit of insubordination, due to the contagion of democracy, might get the upper hand. These and many other motives had, until Pope John came along, prevented even the slightest dismantling of the enormous "pyramid" referred to by one of the Council Fathers during the second session. The result was that those who lived outside this pyramid had very little opportunity of perceiving that the Church was something other than an organization for the strict control of consciences, deprived of any breath of liberty, and that the pope was, even apart from the spiritual purpose of his rule, very different from the princes of the great religious institutions: they thought he was a prince too, in fact the "prince" of the apostles, endowed with all the rights, all the powers and prerogatives which are attributed to the princes of this world.

And so, between the heart of the modern world and the true nature of the Church, which is the true nature of love, there remained, if not a wall, a velvet curtain which muffled the dialogue.

2. THE PASTORAL VOCATION

Pope John must have for long cherished a great desire to see the end of this misunderstanding, so that at last the primacy of love should be seen to shine before men's eyes without the screen of a secular type of authoritarianism. Otherwise how can we explain his choice of a name? It was so unforeseen, and the reasons given were such, that we are led to think that it must have been the result of long reflection, certainly disinterested, but closely bound to the whole story of his experience as a servant of the Church. In certain passages of his "Coronation speech" we seem to detect the discreet and humble reappearance of a long series of murmured protests which obedience had never allowed him to turn into polemical opposition, but which, in his inner soul, determined the shape of his pontificate:

> In fact some expect the Pope to be a statesman, a diplomat, a scientist, a social organizer, or one who is willing to accept all the forms of progress shown in modern life, without any exception. . . . We wish to make this clear, that we cherish as dearest to our heart our task of shepherd of the whole fold.

The other human qualities—learning, intelligence, diplomatic tact and organizing skill—may serve as an adornment and completion of Papal rule, but can never be substitutes. . . .

Note how the personal choice is here shown by his subjective preferences ("we cherish"), and by the objective reference to "Papal rule", which is of its own nature the mission of the Good Shepherd, and which must assume also the visible marks of the Good Shepherd: "great gentleness and humility".

Those who think that Pope John invented his pontifical style day by day, following the good impulse of his heart rather than a precise plan drawn up by his intellect, should re-read the speeches he made during the first days of his pontificate, and they will see that, under the appearances of intuitive improvisation, he set before himself and developed a design that was from the very start perfectly clear to him. Of course every pope has known that he was the universal shepherd of the flock of Christ. But it was not enough to know this or even to desire it. Pope John's vocation was to strip the pastoral character of the pope from all that had been superimposed on it, so as to restore it to its human and evangelical simplicity. He was always devoted to Pius X, the pope who was more like him than any other, precisely because of this simplicity which enabled him in such a different age and in the midst of much greater difficulties, to be the "parish priest of the world". Speaking of him, while still Patriarch of Venice, his words bore a clear note of prophecy:

> With every day that passes we are discovering Pius X anew, and the mysterious riches of nature and grace which far exceeded the singular aspect of his personal characteristic humanity, which caught the popular imagination, but which threatens to diminish his personality every time we hear him hailed as the "country parson" or as the "pious Pope", expressions in which the intended compliment seems to restrict the field of his witness, and of his prophetic genius. (*Scritti e Discorsi*, vol. III, pp. 651–2.)

Before Angelo Roncalli became pope his long diplomatic career had somewhat concealed him from our eyes, which are, moreover, so easily prejudiced against the man who represents to us more the power than the love of the Church. He too, perhaps, although he always sought to find, on the margins of his bureaucratic duties, opportunities for warm-hearted and fervent pastoral excursions, was convinced that he had for ever sacrificed to God the loftiest and purest of his priestly desires. On 3 January 1932 he wrote from Sofia this letter to a friend:

> You do very well not to give up the exercise of the priestly service. Oh, how I envy you for this! I hope the Lord will one day take into account the sacrifice I have been obliged to impose upon myself regarding this, for the last seven years. Oh, what an impoverished life is that of the bishop and priest reduced to being merely a diplomat and bureaucrat!
>
> As time goes on, and as my old Assumptionist Father who helps me becomes less useful because of his infirmities, I feel the need of a young secretary who would help me in so many matters that take up all my time. But when I think that a young priest, staying here, cannot exercise his ministry, I am afraid of the responsibility of calling him. Make the most of the possibilities granted you of preaching, hearing confessions, teaching the catechism and duly celebrating the Mass. All this is precious nourishment for the soul of a priest; it is a continual festival, and a means of winning merit and eternal glory. Generally speaking, a priest—even if he were a Consalvi—without a love for his ministry is savourless and worthless. (*Algisi*, p. 340.)

When he was sent to Venice as Patriarch he was at last able to give expression to his pastoral talent, thus realizing, in the most perfect form, the guiding idea of his whole life. When he presented himself to the Venetians he said of himself, in a lively speech full of serene and robust spirituality:

> The priest: *ecce sacerdos*. From my birth I have never wanted to be anything but a priest. Thus the humble son of the people was granted a wonderful mission that was to be for the people's good. The priest is to strengthen and enlighten souls: he is able to carry out this task because he himself feels the weight

of human frailty. . . . When you look at your Patriarch look for the priest . . . the Pastor: *ecce pastor*. A man of little worth, a humble priest, but above all a shepherd. Since I was a young priest my only ambition has been to be a country parson. . . . I shall get to know you all, but simply, without ceremony, with swift and silent steps. The shepherd's task is this: to count his sheep, one by one. (*Scritti e Discorsi*, vol. I, pp. 17–19.)

3. TRUE FATHERHOOD

"With swift and silent steps . . . to count his sheep, one by one": this well describes the manner of his pastoral zeal. When he became pope how could he continue to proceed with "swift and silent steps"? There was the barrier of the Vatican walls, and above all, the high unscalable wall of the convention which ordered the pope to stay within the city State. Instead he continued to move about, he enjoyed being seen and seeing the people —his sheep—with those bright wise eyes of his that made those he met feel they were old friends.

We are well aware that nowadays a pastoral activity, that is to be effective and modern, cannot do without an objective study of the scene of its labours and a scientific search for the most suitable means. In other times the pastor was at work within an atmosphere which was predisposed to Christianity or, at least, not alienated from it by psychological and doctrinal divisions. Even sinners lived within the framework of a Christian society and, even if they had lost grace, they had not entirely lost faith or the knowledge of the ways by which they could re-establish contact with the Church. But today the Christian message must reconstruct its own human premises, and must, to this end, adopt those tools which reason has found and tried. Pope John had nothing to say against this technique, in fact on several occasions he recommended it. But, in his own case, he contented himself with proving that technique can neither substitute nor foster the pastoral instinct, which must precede all study and all learned considerations, because it is simply the expression of a supernatural fatherhood. And what is this supernatural fatherhood?

It is surely a revelation of the love with which God has loved the world, a love which continues to show itself through the priest, by virtue of his Holy Orders. But, in order to be truly fatherly, love must make use of the resources of instinct, which in the priest must remain always at his disposal, for ever guarded under the clear gaze of abstinence and contemplative solitude. It is impossible to deny that quite frequently this fatherhood is to such an extent felt as something supernatural that it no longer has any natural characteristics: in that case its function is reduced to conventional gestures, bereft of creative impulse, and therefore destined for the conventional atmosphere of convents and for groups of strict parochial piety. When instead the fatherhood is felt as something natural as well as supernatural, that is, when it obeys the impulses both of grace and of nature, then the kindness of God is revealed to all men, a kindness which is severe and loving at the same time, unbending and yet tender, like truth when imparted by a loving mother.

Revelation gives us no guarantee that a pope's heart may be able to fulfil the requirements of charity with the aid of its own affectionate impulses. Charity finds its normal and objective expression in the power of the sacraments and the word of God. When this motherly power of the Church is allied to affectionate interventions prompted by the human heart, this astonishes and moves the whole world, as was the case with Pope John. It was clear that he loved not only good Catholics, but also the separated brethren, and not only those who believe in Christ but all men without distinction.

It was not that he did not take his own authority seriously, or forget its supernatural foundations. His special merit lay in having freed this authority from the rigid and discriminatory forms of its traditional exercise. And so he succeeded in diffusing, within the most rigid institutions, for which he had formal respect, something of a family atmosphere. Because of him the Church has become more friendly, more endowed with that *esprit de finesse*, the sensitiveness which is indispensable for a true understanding of this mortal life.

Pope John's cordiality was not only, as we have already said, a happy natural characteristic. Besides belonging to the spontaneity of a happy nature, it formed part of a moral quality that he had perfected by long and conscious effort. Truth triumphs through charity: charity reveals itself to men through goodness of heart. Those who exercise authority often cease to esteem goodness of heart, almost as if they feared to lose prestige and encourage the indifference of their subjects. It may be true that in civil institutions kindheartedness may be too subjective an element, which may in subjects facilitate a spirit of presumption and bring the law into discredit. But in the Church fatherly kindness is necessary in order that those who obey may not lose the sense of the real reasons for their obedience, reasons which are bound up with the charity of Christ. On 29 June 1942 Mgr Roncalli was writing from Athens, while the war still raged:

> Now the situation has much improved. It would not be quite exact if I were to compare my situation to that of Fra Felice and Fra Cristoforo at the hospice in Milan. But I can assure you that all fourteen works of mercy can be performed here. And the satisfaction felt by the soul, among all this misery and this self-sacrifice in circumstances which still preserve all the phosphorescence of Greek vanity, but which conceal bitter distress and poverty, sometimes becomes pure spiritual joy, the joy which springs from the "*intelligere super egenum et pauperem*", and which convinces us more and more that nothing in the world is more noble and honourable than spending oneself in the service of our brothers. Every time we suffer heat or cold in so doing our sacrifice seems light, for it is certainly by this way, the way of charity, and by no other, that there will be brought about that triumph of truth which in the end will save the world from divisions and conflicts, and give us peace. (*Algisi*, p. 347.)

Intelligere super egenum! Unless it is thus drawn towards the alleviation of human distress the mind of the Church becomes alienated from the spirit of the Gospel. Whatever may be said about the ways by which it will be necessary to reform the pastoral

life of the Church, every reform will still have to be subordinated
to certain laws which are more concerned with the order of being
than with the order of ways and means. These laws may be reduced to two: never to deal with the faithful through the heart
alone, because without the light of the mind the heart is already
corrupt or may be a corrupting influence; never to act only by
the light of the mind, because without the heart the mind can
save no one, and more often destroys.

Intelligent men (the "wiseacres", as he liked to call them)
thought little of Pope John, because he was "too kind-hearted".
But in his case it was the heart that thought, that made its plans:
it was a *mens cordis*, an intelligence of the heart. Every ruler, if
intelligent, has his plans, but it is not always the heart that inspires
them and translates them into action. The heart, as all rulers know,
is a weakness. But in an institution like the Church intelligence
without heart easily becomes fatal. Left to itself the intelligence
draws the pattern and then cuts round it. It matters little if it
cuts through living flesh: there is always the consoling pretext
that the truth must rank supreme. The intelligence of the heart,
instead, considers both the truth and the complications of life,
and adapts itself to one and another with gentleness and firmness,
just as God permits the good corn and the cockle to grow together, thus frustrating the impatience of his zealous servants. It
is the heart that makes the intelligence patient, adapts it to the
needs of men, and respects their liberties while guiding their
actions. So it was that Pope John, without doing violence to
anyone, went forward along the ways of charity, transforming the
Church according to the heart of God, and—and this was the
miracle—according to the heart of man. How can one better
describe such a miracle than by using one of his own delightful
and profound images?

"The bishop is always the public fountain" (*Diario*, 6 Feb.
1939, p. 29). "To my own poor fountain come all sorts of men.
My job is to give water to them all. If I make a good impression
even on the heart of a rascal this seems to me to be an act of charity
which in its own good time will bring a blessing" (*Diario*,
24 Feb. 1940, p. 32).

4. END OF A SPECIAL LANGUAGE

Can it be that through his being so meekly at the disposal of all and sundry the pontifical authority may have lost some prestige? Is it not rather true that he revealed to all the sources of this authority, and therefore its superhuman nobility?

Concerning Pope John's authority Don Giuseppe De Luca, a man who had some intimate knowledge of him, has written:

> John XXIII is tremblingly aware of his unique authority, but not intimidated by it. He knows it, he feels it, but I would not say he suffers from it. He puts all his trust in the Lord, on the one hand, and in the faithful, on the other. Nothing infatuated or fanatical about him; if anything he has an apologetic air, as if he were saying that it is true that he is the Pope, and he cannot deny it, but he did not and does not do it on purpose. . . .
>
> One of the strange secrets of John XXIII, seen by whoever observes and studies him with all the veneration and affection of a faithful Catholic, and in my own case of a priest, but with the sincere desire to see, understand and explain his personality, a personality now so well known to the general public and one which will pass into history—one of his secrets, I was saying, is this: that he forces us to seek in the most unexpected profundities what are after all his dominant qualities. The water of his spring rises God alone knows how far away, underground. . . .
>
> He speaks familiarly with all; he loves to talk and to listen to others' talk. Those who are waiting outside his room will think: My God, whatever can the Pope be saying? But the Pope talks with everyone in the same frank way, about the most simple things, the least sublime; he does not argue, he does not pronounce judgments or answers, he is not always pontificating. He receives and entertains all who come, in the intimacy which is his own. His own story, his humanity, what Ariosto would have called his "good taste in poetry", remain his own secret gift. He does not play the master or the writer, does not claim to be a learned and cultured man. In fact, he is annoyed with those who try this game with him and, even

when it is out of real affection for him and not in order to receive favours or honours but only to give him pleasure, plan undertakings, organizations, institutes, institutions, and other marvels. And so it comes about that in his pontificate he has brought back to life, from long ago, sometimes from centuries ago, certain themes which are among the most august of our two thousand years old Christianity.

He does not interrogate, he does not discourse, he does not even allow the conversation to turn upon those varied and most topical events which are rather like the noise made by the wind of time. He goes on studying in his old way, his mind works slowly and strongly, and all this in the shelter of his soul, a life spent in prayer and the work of his sublime ministry. And in this way his wisdom finds expression, unconsciously, in acts of government, neither more nor less than does his awareness (or better, his knowledge) of his unique authority.[1]

This total avoidance of all duplicity—even of that duplicity which seeks to hide in an art which has the same etymological root, diplomacy—produced that marvel which for a long time left us rather bewildered: I mean the language of Pope John. When we have all his writings at our disposal we shall perhaps be able to reconstruct, at least in part, the story of this great religious event. But, even while we know only what is general knowledge, it is easy to see how, with his coming, a language has ceased to be, a language which had centuries of tradition behind it and which must have weighed sadly upon the humble souls of many of his predecessors. He himself wrote in his *Journal*:[2]

It is commonly believed and considered fitting that even the everyday language of the Pope should be full of mystery and awe. But the example of Jesus is more closely followed in the most appealing simplicity, not dissociated from the God-given prudence of wise and holy men. Wiseacres may show disrespect, if not scorn, for the simple man. But those wiseacres are of no account; even if their opinions and conduct

[1] Don Giuseppe De Luca, *Giovanni XXIII*, Ed. Morcelliana, Brescia, 1963, pp. 17-20 *et seq.*
[2] Page 309: 13 Aug. 1961.

inflict some humiliations, no notice should be taken of them at all: in the end everything ends in their defeat and confusion.

It is generally observed that, while the language of the Bible is still today a perfect vehicle for the intimate language of the soul, which, when it deals with absolute values, is neither ancient nor modern, the language of the popes had acquired the impassive style of official documents, never showing a gleam of fantasy, or realistic illustration by means of parables: it had been lucid without being clear, reasonable without being natural, in short, far removed from the language of common man. It was not that Pope John succeeded in every one of his speeches in freeing himself from the conventional models which have become obligatory in the Catholic hierarchy, but little by little, that is, as he perceived how willingly the people responded to his fatherly improvisations and to his affectionate conversations, he returned to his own native style, inflicting considerable distress on academic formalism, which exists, alas! even in the ecclesiastical world.[3] He took no notice of the faithful admirers of long Latinized verbiage and, brushing aside all the traditional textbooks, he drew his language from his experience of life and from the very idiom of revelation. The Gospel images, however, when reported in the usual way, rarely arouse feeling worthy of their meaning because of the patina of age which now covers them. They need—and this was a stroke of genius on the part of Pope John—a touch of fantasy,[4] one of those slight variations by means of which our love binds together the ancient image and our own living memories, plucking the truth from its original context to insert it into the newly woven fabric upon which the spool of tears and laughter is still moving to and fro.

Among all the other reasons we have for being grateful for

---

[3] We find in a reported account of a general Audience this (really unusual!) interruption: "At this point, as a small child showed some signs of restlessness, His Holiness said affectionately: 'You see, in his own way the little one wants to share in this conversation with the Pope; he wants to speak, but he does not yet know how to make himself understood. Who knows how eagerly he will return here, when he is bigger! But now it is best to try to help him, though not perhaps in the Audience hall.' A general applause greeted the charming episode." (*O.R.*, 1 Nov. 1962.)

[4] An example of this is the evangelical image of the fountain of fresh water, which he frequently used, with variations. "The Church", he said once, "is the old village fountain . . . to which all generations come for water."

what Pope John has offered us, day after day, there is his truly evangelical capacity for restoring mysterious things to the circle of familiar images. With an agility not prescribed in the official rubrics, he would pass from the Latin of the Curia to the dialect of Bergamo; he had both the priest's liking for solemn rites and his own natural liking for homely gestures. His constant intention was to make himself as much as possible a man like all others, and to step down from the frame consecrated by the centuries.[5] His way of abandoning himself unreservedly, on every occasion, to the lively pictures his memory recalled, in such a way that the gravest doctrinal statements were always illustrated with vivid anecdotes, that need he felt to see humble people face to face and speak to them as a man to his fellows, that way of speaking Italian like a country parson, admirably combining an old-fashioned vocabulary with the whimsical appeals of his imagination and his heart: all this has made of him, as regards language also, the pope most truly one of the people, and most dear to the people, that the Church has had in recent centuries.

[5] Mgr Alfredo Cavagna, his confessor, confided to the *Osservatore Romano* on 5 June 1963: "He was seen talking to everyone with the same simplicity, to the learned and ignorant, important personages and humble folk. In his discourses he preferred simple and spontaneous words which could be understood by all, and avoided all oratory which was out of keeping with his own natural style. It was in order to draw closer to everyone that in the first years of his pontificate he attempted to study English. He pointed out to me: 'It is not that I want to make speeches in English, but it does not seem to me very fatherly to greet so many people who only know English and not be able to say a single word to them.' Even during these last months he showed me a Russian grammar, telling me that, as he knew a little Slavonic, it would be easy for him to learn at least some Russian words and show in this way also how much he loved that great people, because he was constantly repeating the words of the divine Redeemer: 'I came not to call the righteous, but sinners'."

"All ordinary things but done in no ordinary way"

Today was a perfect feast; I spent it in the company of St Francis de Sales, my gentlest of saints. What a magnificent figure of a man, priest and Bishop! If I were like him, I would not mind even if they were to make me Pope! I love to let my thoughts dwell on him, on his goodness and on his teaching. I have read his life so many times! His counsels are so acceptable to my heart. By the light of his example I feel more inclined towards humility, gentleness and calm. My life, so the Lord tells me, must be a perfect copy of that of St Francis de Sales if I wish it to bear good fruits. Nothing extraordinary in me or in my behaviour, except my way of doing ordinary things: "all ordinary things but done in no ordinary way". A great, a burning love for Jesus Christ and his Church: unalterable serenity of mind, wonderful gentleness with my fellow men, that is all. (*Journal*, 1903, p. 110.)

"An atmosphere of heaven"

To succeed in my apostolate I will recognize no other school than that of the divine Heart of Jesus. "Learn from me, for I am gentle and lowly in heart." Experience also has confirmed the supreme wisdom of this method, which brings real success.

I shall love my young students as a mother her sons, but always in the Lord and with the intention of bringing them up as worthy sons of the Church and, if I can, as future generous apostles of truth and goodness—and at the same time I shall be cherishing in them the best hopes of our families and of our country.

I shall be particularly careful always to maintain in my house a fragrant atmosphere of purity which may influence my young men and make such a profound impression on them that it will survive in later years, even in the future conflict of their lives. Nothing affected or superficial, but in simplicity of manners and speech the indefinable quality that made the saintly teachers of old and of our own times seem to live in an atmosphere of heaven, and enabled them to do so much good and be true builders of great souls. Lord, help me to follow, if only from afar and in my humble way, these shining examples of great teachers of the young.

The work I have set my hand to is enormous; the corn is

already golden in the fields, but alas! the reapers are few. I will try, with prayers to God and my own endeavours, to inspire in young clerics and priests a love and enthusiasm for this form of ministry which excels all others. I will try to make it attractive, especially to those to whom nature and grace have granted a special aptitude for working with the young. Who knows but that the right word and still more a good example may succeed, and I may soon find myself surrounded with a fine circle of brothers, all eager for the apostolate among young people? I shall do all I can to get the Priests of the Sacred Heart to take up this order of ideals and works. The Congregation was instituted chiefly for this purpose and one must try to increase its numbers, for it was intended that it should permeate the whole diocese of Bergamo with its spirit of apostolic work and ecclesiastical discipline. (*Journal*, 1919, pp. 194-5.)

"Patient and good"

A characteristic of this retreat has been a great inner peace and ioy, which embolden me to offer myself to the Lord for any sacrifice he may wish me to make of what is dear to me. My whole person and my whole life must be imbued with this tranquillity and joy. This comes easily to me now, but future difficulties and opposition may disturb me. I must do my best to preserve this cheerfulness in my soul and in my outward behaviour. One must learn how to bear suffering without letting anyone even know it is there. Was this not one of the last lessons I learnt from Mgr Radini, of revered memory?

One of the similes used by St Francis de Sales, which I love to repeat, is: "I am like a bird singing in a thicket of thorns"; this must be a continual inspiration to me. So, I must say very little to anyone about the things that hurt me. Great discretion and forbearance in my judgments of men and situations: willingness to pray, particularly, for those who may cause me suffering, and in everything great kindness and endless patience, remembering that any other sentiment or mixture of sentiments *à la Macédoine*, as they say here, is contrary to the spirit of the Gospel and of evangelic perfection. So long as charity may triumph, at all costs, I would choose to be considered as of little worth. I will be patient and good to a heroic degree, even if I am to be crushed. Only in this way shall I deserve to be called a true Bishop and be worthy to share in the priesthood of Jesus Christ, who at the cost of his compliance, humiliation and suffering was the real and only Physician and Saviour of all mankind, by whose wounds we are healed. (*Journal*, 1930, pp. 217–18.)

"*Opening a source of blessings*"

I tremble when I think how the Lord will judge me, looking at me by the light of his lantern. But when I ask myself what more I can do to please the Lord, and to make myself holy, I find no other answer than this: continue under obedience as you are now; do your ordinary things, day after day, without over-anxiety, without ostentation, but always trying to do them with greater fervour and perfection.

Be faithful to the pattern of priestly piety: Mass, brief meditation, Breviary, rosary, visit to the Blessed Sacrament, examination of conscience, the reading of good books; but all this with greater enthusiasm of love, with superabundant zeal, like a lamp overflowing with oil.

Do not be concerned about your future but think that perhaps you are drawing near the gateway of eternal life. At the same time be ever more content to live like this, hidden from the world, perhaps forgotten by your Superiors, and do not grieve at being little appreciated but try to find an even greater joy in "being esteemed of little worth".

The circumstances of my ministry, as it has taken shape during ten years in Bulgaria, do not advise or permit me to do anything more than I am already doing—at least for the present. So I must go on living from day to day. I will offer more lovingly to Jesus the life I lead here and the restrictions I have to set on my outward activity and my whole life of more intense prayers for the salvation and sanctification of my soul and the souls of these Bishops and priests, and for the wider diffusion and penetration of the spirit of charity in this country where everything is so harsh; for the edification and religious advancement of the Catholics and for the enlightenment and blessing of this Bulgarian people, so sadly misled and yet so richly endowed with capacities for service in the kingdom of Christ and his Church.

What has Mgr Roncalli been doing during these monotonous

years at the Apostolic Delegation? Trying to make himself holy and with simplicity, kindness and joy opening a source of blessings and graces for all Bulgaria, whether he lives to see it or not.

This is what ought to be. But these are grand words and still grander things. O my Jesus, it shames me to think of them; I blush to speak of them. But give me the grace, the power, the glory of making this come true. The rest does not matter. All the rest is vanity, worthlessness and affliction of the soul. (*Journal,* 1934, pp. 222–3.)

"Gravity and lovable dignity"

What is the result of this spiritual concentration of mine? Nothing remarkable or exciting but, as it seems to me, a consolidation of my principles and positions in the eyes of the Lord and in all that regards my own humble life and my sacred ministry in the service of Holy Church. Even without exaggerating the importance of entering upon this last, possibly rapid and brief, period of my life, I feel something more mature and authoritative in me in relation to all that interests and surrounds me. I think I notice a greater detachment from all that concerns my own future, a more marked indifference "to all created things", a slow and slight blurring of the outlines of things, persons, places and undertakings to which I was formerly more strongly attached, a more evident inclination to understand and sympathize and a greater clarity and tranquillity in impression and judgments. I will be careful to preserve a fine simplicity in my conversation and behaviour, without any affectation; at the same time there must be apparent the gravity and lovable dignity of the elderly prelate, who diffuses an air of nobility, wisdom and grace. (*Journal,* 1940, p. 237.)

"The water of life"

O Jesus, how much I thank you for having kept me faithful to this principle: "From me, as from a living fountain, the humble and the great, the poor and the rich draw the water of life." Ah, I am numbered among the humble and the poor! In Bulgaria, the difficulties of my circumstances, even more than the difficulties caused by men, and the monotony of that life which was one long sequence of daily pricks and scratches, cost me much in mortification and silence. But your grace preserved my inner joy, which helped me to hide my difficulties and distress. In Turkey the responsibilities of my pastoral work were at once a torment and a joy to me. Could I not, should I not, have done more, have made a more decided effort and gone against the inclination of my nature? Did the search for calm and peace, which I considered to be more in harmony with the Lord's spirit, not perhaps mask a certain unwillingness to take up the sword, and a preference for what was easiest and most convenient for me, even if gentleness has indeed been defined as the fullness of strength? O my Jesus, you search all hearts: the exact point at which even the striving after virtue may lead to failure or excess is known to you alone. (*Journal*, 1950, p. 274.)

"*The winning beauty of simplicity*"

"Simplicity of heart and speech!" The older I grow the more clearly I perceive the dignity and the winning beauty of simplicity in thought, conduct and speech: a desire to simplify all that is complicated and to treat everything with the greatest naturalness and clarity, without wrapping things up in trimmings and artificial turns of thought and phrase. "To be simple with prudence"—the motto is St John Chrysostom's. What a wealth of doctrine in these two phrases!

Friendliness, serenity and imperturbable patience! I must always remember that "a soft answer turns away wrath". What bitterness is caused by a rough, abrupt or impatient manner! Sometimes the fear of being underestimated as a person of little worth tempts us to give ourselves airs and assert ourselves a little. But this is contrary to my nature. To be simple, with no pretensions, requires no effort from me. This is a great gift that the Lord has bestowed on me: I want to preserve it and to be worthy of it. (*Journal*, 1952, pp. 278–9.)

"*What a transformation*"

In April last year I sought shelter under the roof of the Sacred Heart at Montmartre in Paris, and May this year finds me here at the foot of the Grappa, Cardinal and Patriarch of Venice. What a transformation in all that surrounds me! I hardly know what to dwell on more: on how "I rejoiced when they said to me..." with all that follows, or on the sense of insufficiency which inspires feelings of humility and trust in the Lord. It is he who has really done all, and done it without my help, for I could never have imagined or desired such greatness. I am happy also because this meekness and humility do not go against the grain with me but come easily to my nature. Why should I be vain or proud of anything, my Lord? Is not "my merit" all "God's mercy"?

It is interesting to note that Providence has brought me back to where I began to exercise my priestly vocation, that is to pastoral work. Now I am ministering directly to souls. To tell the truth, I have always believed that, for an ecclesiastic, diplomacy (so-called!) must be imbued with the pastoral spirit; otherwise it is of no use and makes a sacred mission look ridiculous. Now I am confronted with the Church's real interests, relating to her final purpose, which is to save souls and guide them to heaven. This is enough for me and I thank the Lord for it. I said so in St Mark's in Venice on 15 March, the day of my solemn entry. I desire and think of nothing else but to live and die for the souls entrusted to me. "The good shepherd gives his life for his sheep.... I am come that they may have life, and may have it more abundantly" (John 10. 11 and 10).

My triumphal entry into Venice and these first two months' contact with my children make me realize the natural goodwill the Venetians feel for their Patriarch: they give me great encouragement. I do not want to set myself any new precepts to follow. I shall continue on my own way and according to my own temperament. Humility, simplicity, fidelity to the Gospel in word and works, with unfaltering gentleness, inexhaustible patience and fatherly and insatiable enthusiasm for the welfare of souls. I see that they like to listen to me and that my simple words go straight to their hearts. But I will take great care to prepare my sermons well, so that what I say may not be lacking in dignity and may be more and more edifying. (*Journal*, 1953, pp. 283-4.)

"The whole world is my family"

My first duty: to set my will in order, in preparation for my death, which may be near; the thought of it is never far from me. I shall take care to arrange everything in an orderly manner; even when it is written down, it will still be the will of a poor and simple Pope. I have only a few details to add and these are already substantially accounted for. I want the Pope's example to be an encouragement and an admonition to all the Cardinals. It is quite wrong for any ecclesiastic to die without leaving a will in good order, and not having done so may be a terrifying thought when he is face to face with eternity.

Since the Lord chose me, unworthy as I am, for this great service, I feel I have no longer any special ties in this life, no family, no earthly country or nation, nor any particular preferences with regard to studies or projects, even good ones. Now, more than ever, I see myself only as the humble and unworthy "servant of God and servant of the servants of God". The whole world is my family. This sense of belonging to every one must give character and vigour to my mind, my heart and my actions.

This vision, this feeling of belonging to the whole world, will give a new impulse to my constant and continual daily prayer: the Breviary, Holy Mass, the whole rosary and my faithful visits to Jesus in the tabernacle, all varied and ritual forms of close and trustful union with Jesus.

The experience of this first year gives me light and strength in my efforts to straighten, to reform, and tactfully and patiently to make improvements in everything.

Above all, I am grateful to the Lord for the temperament he has given me, which preserves me from anxieties and tiresome perplexities. I feel I am under obedience in all things and I have noticed that this disposition, in great things and in small, gives me, unworthy as I am, a strength of daring simplicity, so wholly evangelical in its nature that it demands and obtains universal respect and edifies many. "Lord, I am not worthy. O Lord, be always my strength and the joy of my heart. My God, my mercy."

The welcome immediately accorded to my unworthy person and the affection still shown by all who approach me are always a source of surprise to me. The maxim "Know thyself" suffices for my spiritual serenity and keeps me on the alert. The secret of my success must lie there: in not "searching into things which are above my ability" and in being content to be "meek and humble of heart". Meekness and humbleness of heart give graciousness in receiving, speaking and dealing with people, and the patience to bear, to pity, to keep silent and to encourage. Above all, one must always be ready for the Lord's surprise moves, for although he treats his loved ones well, he generally likes to test them with all sorts of trials such as bodily infirmities, bitterness of soul and sometimes opposition so powerful as to transform and wear out the life of the servant of God, the life of the servant of the servants of God, making it a real martyrdom. (*Journal*, 1959, pp. 298-9.)

"*I am in the service of your love*"

We were recently moved and uplifted by reading a homily by St John Chrysostom, which begins with the words: *Moyses, magnus ille famulus.*

We love indeed to appropriate to ourselves the sweet words of St John Chrysostom, because they do so well express our own feelings in this happy hour: "If the presence of a single person, myself, has filled the people with such joy, think of my own happiness when I see you all. Jacob in his old age rejoiced and his soul exulted when he saw again even one of his sons, Joseph, and here am I contemplating not only Joseph, but all of you, just like him. . . . I am in the service of your love."

Two words shine out in this context: joy and service. The joy of brotherhood makes more easy even the most arduous work; and the service of Holy Church gives real joy, the only joy found here below which endures unaltered. So it is well to say with the Psalmist: "Behold how good and pleasant it is, when brothers dwell in unity!" (Psalm 133. 1). But this joy becomes more intense when it springs from the knowledge of having tried to do all one's duty, of having given generous service in one's ministry. For this reason we love to repeat with the Patriarch of Constantinople: "I am in the service of your love." The Pope feels his indebtedness particularly to his collaborators, and towards all his other sons, who have known how to enter into his most sacred preoccupations concerning the Council. It is a sweet bond of union between us, and firmer than any other, because love makes every yoke more light. We are grateful to you for this, and express to you our heartfelt appreciation. . . . "You have sanctified the air around you and turned the city into a church." And just as the mother rejoices when her sons are happy so the shepherd rejoices at the happiness of his flock. (Allocution of 23 Jan. 1962.)

"A tremor passes from the father to his children"

We are glad today to have gathered you all together in this hall, which has now become familiar to Catholics from all over the world.

To the gates of Rome, amid the delights of nature, the faithful come here to greet the Pope, and we love to welcome them and speak with them in all simplicity: our eyes meet, our hearts throb together. Most of the pilgrims are young people. A tremor passes from the old father's soul and is communicated to the children, all equally beloved, who have come not only from neighbouring dioceses and countries, but from all the continents: people of all ages and professions, of differing culture and education, and some even who belong to the non-Catholic religious confessions.

Our heart is touched when we hear the voices of our children of Europe and the Near East, of the Americas, Australia and the islands scattered over the oceans! And when we see, and it is easy to pick them out, the distinguished representatives of Africa and Asia, whose entry into the society of nations brings a new contribution of vitality and fresh youth to the whole human family, we bless and thank the Lord without ceasing.

Is this Audience, is this gathering together of all of you, not an image of the flock which gathered around the Shepherd of the Gospel on the hills of Galilee?

My beloved young people, you represent a living image of this. And today, such is our deep emotion when we think of the mysterious designs of Providence, that we would liken you all to those disciples of Emmaus, who felt the fascination of their divine risen Shepherd, who had joined them as they walked along their road: "Did not our hearts burn within us while he talked to us along the road, while he opened to us the Scriptures?" (Luke 24. 32).

The Pope and the Bishops, and with them the clergy and the people, are all on the same road; it is a continual going and coming on this road of the Council, which is intended to be a general infusion and diffusion of grace, of holy fervour, in the certainty of sowing that which will flower in its own time, according to the laws of providence which await and encourage the free co-operation of man with the great designs of God.

We seize the opportunity of this meeting today, desired by us, my beloved children, and so serene and joyful for you and for us too, to encourage you to share in the sacred joy of the Council, which will truly be the splendour of heaven, the guide to life, and above all the certain and effective beginning of a triumphant apostolate. We express to you, beloved young people, our trembling and joyful hope.

We trust that from the Ecumenical Council, for which we have been preparing ourselves with incessant prayer, may shine a heavenly light, diffused in the majesty and beauty of Jesus the Good Shepherd.

In truth, as the Bible tells us, the Church of Jesus is simply the expression of his loving gift of himself to the whole flock, formed of innumerable sheep scattered throughout the world. (Allocution of 10 Aug. 1962, 58th anniversary of his ordination as priest.)

CHAPTER EIGHT

Travelling Together

I. A "WISE AND GRACIOUS PRUDENCE"

BEFORE Pope John's Christian optimism was expressed as doctrine
with full papal authority in *Pacem in terris* it was, as we have seen,
a moral virtue perfected over a long period of time, and in spite
of the fact that the epoch in which he gathered most of his
experience was one of harsh ideological conflicts and of irritation
and dismay among Catholics. His power of pointing out, in
the midst of the new historical reality, the positive elements which
deserve from the Church not so much the harshness of condemnation as the willingness to take part in a dialogue, is, even more than
a sign of a frank and unprejudiced mind, the result of a virtue
which presides over the practice of all the other moral virtues
and one which Pope John enjoyed to an extraordinary degree:
prudence.

The virtue of prudence is in fact the favourite target of those
determined defenders of truth who consider that this should be
loved so whole-heartedly as to exclude all contact with those
who do not share it or, worse, who oppose it, and all activity
which might subject it to limitations or compromise. Prudence
thus becomes almost fatally—and in opposition to the teaching
of its first great theorist Aristotle, who called it the "strategic
virtue"—the virtue of "not doing", "not saying", "avoiding",
"refusing to meet". A man who, professing to be the minister of
a truth concerned with living, like Christian truth, lets slip an
occasion to affirm it and insert it in the flow of events because he is
afraid of possible harmful consequences, such a man, I say, will
probably deserve to be described as a prudent man among his
contemporaries, but in the eyes of God, and of history, he will
be judged as imprudent. Perhaps the time is near when, recon-

sidering the story of our past, we shall have to correct the official list of "prudent men".

The line separating Christian prudence from merely human prudence is so fine that only one who has the gift of spiritual discernment succeeds in perceiving it. Undoubtedly, Pope John was not prudent in the worldly sense; but he was most prudent according to the spirit. Measured by worldly prudence, he caused considerable bewilderment and confusion of ideas; according to the spiritual sense of prudence he brought about a new order, a new clarity of Christian thought. He was certainly aware that many, even among his collaborators, considered several of his initiatives, particularly that of the Council, dangerous "childish nonsense". But prudence herself taught him to bear all with patience and await the outcome with confidence. A page of his *Journal*, dealing with prudence and written in August 1961, reveals, even while teaching the doctrine, certain of his many personal experiences which it would not be wise to illustrate here with concrete examples:

> The "simple, upright, Godfearing man" is always the worthiest and the strongest. Naturally he must always be sustained by a wise and gracious prudence. He is a simple man who is not ashamed to profess the Gospel, even in the face of men who consider it to be nothing but weakness and childish nonsense, and to profess it entirely on all occasions, and in the presence of all; he does not let himself be deceived or prejudiced by his fellows, nor does he lose his peace of mind, however they may treat him.

This prudence then is not merely "gracious", it is strong and creative: its skill is shown not in setting up barriers but in digging new roads. . . . We will now try to discover how it works, and this will serve to give us a more exact notion of what it was able to do, for the good of the Church, in so short a time.

A prudence without love is not prudence: this truth is insufficiently recognized. Setting aside moral and religious truth, and working by the light of pure reason, it is not always possible to present totally convincing rules of action, but it is possible to draw up categorical prohibitions. When faced with any historical situation, of greater or less importance, the reason must refer to the doctrinal principles guarded by the Church and from them deduce rules that shall be as specific as possible, that is as applicable as possible to the particular situation. But, between the doctrinal principle concerned and the action there will always be a "space", which we may not fill by a process of mere deduction. The response to the particular situation (to the *kairos*, that is, the will of God in the actual moment) must, in the last instance, be intuitively understood, rather than deduced, and even when, as is only right, the answer is in accordance with all the principles, it will nevertheless be something new, often daringly new. The moral structure of prudence therefore includes also this *intellectus*, which is not a discursive but an intuitive intelligence.

It is on this intuitive element that love or selfishness is grafted, giving to the identical rational action of prudence totally contradictory results. Selfishness acts in such a way that intuition is subordinated to more or less conscious personal interests; love acts in such a way that intuition is in the service of absolute values in their inexhaustible universality. Now we see the obvious corollaries. A man who is anxious about his career is, for this reason, imprudent, because he lacks love. A man who is always anxious about other people's opinions is, for this reason, imprudent. A man who, professing to be a Christian, does not every day yearn to save the world, will never be a prudent man in the Christian sense, whatever he may do. His choices will never be dictated by the need for salvation.

The problem of the choice of means, so characteristic of prudence, is a secondary problem: the first is that of the power of intuition whether nourished or not by love. It was only because Pope John loved, only because of this, that he was granted an understanding of the modern man greater than that of the bold analysts of the society of today, greater than that of the patient laborious experts of modern psychology.

2. RESPECT FOR MAN

At the basis of the "dialogue" which Pope John, first as a Christian and then as pope, opened with the modern world, there was then an extraordinary intuitive prudence. And at the source of this prudence there was a great love for men.

> In order to love others to such an extent [Cardinal Suenens said of him] the secret is: to deny oneself. Love, it has been said, is "devoted attention to the lives of others". In order to belong entirely to others, one must banish all thought for oneself. To give yourself you must first forget yourself. John XXIII has left us the memory of one who in his own right did not exist. He placed himself beyond all earthly vanities: self-denial was a habit of his soul. This innate humility allowed him to speak of himself with complete detachment and shrewdness, as if he were speaking of someone else.

This last remark is extraordinarily acute. Pope John treated himself as if he were someone else: inverting the Gospel equation he loved himself as he loved others. That was why he could talk of himself without formal humility. He called himself "humble Pope John" without any striving after effect. To call oneself humble is possible only for those who are absurdly vain, or for those who are so humble that they no longer care about the customary forms of its virtue. One too often gets the impression that virtue, and especially humility, is a difficult game of which you must learn all the rules. Among the rules of humility, for example, is one that you must never speak well of yourself. Pope John's humility was above and beyond the rules of the game: everyone understood that it was real, although some conventional signs were lacking. It was fused with his love of the truth, wherever that might be found, and above any temptation to make use of it.

From this root stemmed his most characteristic moral gift: that of being able to converse with others. As an example one should read these expressions which form part of the speech pronounced on the occasion of his ceremonial entrance into Venice:

> Now I humbly introduce myself. Like every man who lives on this earth, I come from a family and from a clearly defined starting-point: with the grace of good bodily health, and with enough common sense to enable me to understand

things quickly and clearly, with a loving disposition towards men which keeps me faithful to the teaching of the Gospel, respectful of my own rights as of those of others, and incapable of doing ill to anyone; indeed it encourages me to do good to all.

I am of humble birth and I was trained to a contented and blessed poverty, which makes few demands and fosters the growth of the most noble and lofty virtues, a good preparation for the higher ascents of life.

Providence took me from my native village and made me travel along the roads of this world in the East and in the West, bringing me into touch with people of different religions and ideologies, at grips with social problems which are acute and menacing, and meanwhile preserved my serenity, a balanced judgment and a spirit of enquiry. I was always engaged, naturally, with fidelity to the principles of Catholic belief and moral teaching, more with what unites men than with what divides them and provokes conflicts. . . .

These notes give you the modest physiognomy of the man before you . . . who has deserved the title of a man of proven honesty, of an honest man without a stain who is worthy of confident respect. (*Scritti e Discorsi*, vol. I, pp. 16 *et seq.*)

But already, in October 1929, he was writing, using an image which confirms him in our eyes as a biblical character:

I have come back from the holidays to my work. This year's festivities for my jubilee as priest are ended.

I have let them do what they would at Sofia and at Sotto il Monte. How ashamed I feel! Innumerable priests, dead and still alive, have performed prodigies in the apostolate and the sanctification of souls in twenty-five years. And what have I done?

My Jesus, mercy!

But, when I humble myself at the thought of the little or nothing I have achieved yet, I raise my eyes to the future. There is still light in front of me: there is still the hope of some good. So I take up my staff once more, now an old man's staff, and go forward towards all that the Lord will require of me. (*Diario*, p. 14.)

And at the end of his life, when he received the Peace Prize, he used once more his old style of speech, this time in a setting of more grandeur: with his "old man's staff" he had truly arrived very far, but his heart had the old frank simplicity:

"The humble Pope who is speaking to you", he said, "is fully aware of being in himself of very little worth before God: he can only feel ashamed. . . . We can say with all simplicity, just as we think: no circumstances, no event, however great an honour it may be for our humble person, can make us proud, or impair the serenity of our soul."

His careful thought for others' lives kept him free from the more or less specious falsifications to which the proud spirit falls a prey. He found himself in man, in every man; he rejoiced unreservedly in good wherever he found it, no matter whether in friends or enemies; over evil he drew the veil of compassion, the same delicate compassion with which he treated himself, benignly.[1] His power of sharing in all that was human had been refined in humility and love. It was from this foundation that all his daring sprang: he trusted man, not because of a pagan faith in human nature, but because of his Christian awareness that God works in the heart of every creature, fostering his longing for what is good and transforming into good even what is evil. Faith in man, when it is robust, is merely a form of faith in God.

With great benevolence he explained to the faithful in an Audience on 23 January 1963:

> The various things around us generally show four aspects: usually three of these are evil or uncertain: one is clear, limpid, shining. Now, men seem inclined rather to dwell on the first three of these, and so they at once begin to set their imagination, their eyes and their tongue to work, abandoning themselves to inexact or rash judgments, and to criticism, lingering, not on what is actually satisfactory, but on what might conflict with or disappoint their own views. In a word, they seek

---

[1] Who does not remember his visit to the Roman prison? Among the prisoners were two assassins. After having heard the Holy Father, one of them went up to him and said: "Are the words of hope spoken by Your Holiness intended also for me, a great sinner?" For answer the Pope opened wide his arms and clasped him to his breast. "Is that prisoner not the symbol of all mankind, so dear to the heart of John XXIII?" said Cardinal Suenens, recalling this episode when he spoke to the Conciliar Fathers.

more to remain in a state of alarm about what may disturb their customary quiet, or their precarious balance, than to discover what would help them to go forward with speed and serenity.

To dwell on the "limpid and shining" aspect, without forgetting the others, is not improvident optimism; it is dutiful co-operation with the positive forward movement of contingent beings, a movement in which the appeal of the absolute is always, more or less, to be felt.

3. OPTIMISM AS LOVE

Even his visible joy was governed by the desire to encourage optimism in others, especially in those who were sorely tried. Sadness, like error and sin, tends towards ontological regression: it is a psychological symptom of non-being. Is there not perhaps a link between nausea and nothingness? And between nausea and incommunicability is there not, according to an illustrious teacher of our own times, a causal relation? "Others are Hell": this is the sincerest slogan of nihilistic existentialism. Pope John moved in the opposite hemisphere, that of *being*, in which, at the antipodes of disgust and incommunicability, there is joy and there is communication.

On his sixtieth birthday he noted, on a photograph he sent to a friend: "This is Mgr Roncalli at sixty years of age. It is the finest age to be: good health, more judgment, an easier way of seeing clearly into things, with gentleness, and trustful optimism" (*Algisi*, p. 162).

And he wrote in the same year: "My sixty years do not in the least weigh upon the buoyancy of my spirit, which does not care to linger in the past" (*Algisi*, p. 163).

This did not mean he was insensible to the thought of death, or to the profound melancholy sure to be felt by one who held friendship in such honour and the ties of kinship. Here are passages from letters written within the ten years 1936–47:

> When I think of my years, and that at my age Mgr Radini was dying, I sometimes feel the temptation to consider myself

an old man. One must resist this; in spite of outward appearances, one must preserve a bright youthfulness of spirit. This pleases the Lord, is edifying to souls, and is good for us too, for it is our duty to infuse joy and optimism in others. (*Algisi*, p. 161.)

Thanks be to God, I prefer to look forward rather than backward. And I cherish the dearest memories of people and things in order to remind myself of the final reunion which awaits us. Life is rather like a long voyage. We set out waving and weeping as we part from our dear ones. But when we arrive the same people are already in the harbour to await us. (*Algisi*, p. 163.)

For some time past I have been receiving *L'Eco di Bergamo*, although still somewhat interruptedly. It serves to keep me informed of the activities of the diocese, which still interest me most keenly even if, alas! when I think of those departed long ago, and those who day after day set out for the other life, I feel as if I were lingering among the avenues of a cemetery. But I try to react and to preserve my youthful spirit, so as not to fail in the encouragement of the young in years when they give way to pessimism. (*Algisi*, p. 358.)

Every time his imagination was tempted to dwell on signs of death, or old age, or on sad things in general, he reacted, keeping up his spirits with the strength of love, in which his nature, naturally open to all that is good and beautiful, found its expression and inspiration.

4. KEEPING STEP WITH THOSE WHO GO FORWARD

From this radiant spiritual nature sprang his insatiable love of communication with others, his desire to go forward in the company of whoever he happened to meet along the road. And he always remembered and was grateful for every encounter, certain that, in spite of its apparent fortuitousness, every such experience was a part of the embroidery with which God, and God alone, brings to perfection the design of his creation. That is why, as we have already said, to put his trust in man was for him a way of trusting in God. In 1948 he wrote prophetically: "On one turning of the old stairway of the Vatican, to the left of the courtyard of San Damaso, can be seen a fine seventeenth-century painting. Underneath are the words said by Jesus to Peter when he was in danger of drowning: 'O man of little faith, why did you doubt?' These are words of comfort for us all" (*Algisi*, p. 361).

His whole life is marked by this faith in God, and faith in man, in God's name. When he left Bulgaria in 1934 he wrote:

> If I were sure not to be misunderstood, I would like to address a word also to all our separated brothers. The difference in religious convictions with regard to one of the fundamental points of the teaching of Jesus recorded by the Gospel, that is, the union of all the faithful of the Church of Christ with the successor of the Prince of the Apostles, compelled me to observe a certain caution in my relations and my personal contacts with them. This was quite natural, and I think perfectly understood by them too. The respect which I have always sought to show, in public and private, for all and every one of them, my unbreakable silence which hurt no one, and the fact that I never stooped to pick up the stone that was hurled at me from one or the other side of the street, leave me with the frank assurance that I showed them all that I love them too in the Lord, with that brotherly, sincere and heartfelt charity that we learn from the Gospel.

In Turkey he found he had to carry out his mission in extremely difficult circumstances, for two fundamental reasons. The first was the traditional intransigeance of the small Catholic community with regard to the Orthodox, an intransigeance which assumed a nationalistic character when confronted with expressions of Mahometan piety. The second was the new political régime set up in the Turkish peninsula by Kemal Ataturk, who had adopted the programme of Western secularists, and in such a radical manner as to prohibit, among other things, every external manifestation of a religious character, including the use of ecclesiastical dress.

The Apostolic Delegate was not only undismayed by this, but found on this occasion an ideal opportunity to exercise his spirit of conciliation. First of all, he ordered to be taken down from the façade of his palace the words *"qui ex Patre Filioque procedit"*, which were very prominently displayed in order to remind everyone of the reasons for an ancient irreparable rupture, and he substituted for it the words: *"Pater et Pastor."* But the scruples of the Catholic minority were not only theological. A nationalistic spirit supported their pride and induced them to boast of their superiority over the people who were their hosts. Mgr Roncalli substituted Turkish for French in the reading of the Gospel passage *infra Missam* and in the concluding invocations of the Divine Praises.[2] After this the Turks also were frequently present at the Catholic functions, led by their curiosity to hear the language of the Koran in the Catholic Church. Nor was he afraid to express, from time to time, a severe judgment on the historical responsibilities of the Catholics of the Latin rite, who had had such an influence on the initial rupture of Christian unity and its progressive deterioration.

As regards the prohibition of wearing ecclesiastical dress, he first ascertained the impossibility of refusing obedience and then decided to endow this act of despoliation with a certain solemnity and ceremoniousness. After a religious function in the church of St Anthony, he left the church in the midst of all the other ecclesiastics, all in lay attire but, as he had himself suggested, not all alike but each one different from the other. The Delegate's face as he came out of the church, under the amused eyes of the Turks, was anything but the face of a martyr!

In other and graver circumstances too he abstained from taking up a rigid position. He understood that, apart from its exaggerations, the reform set in motion by the great statesman not only responded to the requirements of natural law, but, in the long run, would even favour the fortunes of Christianity.

---

[2] "When he wished to provide a translation of those prayers he realized his difficulty," Algisi tells us (*op. cit.*, p. 141). "How was he to translate 'God' into Turkish? With 'Allah'? But could he translate 'Mary, Mother of God' with 'Mary, Mother of Allah'? The translation sounded strange to both Christians and Turks, and even theologically was not without fault. They had recourse to the name '*Tamré*' (God), which, however, still does not resolve all the difficulties. It was one of the signs of the need for Christians to make an effort of mental adjustment. The recital of the prayers in Turkish soon became obligatory for the Cathedral, but not without some objections on the part of the more narrow-minded Catholics, who criticized that act of courtesy towards the Turks, made just at the moment when the latter had been less considerate."

To illustrate the style and criteria adopted by Mgr Roncalli it will be useful to record a conversation reconstructed, certainly from authoritative sources, by Algisi, between the Apostolic Delegate and the Under-Secretary for Foreign Affairs of the Ankara Government[3]:

> "Being in Ankara for business connected with my mission, I am glad to have this opportunity of offering my respects to the representatives of Turkey."
>
> "And I am glad to make your personal acquaintance and to tell you that the Turkish government has the greatest respect for you and for the great and illustrious tradition that you represent."
>
> "I thank you. I hope that the Turkish authorities will in their turn have been able to take note of the obedience shown by Catholics to the laws of the country, even when these are, at times, unwelcome. The dress I am wearing is a proof of this."
>
> "That is true. On the other hand we wish to assure you of our most friendly respect for the liberty of your ministry, in so far as it does not interfere with the laws of our country . . . even if we dislike titles which signify relations with a religious power which, although venerable, is nevertheless alien to us."
>
> "I understand. This does not prevent this religious power from feeling pleasure in the rise of Turkey, and finding in her new constitution some fundamental principles of Christianity . . . even if we are bound to disagree with the irreligious spirit with which they are put into practice."
>
> "The lay constitution of our State is one of our fundamental principles and is the guarantee of our liberty."
>
> "The Church will be most careful not to interfere with that. But I am an optimist. In everything I look rather for what unites than for what separates. In agreement as we are, on natural principles, we can go forward a little together. For the rest, it is better to be hopeful. Meanwhile, for our own part, we have taken some steps forward: the Turkish language has entered the church. . . ."

[3] *Algisi*, pp. 143–4. The whole chapter VI, *La Turchia di Ataturk*, is most significant in its account of the Nuncio's understanding of the secular character of the new régime.

"We can go forward a little together": here is the justification for a loyal and trustful collaboration, which does not meddle with the question of principles. This inclination to go forward together, in spite of such radical differences concerning the final goal of the journey, was not a spirit of adaptability which, to overcome scruples, makes use of the traditional principle of "choosing the lesser of two inevitable evils". Nor does it make use of the other, equally famous, of the "double effect", which means that one may perform an action not evil in itself, which may have two results, one bad and one good, provided that one's intention was the good end, and that it was necessary to do something. Whatever may be their value in resolving the complicated argument about the legitimacy of collaboration with non-Catholics, these principles do not in themselves give due consideration to the respect deserved by the goodness of the moral and social ideals pursued by man, independently of his ideologies. If a man, or an organization, or a people, have good intentions, and go forward bravely in the name of ideals which are, even partially, good in themselves, they must in Catholics meet with a friendly disposition and a disinterested spirit of service. To subordinate any collaboration or dialogue to a verification of sincerity or to a perfect conformity of intention with the laws of goodness and truth, means in practice condemning oneself to isolation, besides the waste and perhaps final loss of natural goodness. As a general rule: one must trust man, and the power for good that is in him, and above all, the work of grace, which knows how "to draw good from all".

"The world is moving forward: one must take it as it is with an ever young and confident spirit. It is no use wasting time making comparisons. One must think rather that this continual renewal proves the presence of the Lord's grace, always ready to enlighten souls, and direct them towards higher things, and draw good from everything. I prefer rather to keep in step with those who go forward, than to pause and be overtaken" (*Algisi*, p. 315). In these concepts, expressed in a letter dated Istanbul, 24 October 1940, there is already, in a nutshell, the *Pacem in terris*. That they were not, as it were, improvisations, or to be applied merely to problems of the moment, was proved when later on Mgr Roncalli, during his stay in Paris, won the sincere friendship of some of the most distinguished French laymen, such as Herriot and Auriol, and in Venice where, without having recourse to interdicts or censures, he was able to solve the delicate problems connected with the modern and cultural initiatives of the city.

It was in fact in Venice, in February 1957, that there occurred the incident which caused Cardinal Roncalli, so naturally reserved and so scrupulous in obedience, some hours of real bitterness.[4] There were two gatherings arranged to take place in that city, each of which was bound, for a different reason, to attract the attention of the whole nation: the resumption of the Montesi trial, and the Socialist Party Congress. As for the trial, everyone still remembered vividly all the vulgarity and passion with which the organs of public opinion had disturbed the impartial inquiry of justice, fostering political or even ideological interpretations of a sordid crime of the underworld. As for the Congress, no one underestimated the importance which its decisions might have on the future life of the nation. It was right that the Pastor of the city should take the occasion offered by these two events to exhort the faithful to maintain a spirit of understanding and discretion, and above all, to show good will as hosts. But it was enough that in his pastoral letter he expressed good wishes for the Socialist Party for the most arbitrary interpretations to be made throughout Italy. In his words there was nothing that exceeded a sincere feeling of solidarity with "the many brothers who represent all the regions of Italy, working together in a common striving towards the ideals of truth, goodness, justice and peace". Accustomed as he was to attacking at the roots the "war psychosis", and not only the psychosis of armed war, he thought that his gesture was simply one of natural wisdom. It was sad to see him, on the one hand, accused of dangerously yielding to Marxist suggestions and,

[4] See the account in *Algisi*, pp. 279-82. As we know, in order to dispel misunderstandings and perhaps to fall in line with suggestions from higher sources, he said and wrote explanations of this gesture of his: above all these were a charitable move to calm troubled consciences. Speaking at Treviso, he ended with a defence of his conception of courtesy as the beginning of charity: "But without impairing the purity of doctrine there is a wide field and a vast horizon for the exercise of charity; the charity that gives and sacrifices itself, charity that begins with tokens of that respect and courtesy which adorn human society and soon rises to marvellous and heroic expressions of pastoral service."

on the other, with more benevolence, thought to be attempting to win the Socialists for Christ. It was instead simply a desire to see human relations, mere human relations, established among men (it was he who had written: "courtesy is a branch of love"), leaving to other moments and other organs the task of ideological disputes and pastoral approaches. In the light of his pontificate the episode of Venice was to acquire a faintly prophetic character.

In fact, the best was still to come. Everyone knows that the opportunities for free discussion diminish with every step one takes on the ladder of responsibilities. But when he became pope, instead of hiding the lamp of brotherly friendship, he set it high on a candlestick and all the world received light from it.

From that moment on the dialogue between the Church and the world has no longer been the task of the frontier bishops or of those daring Christians who are free from institutional responsibilities: it is the pledged task of the papacy, as Paul VI has himself insisted. The age-old papal monologue has been interrupted: the pope has come down on to the common ground, and has spoken to man face to face, no longer from his throne, and without imparting to all his actions the style of infallibility. Pope John's method remained that which he had learned in his youth, and which he had faithfully employed for so many years. Even in the most ceremonial meetings, he would start talking freely, in his naturally humble way, free from the embarrassment of the "royal plural".

How productive of good this method was is proved by the direct testimony of a man of God, the then Primate of Canterbury, Dr Fisher, who had the courage and the originality to re-initiate the dialogue with the Catholic Church:

> In losing Pope John, Christians everywhere will feel that they have lost a Christian friend. That was his great characteristic. That is how he showed himself to churchmen of all Churches and indeed to those outside the Churches too. It was because of his obvious desire to be friendly to his Christian brethren that I wanted to go to Rome to meet him. An Archbishop of Canterbury had not spoken to a Pope for over four hundred years. Yet when we met, there was no kind of em-

barrassment on either side. Within a minute or two we were talking as old friends talk, freely and sympathetically about our own spiritual experiences as Christians. We talked for an hour without a pause and without a dull moment.

I had been told beforehand that he would do all the talking. He was an old man and, as old men often are, ready to be voluble. But it was not so then. We passed at once to the easy exchanges of friendly discourse. There had been some hints from the Vatican staff that formalities would be strictly and rather forbiddingly observed. I was indeed received with the fullest honours of a formal reception: but that was the end of formality. I am sure that on appropriate occasions he observed all the formalities with great care and dignity. But always he was ready to break out with the force of his own personality, and to make every one of his contacts, official and unofficial, a personal one.[5]

The expression is exact: he transformed all his contacts into a personal experience, even in circumstances of great solemnity and obvious historical importance.

There was always a light burning in his window: the Anglican Primate saw it, went, and found a friend; the whole world saw it, and went to pray beneath his window. The light went out only when his great heart ceased to beat.

[5] B.B.C. European Service, 2 June 1963.

. . . That day must finally come when there will be one flock and one shepherd, because Jesus Christ wishes it to be so. Let us with our prayers hasten the coming of this blessed day: "The way of love is the way of truth."

A legend narrates that Constantine the Great, when leaving Rome for the East, said: "My Rome is Sardica," for he intended to found in what is today the capital of Bulgaria the majestic capital of his Empire of the East. Later on, however, after arriving here, he changed his plan and went on to the shores of the Bosphorus, where he built the great city which has borne his name through the centuries. It has fallen to me to follow the path of Constantine, although in a much more modest way; the way, I mean, from Sardica to Constantinople, from Sofia to Istanbul. However, as I leave for my new destination I carry with me a precious memory of Bulgaria. I have begged the Holy Father to be good enough to change my archbishop's title to that of a wonderful place, a delightful place in Bulgaria. From now onwards I shall no longer bear the name of Archbishop of Aeropolis, but that of Archbishop of Mesembria. In this way I shall have something to remind me every day of Bulgaria, a memory which will stir my heart every time I raise my hand to bless the people in solemn moments, and every time I set my signature to a document.

But you also, brothers, on whom my blessing rests, do not forget me; I wish to remain your friend for ever, the firm and loving friend of Bulgaria.

According to a tradition still preserved in Catholic Ireland, on Christmas Eve every house sets a light in the window, in order to let Joseph and Mary know, in case they are passing by that night, looking for shelter, that inside there is a family, awaiting them around the fire and around the table laden with the gifts of God. Dear brothers, no one knows the ways of the future! Wherever I might go in the world, if someone from Bulgaria should pass by my house, at night, in distress, he will find a lamp lit in my window. Knock! Knock! I will not ask you if you are a Catholic or not; it is enough that you are my brother from Bulgaria: enter! Two brotherly arms will embrace you, the warm heart of a friend will welcome you. For such is the Christian charity of the

Lord, expressions of which have sweetened my life during my ten years' sojourn in Bulgaria. (Farewell speech to the Bulgarian people, Nov. 1934.)

"I love the Turks"

It is my special intention, as an exercise in mortification, to learn the Turkish language. To know so little of it, after five years in Istanbul, is a disgrace, and would indicate scant understanding of the nature of my mission here, if there were no reasons for excuse and justification.

Now I will begin again with renewed energy; the mortification will become a source of satisfaction to me. I love the Turks, I appreciate the natural qualities of these people who have their own place reserved in the march of civilization. Whether I succeed or not in learning the language is of no consequence. My duty, the honour of the Holy See, the example I am bound to give: that is enough. If I were to succeed only in holding to this firm resolve I should consider I had gathered great and blessed fruit from my retreat.

Every evening from the window of my room, here in the Residence of the Jesuit Fathers, I see an assemblage of boats on the Bosphorus; they come round from the Golden Horn in tens and hundreds; they gather at a given rendezvous and then they light up, some more brilliantly than others, offering a most impressive spectacle of colours and lights. I thought it was a festival on the sea for Bairam, which occurs just about now. But it is the organized fleet fishing for *bonito*, large fish which are said to come from far away in the Black Sea. These lights glow all night and one can hear the cheerful voices of the fishermen.

I find the sight very moving. The other night, towards one o'clock, it was pouring with rain but the fishermen were still there, undeterred from their heavy toil.

Oh, how ashamed we should feel, we priests, "fishers of men", before such an example! To pass from the illustration to the lesson illustrated, what a vision of work, zeal and labour for the souls of men to set before our eyes! Very little is left in this land of the kingdom of Jesus Christ. Debris and seeds. But innumerable souls to be won for Christ, lost in this weltering mass of Moslems, Jews and Orthodox. We must do as the fishermen of the Bosphorus do, work night and day with our torches lit, each in his own little boat, at the orders of our spiritual leaders: that is our grave and solemn duty.

My work in Turkey is not easy, but it is coming along well and gives me great consolation. I see the charity of the Lord here, and the clergy united among themselves and with their humble pastor. The political situation does not allow me to do much, but it seems to me there is something gained if at least I do not worsen it through my own fault.

My mission in Greece, on the other hand, is so full of vexations! For this very reason I love it even more and intend to go on working there with heart and soul, forcing myself to overcome all my repugnance. For me it is an order: therefore it requires obedience. I confess I would not mind if it were entrusted to someone else, but while it is mine I want to honour the obligation at all costs. "They who sow in tears shall reap in joy." It matters little to me that others will reap. (*Journal*, 1939, pp. 233–5.)

"The good side of people and things"

My own temperament inclines me towards compliance and a readiness to appreciate the good side of people and things, rather than to criticize and pronounce harsh judgments. This, and the considerable difference in age, mine being more full of experience and profound understanding of the human heart, often make me feel painfully out of sympathy with my entourage. Any kind of distrust and discourtesy shown to anyone, especially to the humble, poor or socially inferior, every destructive or thoughtless criticism, makes me writhe with pain. I say nothing but my heart bleeds. These colleagues of mine are good ecclesiastics: I appreciate their excellent qualities, I am very fond of them and they deserve all my affection. And yet they cause me a lot of suffering. On certain days and in certain circumstances I am tempted to react violently. But I prefer to keep silence, trusting that this will be a more eloquent and effective lesson. Could this be weakness on my part? I must, I will continue to bear this light cross serenely, together with the mortifying sense of my own worthlessness, and I will leave everything to God, who sees into all hearts and shows them the refinements of his love. (*Journal*, 1948, p. 271.)

"*Respect for the French*"

I must have a great understanding and respect for the French people. My prolonged stay with them enables me to appreciate the very noble spiritual qualities of this people and the fervour of Catholics of every school of thought. At the same time, however, it has enabled me to see their failings and excesses also. This means I have to be very careful in what I say. I am free to form my own judgment, but I must beware of any criticism, however slight and friendly, that might wound their susceptibilities. Oh, this never doing or saying to others what we would not wish to have done or said to us! We are all rather remiss about this. Great care then to avoid the slightest expression that might lessen the effectiveness or the dignity of our conduct. I say this for myself, but I must be the guide and example of those around me, my collaborators. In every case, a caress is always better than a scratch. (*Journal*, 1952, p. 279.)

"*Greetings*" to the Socialists

Another congress of vaster proportions, if not of equal significance, will be held in these days in Venice, with representatives from all the regions of Italy: the Congress of the Socialist Party.

From the fact that I speak to you of it serenely and respectfully, as a good Venetian, who holds hospitality in great honour, and moreover one who holds to the Pauline teaching that the bishop must appear to all "hospitable and kind", you will understand that I appreciate the exceptional importance of this event, which is of considerable significance for the immediate future of our country.

It is, I am willing to believe, inspired by the effort to arrive at a common understanding of what is most worth while in the effort to improve living conditions, and social prosperity.

It is always somewhat painful, sometimes very painful, for a shepherd of souls to have to take notice of the fact that many honest and noble minds remain insensible and unresponsive, as if under darkened skies, ignorant or apparently forgetful of the fundamental principles of this divine message which, even amid the weaknesses of men and epochs, were the life blood of twenty centuries of history, of science and art, to the honour of the nations of Europe: minds that think they can achieve the reconstruction of the modern economic, civic and social order on an ideology which is not inspired by the Gospel of Christ.

However, now that we have made our position as spiritual leader clear, as is customary among courteous people, there still remains the heartfelt wish that the children of Venice, welcoming and friendly, as is their wont, will do their part to ensure success to the gathering of so many brothers from all the regions of Italy, for the sake of a common effort towards ideals of truth, goodness, justice and peace. (*Algisi*, pp. 280–1.)

CHAPTER NINE

"The People of God"

I. THE CRISIS OF CHRIST'S PEOPLE

"MAY your priesthood be a source of joy to Holy Church!"
When Pope Pius X said this, placing his hands on the head of the
newly ordained priest from Bergamo, on 11 August 1904, he
did not know how prophetic were his words. Few periods in her
history have given the Church more joy than she was given during
the reign of Pope John.

The age we are living in is still a harsh age, which does not
grant to anyone, and least of all to the guardians of the Christian
tradition, either the calm enjoyment of what has been inherited
from the past or an easy and consoling vision of the future. If
we had to judge the heart of the Church from the voices and
faces of some of her children, we should find her disconsolate
and afraid. Pope John knew this and, as we have seen, was engaged not so much in keeping up his own spirits so as to strengthen
the pessimists as in trying to find and point out to others that
within the tangle of forces agitating the present age there could
be discerned the firm lines of Christian renewal. His pontificate
was needed to make us realize once more, what we can now never
again forget, that the Church "has only just begun to be born".
The expression is his own, and goes back to his years in Istanbul,
years in which he saw the decay of "many things that had been
the adornment of Catholicism". Having lived for so long in
places—Bulgaria, Turkey and, why not? Paris—in which
Catholicism is the religion of a minority and has apparently more
in common with the ruins of the past than with the new structures upon which the future is taking shape, helped him to see the
solution, for himself, and in the end for the advantage of the
whole Church, of the crisis of Catholicism. He began by taking

note, without a great deal of historical research but with a great
power of intuition, of two facts, which will be common knowledge in the Church of the future: the normality of the situation
in which the Christian minority finds itself, and the mystical,
and not political, means by which Catholicism will triumph.

It is difficult for Catholics thoroughly to investigate their
actual position in history without being dismayed. Just as, when
a limb is amputated and the nervous reflexes continue, giving
the impression that the limb is still attached and moving, in the
same way certain Catholic groups behave in modern society as
if their historical organism had never suffered any amputations:
the reflexes are still those of a majority party! Their pride has
not the stamp of genuine feeling, because it has not undergone
the test of truth; it is based upon factual data which are no longer
true and which are artificially kept alive through an effort of the
imagination. Such people speak of the Italians as a Catholic
people, almost as if, to justify such a statement, it were enough to
quote the statistics of baptisms, while totally ignoring the open
disbelief of the majority. They speak of the Christian civilization
of the West as if, for some centuries now, the most characteristic
developments of Western civilization had not been terrifyingly
anti-Christian. Their conscience is not completely adult because
it has never confronted the reality of things with total sincerity,
and still less has it faced those problems which so painfully arise
from this state of things. Why has the gap between the world of
working men and the truths of Christianity become so wide?
Why has the development of the process of industrialization left
the mentality of the masses so denuded of religious concepts? And
why has the apostolic zeal of the Church for so long suffered
almost without resistance the progressive crumbling away of the
"Christian people"? Why does the Christian community, once
sociologically compact—Angelo Roncalli was the son of a community of this kind—for many years now, and in some places
for more than a century, been steadily losing its support among
the working classes, while preserving a hard core which is prevalently bourgeois in formation?

Until one has been moved by the gravity of these problems

one must remain, in the eyes of history, an accused party, and as such one will react against these facts with irritation or dismay. But these problems become less acute and painful when one constantly bears in mind the qualitative superiority of Christianity in comparison with any sociological organization, and the mystical, not political or cultural, role of the Christian as compared with any other form of community. One must also observe the various ways, invisible and compassionate rather than visible and violent, by which salvation overflows from the community of believers to that of unbelievers. Numerous problems seem already to have been solved, for example, in this passage from Mgr Roncalli's *Diario*, dated 25 October 1940:

"According to Sunday's census, Turkey has 17,869,901 inhabitants. My own humble name is numbered among these. May the Lord grant equal grace and mercy to all these souls who have been counted with me. Almost all the thirty cities of Turkey who have more than 20,000 inhabitants were in ancient times the centres of bishoprics. My soul is moved by these memories of so much history and life" (p. 30).

To preserve such serenity, in a country now totally de-christianized, he must have had a lively sense of the all-powerfulness of grace—which can save even unbelievers—and an understanding also of the designs of God, which are served by the failures as well as by the triumphs of the visible Church.[1] In the same city, little more than two years earlier, during Epiphany 1938, the Apostolic Delegate had said to his few faithful:

> Observe this land of Turkey. This was the theatre upon which the adventurous life of the Church was played for so many generations: here the ancient dioceses were as numerous as the stars in the sky. Now all has disappeared; it is hard to identify the ancient localities, it is hard even to name them. Therefore we see that in the Lord's plans all that is material, and by its own nature changeable, is of no importance. We must cling to it because of the link which binds it to what is

[1] I think I detect a thoughtful and trustful presentiment of future events in this greeting to a pilgrimage of Portuguese Catholics (Audience of 24 Oct. 1962): "Return to your homes, to your own people, and say that the Pope is near to you all; say that he scans the far horizons with a father's anxiety."

more sublime, and more sure. We must therefore venerate these places, even in their devastated condition, the memorial monuments, even if in ruins, and the relics, especially if they are illustrious, but we must not dwell on all this. The kingdom of Jesus is for the good of all men; but it is not dependent on what even in true religion is material, exterior and transitory. Jesus of Nazareth fixed the fundamental lines of the Church herself, but did not bind her to conditions of place and circumstance. The storm sweeps over; it shakes the sturdiest buildings, devastates, transforms everything. This does not matter in the least. In the Lord's plans everything serves his glory, everything bears out his teaching, which purifies and renews the generations of mankind. (L. Capovilla, *op. cit.*, pp. 193–4.)

Here we have touched one of the most delicate points of the spirituality of Pope John.

2. SOCIOLOGICAL OPTIMISM

How is it that he never seems to have felt those pastoral anxieties which have given such intensity, and at the same time such power, to the testimony of many bishops and priests, especially in the last twenty years? And how is it that the knowledge of massive unbelief never inclined him in the slightest degree towards historical pessimism? His language, even in its frank realism, was not very different from that of the organized Christianity of old times. It is true that, in an exhortation to the clergy of Venice, on 10 August 1954, he wrote:

"It is well said that geography and statistics are the two eyes of history. This is true of past events, but even more true with regard to the practical needs of unceasing pastoral care" (*Scritti e Discorsi*, vol. IV, p. 52).

But these recommendations to use modern methods to find out the actual religious condition of society are not to be compared with the profound and cruel analyses by means of which France, for example, in the post-war period, convinced herself that she was a *pays de mission*.

Even his scholarly researches seemed to prefer fields less

darkened with passion and still lit by the piety of a people who had remained compact in their faith.[2] It is possible that he never fully shared the adventurous zeal—exposed to most insidious temptations—of the worker priests:

> I have been told an anecdote about the worker priests. It is very significant. "You are a priest," some workmen said one day to one of these good honest priests who had put on over-alls to work at their side: "This is no place for you. Here is a bit of spare ground for you: we will help you to build a chapel hut. We will bring our wives and children to it and, who knows? perhaps we will come too. This is what we want from you: your Gospel and your altar, nothing else."[3]

His vision of the priesthood had remained unchanged from that formed during his long training as a seminarist and his first pastoral experience with Mgr Radini. How was it then, that he was able to understand the modern world so clearly and fulfil its expectations with such courage as not to disappoint even pioneers of the most daring pastoral reforms?

It is probable that Mgr Roncalli kept free from sociological and pastoral pessimism not because he did not, substantially, share the same conclusions and plans, but because he felt in that realism, made up of figures and technical terms, a certain lack of super-natural spirit. It is probable that in him this sensation never be-came self-conscious or deliberately supported by research, and that, with his wholly instinctive realism he felt that the so loudly trumpeted decadence of Christianity was not so real after all! Perhaps the tragedy of dechristianization had been graver in those ages when it went unnoticed; perhaps the so-called Christian peoples, compared with whom the world of today appears to be

---

[2] The mere mention of four works by Pope John shows the general character of his historical interests: *Gli inizi del Seminario di Bergamo e S. Carlo Borromeo*, Bergamo, 1939; *La "Misericordia Maggiore" di Bergamo e le altre istituzioni di beneficenza, amministrate dalla Congregazione di Carità*, Bergamo, 1912; *In memoria di Mons. Giacomo Maria Radini Tedeschi*, Bergamo, 1916; *Gli Atti della Visita Apostolica di San Carlo Borromeo a Bergamo* (1575).

[3] In *Scritti e Discorsi*, vol. III, p. 96. The passage is taken from a speech to the *Assistenti delle ACLI*, 24 July 1956. Perhaps it should not be taken as a peremptory and direct judgment of the Worker Priests. It shows, however, that he had little confidence in the pastoral methods used by the most advanced wing of the Catholic Church.

so dechristianized, were a phenomenon more sociological than genuinely religious.

The word "people" has two meanings: the first is the common meaning, which has for its content the citizens of a single territorial community, either independent of any distinction of class, or with a more or less polemical exclusion of the ruling classes. The second meaning is truly theological, and has for its content the community of those who believe in Christ the Saviour and await his return. Has there ever been—and this is an interesting question—a time when these two meanings were included in the same term? Apparently yes. There were a few epochs when, in some parts of the world, every citizen was a Christian simply by virtue of his citizenship. Ecclesiastical and civil institutions had, more or less, the same subjects, so that these could, in some sectors, arrange an interchange of functions: the priest was an officer of the State, who kept the register of births, and the civil power gave legal status to the precepts of the Church. It was right, in those days, to speak of Christian peoples and Christian nations. The clergy, because they were, and are, in the ecclesiastical order a ruling class, found themselves naturally allied, generally without ill-will or ulterior motives, with the ruling class of the civil order. Does this combination belong to the nature of things? Or is it an accidental product of history? The true hypothesis is the second. The identification of the sociological notion of a people and their theological character is erroneous.

To judge from Pope John's own words, it would seem that he felt a certain nostalgia for a world organized in accordance with a twofold and harmonious hierarchy, religious and civil. His language has, at least formally, the overtones of triumphal expectation. But within the context of traditional concepts and words there is clearly circulating a new idea, that which during his pontificate inspired him to such bold initiatives.

He was sure that, in comparison with the Church of other glorious epochs, the Church of today "has gained in spirituality and depth". The triumph of Christ today is not shown in splendid and magnificent processions, but in the ever more numerous signs "of souls tired and disappointed by vanity turning towards the purest source of truth and life". The masses, it is said, are dechristianized. This is true and sad. But, before drawing up the melancholy balance sheet we should ask ourselves how far they were ever christianized, or if they ever were a Christian people. In order truly to form part of the people of Christ there must be a mature faith. And there is no truly mature faith without the knowledge and possibility of choice. When, after Peter's speech on the day of Pentecost, three thousand persons asked to be baptized, this seemed to be a collective choice, but in reality it was a personal choice made by each; every one of the converts knew what he had chosen. But when Clovis bowed his head under the hand of St Remigius, and with him the whole tribe of the Franks allowed itself to be baptized, there is no reason to believe that any of these converts knew what they were doing. From then onwards the tribes became Christian merely to follow the example of their head. The patient teachings of the catechumens, which made the Christian community of the first centuries so rich in faith and instruction, disappeared almost entirely. The knowledge that the act of faith was a difficult choice which pledged all future loyalty, equivalent to a *metanoia*, a conversion, became almost an aristocratic privilege. People became Christians as naturally as they were born.

Possibly in the uneducated masses this collectivist passivity has always survived. It was contained within the Christian framework as long as the sociological premises remained; when the social transformation broke the ancient mould the masses became dechristianized by the same process by which they had been christianized, that is without being fully conscious of their "perversion".

Therefore, when we speak of the decay of Christianity, we attribute perhaps too much importance to a sociological process which does not really touch the essential truths of the Christian message: it merely modifies the conditions in which it can be effective. Pope John showed that he was not deluded in his belief that, far from falling into decay, Christianity has today possibilities of diffusion and incarnation never known in the past. Step by step as, by means of culture and technical skill, the masses acquire a knowledge of the choices set before them, and on the social plane assume a role that is no longer passive as in the past but active and self-conscious, they may become the people of God and approach the truths of the Christian faith with that integrity of psychological capacity without which the act of faith brings about no real spiritual revolution. The human process of elevation of the masses, which caused the breakdown of the Christian sociological organization, may predispose the people to a conversion, undoubtedly not so totalitarian as that of the German tribes, but more self-conscious and more human. Then the leaven will be seen as something different from the lump without being separated from it: the people of God will be seen to be different from the peoples who are governed and led by human laws: they will then be a sign raised among the nations, without ever identifying themselves with any particular nation.

3. TO PREPARE A PERFECT PEOPLE

Without breaking with the past, without even abandoning its language, Pope John began his pontificate with these ideals in his heart:

> God grant that both Johns may make their voices heard in the universal Church, through our very humble pastoral ministry. This is our heart-felt wish: "to make straight his paths, so that the crooked may be made straight, and the rough ways may be made smooth, and all flesh may see the salvation of God."

> The mission of the humble Pope John is to "make ready a perfect people".[4]

Christianity will be less and less a phenomenon of the masses and more and more the phenomenon of a people: there will be, in the eyes of all, a "people of God", that is, unarmed, and rich only in their own spiritual gifts and weapons. The almost hasty eagerness with which Pope John, first through the Roman Synod, and later through the Council, took steps to reform the Church in accordance with a truly pastoral spirit, suffices to demonstrate that this had been the idea dominating his whole life. He was still

[4] Christmas message of 23 Dec. 1958.

Patriarch of Venice when, during a congress at La Mendola in July 1956, after having described in vivid terms the "colourless and wearisome old age" of churchmen with a bureaucratic mentality, he exclaimed:

"On the other hand how beautiful and how happy is the youth of priests inspired by the sublime purposes of the sacred service of Holy Church, which spreads wide her wings over the innumerable 'people of Christ'."

The conditions for restoring the holy people of Christ are manifold: from theological re-statements (and in the Constitution *De Ecclesia* the chapter on the "People of God" has had wide and fertile results) to canonical re-statements (the Roman Synod, in the intention of Pope John, was to be an example of the reconstruction of the diocesan pastoral college), and to ascetical and pastoral directives. God granted to him the special gift or *charisma*, which has influenced the whole Church, of drawing to himself the masses, for so long inert and separated from the Church because of pastoral neglect and political prejudices. And he pointed out the way to raise the masses to a conscious and joyful response to God's Church with the example of his pastoral fervour, which in the last months of his life had been made more eager and productive of good results by his awareness of his success and of his approaching end.

Already in the first months of his pontificate he was able to note the sudden re-stirring of Christianity in the Roman people, indeed in the whole world, and he spoke of this on 23 December 1958 without any veil of false modesty. It was enough for him to go out from the Vatican, and break a tradition of distant and hieratical immobility, for the joy of faith to flower once more in the depths of the people's soul.

> In the intimate, although imperfect knowledge which we have of ourselves, and in the humility of our soul, we feel the need to take note that it is not simply because of the human and friendly conduct of our humble person that we have been able—as you so kindly tell us—at once to win the affection of peoples and governments, which has been particularly evident in the immediate outbursts of joy and respectful affection on

the part of the people of Rome. It is also because there has been a renewed outpouring of the grace of the Holy Spirit, which was promised to the Lord's Church, and which finds a constant flood of new expressions which arouse much pious wonder around us. .... And it is a special joy to see how the great crowds that seek us, call us, and applaud without ceasing, is formed above all of young people of every sort, thrilled with devoted admiration and lively and innocent enthusiasm, as if they wish to assure us that they, the young, are more ready and more worthy than the old or the mature to defend and do honour to the inheritance of Christ, the glorious and immortal King of all peoples and all ages.

In an exhortation, written on 25 April 1959 and intended for the clergy gathered in the basilica of St Mark's in Venice, to honour the remains of Pius X, he described very vividly the ideal bonds which unite the people to the priest. At a certain point, when enumerating the qualities of the holy pope, he seems involuntarily to be drawing an intimate portrait of himself.

Why do the people pray to this saint? Why do they seek him? Why do they love him? The answer is easy. There was in him the wonderful combination of those positive gifts which are the particular characteristics of every social class. As sincere as the children of the countryside, as frank and robust as the workers in our factories, as patient as our fishermen, as gentle as the shepherd of a flock, as noble and austere as the descendants of the greatest families, friendly and just as a teacher or a magistrate, good and generous as we imagine the saints to be, and as they are.

In order to reconstruct the Christian people according to the new capacities which they now possess, we must have pastors of a universal appeal and of a natural nobility, rich in attractive power as well as in moral worth. They must be set before the eyes of the people in all its variety of class as a term of reference, near to all but bound to none. They must, in short, offer to men, who are the prisoners of their natural conflicts, the possibility of a religious escape from all this, of that peace of the soul which all, even atheists, desire. Once we have guaranteed this transcendence of religion above everything else ("Christ did not go in for sport or politics") the pastor, whether he be pope or a simple priest, will see the people approaching him with ever diminishing diffidence and with growing enthusiasm.

Is this intuition of Pope John's a true one? He proved it, we may say, upon himself. His behaviour towards the civil authority and with regard to political conflicts, in which he never allowed himself to be involved, his teaching, always about religion and directed towards peace, his joy in making direct contact with the people: all this helped to make the people's love and confidence flow out to him, with a swiftness that seemed miraculous. He noted in August 1962:

> The large Audiences (in preparation for the Council) were very useful for this purpose. They were perhaps too crowded, as they included representatives from every country in the world, full of spiritual and religious fervour, and a sincere and pious enthusiasm which is edifying and encourages optimism. What seems clear and providential is that all these crowds of Italians and still more of "foreigners" who come to Rome know at once how to distinguish between the sacred and the profane; that is, Rome the capital of Catholicism and the seat of the universal Roman pontificate, and the Rome of ancient ruins and the whirlwind of secular and . . . worldly living which rages even on the banks of the Tiber. All this, however, with mutual respect among the various human elements, and no unfriendliness between Italians and non-Italians. (*Journal*, p. 321.)

4. POPE JOHN AND THE COMMON PEOPLE

But what moved, consoled and convinced him most was his experience of direct encounters with the people of Rome.[5] When,

[5] Particularly during the last year the Pope seemed to cherish, as a sign from God, these warm-hearted meetings with his people. "Every Sunday", he said at Loreto, "from our window in the Vatican palace, for the mid-day Angelus, we see in St Peter's Square a throng of people which gives me so much comfort and joy. The Pope's voice, trembling with joy, repeats: *Angelus Domini nuntiavit Mariae*, and the crowd, assembled from all over the world, calls back: *Et concepit de Spirito Sancto*. In this way the earth shares in the happiness of Heaven in a single throb of love and praise for our Divine Saviour and his and our Blessed Mother."

In an Audience of the 27 March 1963 he rejoiced because—we quote from an account in the *Osservatore Romano*—"in Rome the Pope is not a hermit, forgotten by all. Even if, because of well-known circumstances, in the last decades of the last century and the first

during the Sundays in Lent, he visited many parishes on the outskirts as well as in the old centre of ancient Rome, he was able to
perceive the latent expectations of the ordinary people, accustomed to thinking of the clergy—just imagine the Pope!—as the
ally of the powers that be, who exploit and ignore them. Everyone
understood that it was simply fatherly love which brought him
to them and kept him talking to them. The political parties
hastily gave up any public attempt to discredit or exploit the
popular enthusiasm, realizing that it was so sincere and so strong
that it would have rejected any eventual intention to exploit it
for electoral purposes. The most objectionable political banners
were taken down in those quarters of the city through which he
passed: the people of the *borgate* (the poorer suburbs) found again,
for a space, that moral and religious unity for the preservation
of which they lack even the most indispensable civic organizations.

How can we describe those Sunday drives, their almost
Eastern joyousness, and Pope John's speeches, truly delivered as
one of the people speaking to the people? And yet these were
circumstances heavy with future consequences. Not only did the
people of Rome thus find their true selves again (the same people
who were later to await Paul VI on his return from the Holy
Land, an immense crowd of silent, noble people) but Pope John
too, as we learn from reliable witnesses, rediscovered, on these
Sunday drives, an almost forgotten aspect of the pontifical
dignity.

I have traced, in the newspapers of 1963,[6] two accounts which
best describe the circumstances and the direct encounters of Pope
John with the crowds during those Lenten visits.

The first is dated 3 March 1963, in the quarter of the Quartic-
ciolo, perhaps the most ill-famed suburb on the outskirts of Rome.

of the present, he was obliged to remain almost secluded in his residence, now he can
easily permit himself, every now and then, an excursion from the Vatican and a visit,
however modest, to his people. At times, on these occasions, wonderful and moving things
occur. As soon as it becomes known that the Pope is going to pass by, and will go to
such and such a place, there is a rush of enthusiastic faithful, and faces, hearts and voices
are full of joy. It is the deep and whole-hearted exultation of the children of God. Take
note that the Pope is not going there to distribute tokens of his supremacy, presents,
money or things considered necessary for life on this earth. No, he brings and gives the
Lord's blessing."

    [6] The accounts given by A. Sterpellone in *Il Messaggero* are particularly detailed and
vivid. I have made use especially of his reports of 4 and 25 March 1963.

The whole population of the zone was awaiting the Pope in the great square in front of the church, and within the newly white-washed walls of the church. When the Pope went up the steps to the altar, the crowd burst into an explosion of joy. The Pope began to speak, but his first words broke against that barrier of uncontrollable voices and enthusiasms.

"But", said the Pope, "if we are to understand each other, it is necessary for you to keep silence while I speak. I have come a long way to speak to you. But now you want to do all the talking. If this goes on, mind, I shall go back to the centre. Absolute silence is necessary. Try to discipline your tongues, if you wish to gladden your hearts."

The prelates looked around them in dismay. The happiness of the people was so great as to lead them to disobey even the Pope. But he alone understood how matters stood, and he did not get flustered: he went on speaking and smiling. He spoke of the prize recently awarded him by an international body for his work in favour of peace in 1962:

"The Pope's greeting", he said, "is always this: *Pax vobis*, peace be with you. These words were pronounced by God's own Son, they are indeed a precious greeting. Now it is not only churchmen who hail the Pope as he passes by and return this greeting of his, but Heads of States too. The Pope has shown himself grateful and courteous before this award they have been pleased to grant him. We know no other peace but the peace of Christ, won by the blood of Christ and preached for so many centuries by the Church."

The Pope then spoke to them confidentially:

"These visits outside the Vatican, in the parishes of my diocese, for this Roman Lent, are a great joy to me. The Pope is a recluse in his great palace; all the world comes to see him, but he is a recluse, he lives in two or three rooms at most, all enclosed. Let the Pope come out a little, at least for Lent, to inspire you with Christian ideals, and to help us all in our sacrifices."

Then he returned to the theme of peace:

"Peace does not imply only the responsibility of those who hold in their hands the destinies of the world; it is also the duty of every one of us to make peace with himself, with his own conscience, and with God. It means peace in families: the Pope rejoices when he finds himself among those of his parishioners who are of humble social conditions, because he too was born of a humble family."

He concluded:

"We must spread abroad the spirit of peace. It must also be accompanied by sacrifice, which will be unfailingly rewarded hereafter. I am confident that the Lord will fulfil the hopes and expectations of the world, which is longing for peace."

Probably the Pope would have liked to go on talking with the people, but there was all that "murmur", as he called it, and so he ended in some haste.

On 24 March he went to Ostia, never before visited by a pope. Around the church of Ostia-Lido, dedicated to the Queen of Peace, a great crowd gathered, greeting him with tremendous applause. The Pope was happy; behind the crowd he could catch a glimpse of nature, the sky, the sea, a source of spiritual serenity.

"For the first time", he said, "the Bishop of Rome has the joy of seeing his children of the marine quarter."

He described the enthusiasm which greeted him as "lively devotion, an expression of youth, and of profound conviction".

"Nature", he continued, "fosters this feeling of youth, this expansion; the sky and the sea are here. Nature is an element of tranquillity. But we have come here, not to enjoy a beautiful spectacle but to invite you to recollect your souls."

He then referred to certain manifestations of barbarism which may find their expression in the wake of sporting events—evidently he was referring to the incident which had occurred at Los Angeles in connection with the boxer Moore—and reminded them all of the teachings of Christian peace. He commented on the Gospel passage for the day, dedicated to the miracle of the multiplication of the loaves and fishes:

"Christ did not go in for sport or politics, but what he said touched the hearts of all; he miraculously satisfied the hunger of the crowd who followed him and needed food. But above all he fed men's souls."

Turning to the young men he said:

"All this youth around me, how can it busy itself only with the things of this world?"

And he encouraged them to rise to greater heights, to the greatest height of all, the priesthood.

He got back into his car and proceeded along the road to Fiumicino. The travellers who were going and coming, crowding around the airport, saw the long cavalcade drive underneath the projecting roof and wondered what great personage was passing through. Then they saw him, behind the glass screen of the car which was going at a walking pace: the Pope was blessing the people, was observing the buildings,[7] the constructions, the aeroplanes on the tarmac, the crowds thronging the terraces, and the chapel of Santa Maria degli Angeli. Then, on to the motor way, towards Rome, under the declining moon.

By the side of the road were long lines of cars, immobile, and people who were surprised and happy to see the Pope. At the village of San Francesco, near Acilia, the papal procession was blocked by the people. The Pope had the cover of his car thrown back, rose to his feet, and waved his travelling hat:

"I give you a great blessing", he said, "it is the first time I have met with such a welcome, such a gathering on all sides. This gives me great joy, but also makes me a little sad, because I cannot stay longer with you."

The people had gathered closely around him, and in their joy had surrounded the car, thwarting all attempts at formality, which some officials were attempting to save *in extremis*. But everyone, even the policemen, were amazed by the spectacle, and allowed the Pope to speak to the people and the people to cry out all their joy to the Pope. Above their heads they waved a poster: "*Al Papa je volemo bene, co' tutto er core*," it said: "we love the Pope with all our hearts."

A triumphal Lent, in short, for the heart of the Pope: nobody beside himself knew that this triumph was also his last farewell. On Easter Day, 1 April, he addressed a very special message

---

[7] We know from a sure source that he intended to go by air to Milan, Bergamo, Venice, and if possible to Istanbul and the Holy Land. The trip to Fiumicino was, so to speak, exploratory.

of thanks to the Romans among the crowd which thronged St Peter's Square:

> You have well deserved the presence of your bishop in your various parishes during the Sundays of Lent. These spontaneous, touching meetings have diffused serenity, re-aroused good intentions, and strengthened good will. What an unforgettable spectacle it was when you, young fathers of families, raised your little children high in the air, as if you were saying: "Here is the Rome of tomorrow!" In those moments our arms were opened to you, but our voice could not fully express the tenderness of our heart.

For Christmas the year before he had said, this time to the whole world:

> Our heart enters your homes, all lit by the joyful expectation of the divine Saviour's birth, and swells with tenderness, to greet you and express our fatherly hopes for you. We would like to be able to linger at the table of the poor, in the factories, in the homes of scholars and scientists, by the bedside of the sick and old, wherever men pray and suffer, work for themselves and others, labour fervently with the work of their hands, or in the training of heart and mind. Yes, we would wish to lay our hand on the heads of the little ones, to look the young in the eyes, to encourage the fathers and mothers to do their daily duty. To all we would repeat the angel's words: "I bring you good news of a great joy: your Saviour is born."

It is not surprising that the people, and especially the ordinary people, gathered around his deathbed with a unanimity such as no one could recall. He had rediscovered the "people of God", by the simplest means: with the words of the Gospel and with his naturally affectionate ways. In those sacred hours, and from his agony till his burial, the whole Church could measure, with astonished eyes, how great had been the spiritual revolution brought about by Pope John.

While the sociological structure of Christianity is crumbling, and the people are engaged in erecting worldly structures and in the pursuit of worldly ideals, the Church is undoubtedly losing its political power and influence. But perhaps it is acquiring the power to reconstruct, within purer and more evangelical terms, the royal people won by Christ. In fact, these people are already here, at our disposal, but, in the confusion of their dispersal, they need a pastoral care more appealing to their hearts, now so changed, they need a liturgy adapted to their new conditions and a theological language less archaic, more akin to their own realistic and rational idiom. And it was to preserve in their integrity the right means of restoring the people of God that Pope John summoned the Council, and bequeathed to us his example and his fatherly and vigorous warning:

No, we cannot boast before God. But if these continued demonstrations of affection for our humble person are not an illusion of our self-love, but a phenomenon which corresponds to the reality of the resounding words with which we began the sacred rite, and if we really find ourselves in the presence of the "Lord's testament", which continues to attest his assurance of his presence and assistance to his people, do you not think this would be the moment to stir up more and more our courage and our religious fervour, and our efforts to apply more faithfully the first divine precept, as the basis for human and social order, for the preparation of the kingdom of God on this earth?

While in various Italian cities and in other European countries active Catholics, bold bands of youthful enthusiasts, have been commemorating the *Rerum Novarum* of the great Pope of the working people and joyfully celebrating the new conception of Christian democracy, I, who am not yet prepared for apostolic work, thought that the best way for me to celebrate the great event and offer my own modest tribute of praise and ardent enthusiasm for the great idea was to cling more closely to Jesus in love and prayer. I prayed with fervour before the Blessed Sacrament, the real Bread of heaven which will give true life to the world; at the feet of the white Immaculate Virgin, in the pretty flower-adorned chapel of the young North American States and, most fervently of all, before the beautiful statue of the Sacred Heart of Montmartre, an affectionate tribute from penitent and devout France. Oh, how beautiful and majestic Jesus is in the Blessed Sacrament on the precious altar, such a loving figure amid his rejoicing saints and adoring angels! The social question is a question of life, not simply material but spiritual life. Amidst the agitation of thinking people and the lamentations of the poor, the earnest work of apostolic souls, the struggles, the disillusions and the triumphs, I find my attention and my interest are held and my fervent wishes and labour fully pledged when, in the background of this great picture, I seem to see Jesus, like the sun in spring-time, rising above the vast sea; his face is mild and serene, his arms opened wide, his Heart on fire with a flame that surrounds and suffuses everything. You, O divine Heart, are the solution of every problem, *solutio omnium difficultatum Christus*; all our hopes are in you, to you we look for salvation.

O Jesus, come back into our society, our family life, our souls, and reign there as our peaceful sovereign. Enlighten with the splendour of faith and the charity of your tender Heart the souls of those who work for the good of the people, for your poor; impart to them your own spirit, a spirit of discipline, order and gentleness, preserving the flame of enthusiasm ever alight in their hearts.

O Jesus, if one day I can do any good, here I am in the ranks of your fighting men. Oh, may my preparation in your school be

really serious, profound and productive of excellent results, because it is easy to lose a sense of direction. May that day come very
soon, when we shall see you restored to the centre of civic life,
borne on the shoulders of your joyful people! (*Journal*, 1903,
pp. 125–6.)

"The problem of the conversion of the world"

My priesthood means not only sacrifice for the sins of the
world and for my own sins but also an apostolate of truth and
love. My vocation leads me to this. The thought of the little I
have done till now and the pardon I have received from the Lord
for my past failings must induce greater fervour.

"Mercy and truth, the universal ways of God." It is here I
must distinguish myself. I must not be a teacher of political
science, of strategy, of human knowledge: there are teachers
galore of these subjects. I am a teacher of mercy and truth. And
by teaching these I shall also contribute a great deal to the social
order. This is stated also in the Psalms: "Mercy and truth have
met together: justice and peace have kissed." My teaching must
be by word and example: therefore principles and exhortations
from my lips and encouragement from my conduct in the eyes
of all, Catholics, Orthodox, Turks and Jews. "Words move but
examples draw."

"The wicked shall be converted to thee." The problem of the
conversion of the irreligious and apostate world presents one of
the mysteries which weigh most heavily on my soul. However,
the solution is not my business but the Lord's secret. On my
shoulders, on the shoulders of all priests, all Catholics, rests the
solemn duty of working together for the conversion of this im-
pious world and for the return of heretics and schismatics to the
unity of the Church, and the preaching of Christ to the Jews who
put him to death. We are not responsible for the result. Our sole
comfort, but it is enough for our peace of mind, is knowing that
Jesus the Saviour is much more anxious than we are for the salvation of souls; he wants them to be saved through our co-operation, but it is his grace alone, working in their souls, which saves
them; and his grace will not be lacking when the moment comes
for their conversion. This moment will be one of the most joyful
surprises of our glorified souls in heaven. (*Journal*, 1940, p. 250.)

"Christ borne on the shoulders of the people"

The taking possession of the archbasilica of the Lateran, "the mother and head of all the churches of the city and the world", meant in ancient times the most solemn investiture of supreme power in the ecclesiastical government of Rome which ruled the whole world.

In fact, the Pope, after accepting his election by the Cardinals, does not need this special investiture, as he has already immediately become the bishop of Rome and the successor of St Peter in the universal government of the Church. But we know that even in the greatest affirmations and manifestations of the spiritual and supernatural order the human eye has always wanted and still wants to play its part. Peoples, times, and tastes change. The grand processions which in ancient times accompanied the newly nominated popes from the Vatican to the Lateran, along the "Pope's Way", almost the same road that we followed this morning coming here, would now no longer be understood. The descriptions given by the author of the *Ordo Romanus XIII,* 1271–76—of the times of the Popes Blessed Gregory X of Piacenza, Blessed Innocent V of Tarantasia, and Pietro Ispano, the XXIst of the series of Johns, from whom in all humility we took our name (1272), may seem outdated.

And yet all is not changed. The ancient procession with everyone on horseback: twelve standard bearers with their banners, groups of lay dignitaries, of choristers, of ecclesiastical dignitaries, bishops and archbishops, of Cardinals, and finally the Pope, no longer pass in front of the magnificently adorned Capitol, nor do they pause to receive from the Senator of Rome the homage of the City: but the various dignitaries who represent the civil order who in Rome today direct the government of public affairs, of cities, regions, and of the entire nation, are still present to confer dignity and meaning, under the golden vaults of this temple. They have come here to this great ceremony of the enthronement of the new bishop of Rome as heir and successor of the Prince of the Apostles, the Head of the universal Church.

Oh, what a wonderful vision is presented by our most sacred archbasilica, which truly in the words of the Holy Father Pius XII, *"praerogativa dignitatis praeclarorum eventuum memoria, antiquitatis monumentis praefulget"*!

Oh, how pleasant it is for upright men, inspired by the spirit of Jesus, to take part in peaceful and uplifting occasions, such as this most happy occasion we are now celebrating, which, tempering the harshness of life, calms those anxieties which the vicissitudes and adversities of every day multiply about our paths, and induce us to forgive, to understand and to love; they give us renewed courage for the performance of our duties and respect for the rights of others, in harmony with what we believe to be our own legitimate rights.

The new Pope's procession has, along the way, lost the pomp of the great old days, but how much it has gained in spirituality and in profound meaning!

People no longer look to the Pope as to a prince, adorned with the symbols of his external power; they look to him as a priest, a father, a shepherd. A modern sociologist, a fervent and profoundly pious Catholic, at the beginning of our own times, which are so much agitated by problems of social order and disorder, expressed the wish that the twentieth century would see Christ returning in triumph, borne on the shoulders of the people.

Alas! Christ has not yet returned in the fullness of his triumph. But the signs that souls tired by vanity and disillusionment are turning to the purest source of truth and life are multiplied before our eyes, and this widespread participation in the Church's joy at the succession of men called to the loftiest and most solemn apostolic ministry is a sure indication of spiritual progress and copious blessings. (*Discorsi Pg.*, I, pp. 36–38, 23 Nov. 1958.)

"*Do not look for new and untried ways*"

The figure of St Pius X, invoked as another heavenly protector of the Ecumenical Council, stands out from the events and circumstances which in his own times led to the formulation of bold and tendentious judgments, and makes us all the more convinced that we are not to look for new and strange ways of achieving the salvation of man and the defence of his rights, or let our fancy suggest easy deviations which we hope will take the place of what is rooted in the very essence of most solid institutions, and is supported by centuries of experience. This means that we must: seek first in the East to draw closer together with our separated brethren, then seek a *rapprochement* and the perfect reunion of so many with the ancient Mother of all; in the West we must aim at the generous pastoral collaboration of both clerical bodies, under the observation and direction of the bishop, who is the shepherd of all the sheep.

The memory of how St Pius X, and we saw this with our own eyes, was saddened by the acclamations of the crowd on the day of his coronation, is indicative of his mind and character.

He loved people, understood the exuberance of their feeling, and was willing to share their joy. But his bowed head, the slow, slight gesture of his hand raised in blessing, his eyes reddened with tears, his smile that was so slow in coming, remained in the memory of all who were present at that ceremony of 9 August 1903, to reveal the inner self-control of that Venetian priest, whose goodness of heart was soon understood by all in its true significance.

In everything the priest must show a sense of moderation, of graciousness, of friendly courtesy. You understand us. The faithful do not like to see you absorbed in practical matters, as if you had to solve every problem within one generation; and they do not appreciate the priest who shows himself too hot-tempered and biased. You must know how to wear the noble and distinguished clerical garb on every occasion with great dignity: it is the image of Christ's tunic; the priest must be "clothed in Christ" (*Christus sacerdotum tunica*); your dress is the shining mark of the interior robe of grace.

It is a great merit to control yourself "in days of wrath", so that friends may find in you the moderators of even their most generous passions, and enemies also, if you should meet with any, may judge you to be men of proven honesty.

Beloved sons! The world still feels, always feels, the appeal of goodness and holiness. You are witnesses of this in these days of the presence in Venice of Pius X.

Why do the people pray to this saint? Why do they seek him? Why do they love him? The answer is easy. There was in him a wonderful combination of those positive qualities which are the particular characteristics of every social class. As sincere as are the children of the countryside, as frank and robust as the workers in our factories, as patient as the fishermen, as gentle as the shepherd of the flock; noble and austere as the descendants of the greatest families, friendly and just as a teacher or a magistrate, good and generous as we imagine the saints to be, and as they are indeed.

Let us all persevere in this search and in this love for human and Christian values, natural and supernatural, and let us beg the Lord to make us long more and more for this harmony of energies and enthusiasms. The people will follow us, not because they seek us, or to stay with us, but to join us in seeking union with Jesus Christ, who is the "shepherd and bishop of our souls" (cf. 1 Peter 2. 25). (*Discorsi Pg.*, vol. I, pp. 903-4.)

"My own hands extended in blessing"

At dawn on this feast of St Lawrence, at a quarter to six in the morning, I said the Divine Office on the terrace looking towards Rome.

My heart is touched when I think of this anniversary of my ordination as a priest—10 August 1904—in the church of Santa Maria in Monte Santo, Piazza del Popolo. The prelate who ordained me was Mgr Ceppetelli, Vicegerent of Rome, Archbishop and titular Patriarch of Constantinople. I remember it all, at a distance of fifty-seven years. Ever since then I have felt ashamed of my worthlessness. "My God, have mercy."

This form of spiritual retreat has a purpose beyond the usual scope. My heart rejoices at the memory of all the Lord's goodness, in spite of my shame that the effort I have put into my work for him has been so disproportionate to the gifts I have received. This is a mystery which moves me deeply and makes me afraid.

After my first Mass over the tomb of St Peter I felt the hands of the Holy Father Pius X laid on my head in a blessing full of good augury for me and for the priestly life I was just entering upon; and after more than half a century (fifty-seven years precisely) here are my own hands extended in a blessing for the Catholics, and not only the Catholics, of the whole world, in a gesture of universal fatherhood. I am successor to this same Pius X who has been proclaimed a saint, and I am still living in the same priestly service as he, his predecessors and his successors, all placed like St Peter at the head of the whole Church of Christ, one, holy, catholic and apostolic.

These are all sacred words, which have a loftier meaning than that of any unimaginable self-glorification of my own, and they leave me still in the depths of my own nothingness, though I am raised to the sublime height of a ministry which towers far above the loftiest human dignity.

When on 28 October 1958, the Cardinals of the Holy Roman Church chose me to assume the supreme responsibility of ruling the universal flock of Jesus Christ, at seventy-seven years of age, everyone was convinced that I would be a provisional and transitional Pope. Yet here I am, already on the eve of the fourth year of my pontificate, with an immense programme of work in front of me to be carried out before the eyes of the whole world, which is watching and waiting. As for myself, I feel like St Martin, who "neither feared to die, nor refused to live".

I must always hold myself ready to die, even a sudden death, and also to live as long as it pleases the Lord to leave me here below. Yes, always. At the beginning of my eightieth year I must hold myself ready: for death or life, for the one as for the other, and I must see to the saving of my soul. Everyone calls me "Holy Father", and holy I must and will be. (*Journal*, Aug. 1961, pp. 302–3.)

Talks from the window (To the Romans, 11 October 1962)

Dear children, my dear children, I hear your voices. Mine is one voice alone, but it resumes the voices of the whole world; here in fact the whole world is represented.

Even the moon seems to have hastened out this evening. See where she is on high, enjoying this spectacle. We are at the close of a great day of peace, yes, of peace; "Glory to God, and peace to men of good will" (cf. Luke 2. 14).

We must often remember these good wishes. Especially when we can see that we are really caught up and united in the light and sweetness of the Lord we say: "This is a foretaste of what ought to be the life of every day, and all days, and the life which awaits us for all eternity."

If I were to ask you, if I could ask every one of you: "where do you come from?" the children of Rome, who are represented here in a special way would reply: "We are your nearest children, you are our bishop, the bishop of Rome."

Well then, children of Rome, you feel you truly represent the Rome that is the "mistress of the world", as by the will of Providence she has been called to be, for the diffusion of truth and Christian peace.

In these words there is the answer to your homage.

My own person counts for nothing: it is a brother who speaks to you, a brother who has become your father through the will of God. But everything, fatherhood and brotherhood, it is all the grace of God. Everything!

Let us continue to love one another, to love one another in this way; and when we meet let us go on thinking only of what unites us, leaving aside whatever there may be which might cause a little difficulty.

We are brothers! The light that shines above us, that is in our hearts and consciences, is the light of Christ, who truly wishes to rule our hearts with his grace.

This morning we have enjoyed a vision which not even the basilica of St Peter, in the four hundred years of its history, has ever contemplated before.

We belong then to an epoch in which we are sensitive to the voices that come from above: and so we want to be faithful and follow the way which blessed Jesus taught us.

Now I give you my blessing. I beg our holy Immaculate Lady, whose supreme prerogative we celebrate today, to join me in this blessing. I have heard some of you recall Ephesus and the torches lit around the basilica of that city, on the occasion of the Third Ecumenical Council, in 431. Some years ago I saw with my own eyes the monuments of that city which record the proclamation of the Dogma of the Divine Motherhood of Mary.

Now, praying for her assistance and all together raising our eyes to Jesus, her Son, and thinking of what you and your families possess of joy, of peace, and also in some measure of sorrow and trials, receive with willing hearts this blessing from your father. In this moment the sight before me is such as to remain for long in my mind, as it will remain in yours. Let us do honour to the impression made by so precious an hour. May your sentiments ever be such as now we express before Heaven and earth: faith, hope, charity. The love of God, love of our fellows: and then, all together, sustained by the peace of the Lord, forward in all good works!

When you return home, you will find your children; caress them and say: This is a caress from the Pope. You will perhaps find some tears to dry. Have a word of comfort for those who suffer. May those in trouble know that the Pope is with his

children especially in hours of sorrow and bitterness. Finally, let
us all especially remember the bond of love, and singing, sighing
or weeping, but always full of faith in Christ who helps and hears
us, let us go serenely and confidently on our way.

To my blessing I now add my good-night wishes, reminding
you not to stop short at a mere beginning of good resolutions.
Today it may well be said that we start a year which will bring a
great flow of graces. The Council has begun and we do not know
when it will end. If it does not end before Christmas, because perhaps we shall not have succeeded in saying all we wish about the
different themes by that date, it will be necessary to meet again.
Well, finding ourselves again "of one heart and mind" will
always be a joy to our souls, our families, Rome and the whole
world. So we welcome these days: we await them with great joy.
(*Discorsi Cn.*, 1962, vol. IV, pp. 60–63.)

(28 October 1962)

My dear children,

When the father speaks he wishes to diffuse affection and
confidence; and his words have a loftier and more profound
resonance when his eyes contemplate, as mine do now, the variety
and beauty of a festive garland of children.

Today four years have gone by since the Lord, in the goodness of his heart, chose to entrust to me the succession to the
apostle Peter, and by so doing to kindle in my soul an even greater
love for the whole human family.

They have been four years of prayer and service, of meetings
and talks, of happiness and of some suffering too; but every day
has been spent in the willing readiness to do the divine will and in
the certainty that all things are working together for the good of
all.

Today, on this feast of Christ the King, I feel my soul touched
with something that gives me an even greater serenity. In fact the
words of the Gospel continue to give their message: it resounds
from one end of the world to the other, and finds its way into all
hearts.

Dangers and sorrows, human prudence and wisdom, all must
be dissolved in a canticle of love, in a renewed prayer imploring
all men to desire to set up the kingdom of Christ: "a kingdom of

truth and life, a kingdom of holiness and grace, a kingdom of justice, love and peace" (see the Preface of the Feast of Christ the King).

Throughout the world there is a fervour of activity to construct and restore, and to make the divine light shine more brightly upon men. Proof of this is seen in the international associations and congresses of various forms and proportions which offer the spectacle of a new spirit which is penetrating the minds of politicians and economists, scientists and men of letters.

Beloved children, let the efforts of every one of you, of us all, be an example to all, in teaching and renewing in individuals, families and society the splendour of the face of Jesus.

Our Lord Jesus Christ, when he offered himself as a willing and stainless victim on the altar of the Cross, restored man to his heavenly Father's embrace, and opened the way to real progress, which ennobles and sanctifies human civilization.

With these feelings of confidence, imploring God to dispel from the horizons of international life all the clouds which overhang it, I bestow upon this Sunday gathering for the *Angelus*, upon every one of you and all your dear ones, the Apostolic blessing: the promise of grace and strength in the sorrows and difficulties of life, and the hope of great happiness. (*Discorsi Cn.*, vol. IV, pp. 89–90.)

(2 December 1962)

My dear children,

I thank you for your presence and for the significance you have wished to attach to it: your good wishes for my health and for the blessing of God.

The good health which for a moment threatened to depart is about to return, in fact is already returning. Therefore as, like good children, we traverse this earth all together, let us pluck up our courage: each to the performance of his own duty, knowing that there is One who sees us all, strengthens us and awaits us.

Today begins the sacred season of Advent, in the light of Mary Immaculate, the beloved Mother of Jesus and our Mother too, whose Feast we propose to celebrate at the end of this week. All this is already the radiance of Bethlehem, the radiance of Holy Christmas.

Dear children, we wish you already happy Feast days. May they be Feasts of goodness, happiness, peace for all, and for the whole world. Amen, Amen. (*Discorsi Cn.*, vol. IV, pp. 150–1.)

(5 December 1962)

My children, Providence is with us. As you see, from one day to another there is progress, not progress in regression but in slowly rising again. Illness, convalescence: we are now in convalescence.

The joy of the present meeting is a source of happiness, a token of the health and strength which are returning.

A new spectacle today: the Church represented in its entirety. Here is the episcopate, here is the priesthood, here are the Christian people. So the family is complete, the family of Christ.

My children, let us bless the Lord for this joy and this unity. Let us go on trying to help one another, as every one of us proceeds on his way.

We are in the Novena of the Immaculate Conception. I do not wish to leave you on this day without calling you all together around our dear Mother, and with you imploring her again as our mighty advocate and heavenly inspiration of all our activity.

The Council is suspended for a while; but we shall always bear in our heart the sweetness and joy of such a perfect union of all; and not simply considering ourselves as representatives of the clergy and people but as representing the various races of mankind, of the whole world, because the whole world was and is redeemed by our Lord Jesus Christ.

To her then, our Mother, we commend the Holy Church, our families, our lives, and our health, because this too helps us to serve the Lord.

There is a prayer in which the various thoughts here expressed are recorded and included.

Venerable Brothers of the Episcopate, and all who are represented here, dear and true brothers in the sphere of the social order, from the highest degrees to the lowest and humblest, but all brothers and all of the same family, I invite you to recite, with one voice, this most beautiful prayer, suggested by the Church.

"We fly to thy patronage, O holy mother of God; despise not our petitions in our necessities, but deliver us ever from all dangers, O glorious and blessed Virgin."

Dear children, another blessing. . . .

The joys of the soul, like this which we are all sharing together, are a source of lasting joy, strength and courage. Amen, Amen! (*Discorsi Cn.*, vol. IV, pp. 151–2.)

The Pope's Rome

In your dear persons the Pope greets the Rome of the twentieth century, which from her ancient quarters around the ruins of the city of the Caesars, from the basilicas of the Christian era, from the churches and sacred monuments, has stretched beyond her walls towards the hills and the sea, along the course of the Tiber and the course of the Aniene.

To this vast animated expanse, where the Romans live their lives, to the houses and buildings where they work and suffer, go the Pope's thoughts every morning, and several times a day, borne on the wings of prayer, the universal embrace of his prayer in which he wishes our own beloved diocese to have the place of honour.

We love this sacred Rome! When from the Apostolic Palace, from the Torre San Giovanni, or Castel Gandolfo, we contemplate the growing residential centres, our heart trembles with joy, and anxiety. For a bishop it is not a question of available building space, of costly or cheap accommodation: it is a question of souls. It is a problem of sacred buildings and their subsidiary organizations, which must ensure the vigour of worship and religious instruction, the life of generous and manifold associations and social aid. The church is everyone's home, and the organizations which spring up beside her belong to all, and are at the service of every family.

What profound joy I have felt during so many opportunities these four years of meeting with the faithful of the ancient city and its modern outgrowths!

Again the day before yesterday, when we went to venerate the Roman saint, Gaspare del Bufalo, at Santa Maria in Trivio, in one of the most characteristic sectors of Rome, our heart rejoiced and touching memories were recalled.

Forty years ago, along the same roads we followed on Friday, we used to pass to go from Santa Maria in Via Lata to the Piazza di Spagna. Today the activity and the speed of traffic have increased immeasurably. But the Romans still have the same faces, and something lovable about them which makes one say: "Yes, they are good-hearted and sensitive to the appeal of heavenly things." And when we see so many hands waving to us, so many arms outstretched from the buses, the shops, the windows, we seem to hear everyone say about us: "We love this man whom Providence has brought from the holy and noble life of the country-side to the splendour of the Roman pontificate." (To the *Consiglio Comunale* of Rome, 3 Jan. 1963.)

Christmas for all, Christians and non-Christians

The Pope, as everyone knows, says the whole rosary every day. This morning I have already said the first part, the Joyful Mysteries. And you know that for the third Mystery, in which we contemplate the birth of Christ, his prayer extends to embrace all children born in the last twenty-four hours, whether they be Christians or not, since our Lord Jesus Christ came on earth and offered himself, a victim of infinite worth, for all. The world-wide range of our prayer and purpose reminds us that the Pope is not only the Head of the Church, our true and perfect inheritance from Christ, but, as all belong to Christ—"I will make the nations your heritage, and the ends of the earth your possession"—he is also a father to all mankind.

All belong to our Lord Jesus Christ, our Brother, all share in the Redemption he wrought. It is true that there are those who have not yet received this grace, through reasons of an external character, for which they are not responsible: in any case there is the great family of men, not all of whom are Christians. There is that of the whole created universe, which is the work of God and dependent on him.

The great Ecumenical Council—now in moment of pause, but which will soon take up once more its various forms of activity, so as to be able to begin its concluding Session in September—is dealing with various and grave questions. In the work we have so far accomplished, we have more than once received the confirmation that while we must, certainly, think of Catholics, who are so greatly privileged, and so near to Mary and Joseph beside the cradle of our Redeemer, yet we must care for all the others too.

For these too, in fact, Jesus came and dwelt among us; to them he imparted his great lesson of work and obedience; for them he gave the Gospel, which has been the rule of life and the source of civilization for twenty centuries. (*Discorsi Cn.*, 1962, vol. IV, pp. 175–6.)

CHAPTER TEN

The New Age

I. THE "TRANSITION"

THE prophetic nature of the personality and teaching of Pope John is shown in both those spheres in which the revealing power of prophecy is generally manifest: the vision which restores its transcendence to the mystery of the kingdom of God, and that which intuitively understands and emphasizes, in man's temporal affairs, those possibilities which elude most observers and which are, nevertheless, the vital portion of the present and will be clear to all when what has survived of the past has disappeared.

"On the morrow of his election Pope John may have seemed to be a 'transitional Pope'. And this he certainly was, but in an unexpected way which the expression, in its habitual meaning, does not suggest. When history has been set in its proper perspective men will undoubtedly be able to say that he opened a new era for the Church, and prepared the passage from the twentieth to the twenty-first century."

When Cardinal Suenens in this way solemnly recognized before the Council the historic significance of the person of Pope John, he was only giving voice to the general feeling of the Catholic Church, indeed of the whole world. I shall try to content myself with a brief outline, in order to trace the most obvious elements of this transition from one epoch to another, and so give to what I say an objective clarity, unblurred by those legitimate but debatable conjectures which always spring, for our peace and our encouragement, from prophetic influences.

There were probably some who thought that, once the light had gone out in Pope John's window, the great phenomenon of universal emotion and soaring hope would rapidly shrink to reasonable proportions, as if the sense of something historically new projected into the modern consciousness by Pope John were nothing else but the ingenuous product of a collective psychology. But instead, even after his burial, the history of the Church still seems ruled by the same inspiration. There was a general desire to safeguard an unhoped for and precious inheritance. The tomb in the Vatican vaults was hardly closed when a man, upon whom the patriarchal eyes of Pope John had so often lingered in silent predilection,[1] raised his voice aloud in the midst of the universal anxiety:

> We must not look behind us, we must no longer fix our gaze on him, but upon the horizon which he has opened before the onward march of the Church and of history.
>
> Prophecy is a difficult art, but, in this moment, it seems to be made more easy, almost self-evident, in the signs given us by the Pope whose death we mourn. John has laid down some guiding lines for our way, and we shall be wise not only to remember these but to follow them.

The conclave had no hesitations. Paul succeeded to John, by virtue of a supernatural design which had become, in all men's eyes, as peremptory as the word of God. And Paul has let slip no opportunity of acknowledging, in the eyes of the world, the law of continuity which binds him to John.

So the intuition of the novelty of this hour in history has not gone down into the grave; it shines from the same candlestick. Was Pope John aware of this new element? When we read attentively his writings and his speeches, and think over the amazing series of his initiatives, we have the impression that in his mind he was slowly moving in the direction of a new dawn, first barely perceived, later contemplated with inner certitude and

[1] There are many and authoritative witnesses to this, first of all Mgr Loris Capovilla. Cardinal Roncalli thought he had, as it were, taken the place meant for Mgr Montini. Once he became Pope, he made no great mystery of his preferences and previsions. Tommaso Gallarati Scotti gives an interesting account in the *Corriere della Sera* of 2 July 1963: "I remember once when I was with the Patriarch of Venice, with others who could corroborate my testimony, in those days immediately preceding the death of Pius XII, he spoke to us with his usual serene simplicity and detachment from self, of a possible Conclave in the near future. He uttered these remarkable words: 'I am only a Cardinal, I am not the Sacred College, but I know that it is very probable that, faced with the problem of the succession, the choice may be made in your city, Milan, in the person of your Archbishop.'"

joy.[2] "The new day has barely dawned", he said in the conclusion of his speech inaugurating the Council, that is, the speech in which he proposed, with all the marks of supernatural certainty, the lines of renewal for the Church, in the heart of a renewed world.

2. THE END OF AN ERRONEOUS PESSIMISM

It is the general conviction of the theologians and Conciliar Fathers that the Church, in her historical form, is turning from an attitude which sought with some success to ensure loyalty to herself to an attitude which seeks to ensure also her own fulfilment of the expectations of the world. But this change of orientation would be without justification, and above all could not take place with prudence, if it were not founded upon a new examination of the world and a new appreciation of its values. Pope John's merit is to have understood the modern world in what is, so to speak, its fundamental sense of purpose. He understood the world, and judged it, and his judgment was not a condemnation. Pope John's verdict on the essential character of the world of today has put an end to a problem which for centuries has wearied and hampered the missionary heart of the Church, and because of this, all our hearts. What is this?

Our Catholic education has in recent centuries, and not always with the necessary discrimination, associated the mystical dialectic between the Church and the world with the dialectic, of a historical-sociological order, between Christianity and the modern world. According to the former, the world is inevitably, in the eyes of the Church, ambiguous. The two propositions: "the world is good", and "the world is bad" are both true for the Christian. It is not possible for the Christian to choose between optimism or pessimism, as if they were alternative terms. His vision of the world necessarily postulates both the optimistic approach to created reality, and the ruthless struggle against the passions which in fact rule the history of men.

Without a doubt there exist, within every Christian com-

[2] This prophetic vision of the new day is affirmed also by Paul VI, who in his letter to the Cardinal Deacon, on 12 Sept. 1963, expressed the hope that "the shining day which he saw dawning with the Ecumenical Council may not be late in coming".

munity and throughout the history of the Church, a variety of special gifts which correspond to this. There are, and there have been, saints whose supernatural mission has been to testify, with their own lives, to the wickedness of the world. Are not the martyrs, for example, the blood-stained signs of the irreconcilable enmity between the kingdom of God and the kingdom of this world? And the great ascetics, who, in the age when the Church came to terms with the powers of this world, withdrew into the wilderness of the Thebaid or into hermitages, were they not also witnesses of the other-worldliness of the kingdom of God? The special *charisma* of Christian pessimism is indispensable if the Church is not to lose faith in the mystery of the Cross: the powers of darkness are still at work, the mystery of wickedness is active, and not only in its invisible outposts, but also in the visible outposts of political struggles and scientific researches. It is certainly true that in the New Testament the dominant note is one of pessimism: hence the perennial "other-worldliness" of Christianity, upon which it is all the more useful for us to meditate, the more compulsive our need to engage in the building of the earthly city.

Nevertheless, this genuine pessimism comes up against an impassable barrier in the extraordinary optimism of Christianity, which also, if well understood, is quite other-worldly. What is history if not the development, within time, and as a result of the creative freedom of man, of the world created by God and blessed with his approval? When he had created them God saw that all things were good. That original approval has never been cancelled, even if God, as Scripture forcefully puts it, has sometimes 'repented' having created man. The goodness of things has the same sturdy power of resistance as their ontological strength. From the morning of the creation till now the pleasure God felt at his own handiwork has been running through the universe as blood runs through the veins, as streams flow down from the heights. Even sin did not destroy it: certainly grace restored it and gave it new life. God enjoys his creatures: God enjoys the world, now lit by the Resurrection radiance. From the biblical psalms to the *Canticle of the Creatures* and the *Phénomène humain*, the flow of cosmic and historical optimism has never quite dried up. Indeed, it seems that from time to time, in response to some particular historical need, God sends us champions of Christian optimism, such as St Francis or St Teresa of Lisieux, or finally, and with a power of historical irradiation, Pope John. The world needed to feel itself loved: that is all. And God sent it a heart that could love it and respect it in all that it still retains and fosters of the ancient creative act. The pleasure of the Father Creator communicated itself to the heart of a Pope who, in his turn, without denying anything of the terrible presence of evil, took pleasure in the modern world. "He saw that it was good" in many of its creations and aspirations: he saw that it was good and he rejoiced in it. And the world was overcome with gratitude and surprise. But the essential conflict remains: in every good thing the reflection of evil is to be seen; every flower transforms into attractive petals an evil sap that flows below the sods of Creation. Hence the necessity of a Christian militia, not so much against the modern world because it is modern, as against the world because it is the world.

This is what is not understood by those who, starting from this structural antinomy, believe that they can transform it into another antinomy: that between the Christianity which took its shape in past centuries and the world which is taking on a new shape in this century of ours, so tragic and yet so grand. And this is a fatal error: Pope John solemnly disowned it.

There was a moment, during his speech at the opening of the Council, when we could not believe our ears. Even in its opening sentences the speech seemed to us to be giving expression to an inspiration which had been held back for many years and which finally broke silence in the circle of the bishops' Assembly, that is to say, in the visible structure of the invisible mind of the Church. Among all the speeches of a Pope, that which gives the Apostolic College sitting in Council its instructions for enquiry and definition is certainly the most authoritative. And it was understood that the proposals of Pope John, in spite of the natural and impulsive way in which they were presented, had been thought over for a long time, one after the other, and considered also with the knowledge of the powerful influence they might be expected to wield over the future: but above all they were proposals by means of which, subject to due considerations of prudence, the holy old man wished to give concise and urgent expression to his serene judgment on the modern world:

> In the daily exercise of our pastoral ministry our ears are sometimes assailed by the insinuations of certain souls who, although burning with zeal, are not furnished with a super-abundant sense of discretion or moderation. In our modern times they see only betrayal and ruin; they go about saying that our epoch, compared with the past, is steadily worsening; and they behave as if they had learnt nothing from history, which is nevertheless the mistress of life, and as if at the time of the earlier Ecumenical Councils everything had been working for the triumph of the Christian idea and the Christian life, and for the true freedom of religion.
>
> But we feel we must differ from these prophets of woe, who are always foretelling tragic events, as if the end of the world had come.
>
> In the present order of things, kindly Providence is leading us to a new order of human relationships which, through the work of men, and for the most part even in excess of their hopes, is directed towards the fulfilment of their noblest and most unhoped for plans. He orders everything, even the diversities of human nature, for the greater good of the Church.

That was not the voice of Angelo Roncalli, it was the voice of the Church, "the voice"—again his own words—"which rings out from the Conciliar gatherings held, in East and West, from the fourth century to medieval, and thence on to modern, times; a voice which acclaims, in a glorious crescendo, the triumph of that divine and human society which is the Church!"

"In our own time the Bride of Christ prefers to make use of the medicine of mercy rather than of severer remedies; she thinks that, rather than issue condemnations, she should try to satisfy the needs of today, by proving the truth of her teachings."

We may say quite simply that with these words of the Pope a whole era of the history of the Church is solemnly, with the approval of the whole ecclesiastical authority, declared closed, and that from that moment the Church has achieved a new consciousness of herself. The Conciliar assembly, receiving such a peremptory warning, far from feeling dismay, rejoiced to hear itself thus freed from a fear complex, and from perplexities concerning possible schemes for the future. The central perspective lines of the Council had been fixed, even if on the canvas the lines seemed confused and contradictory. That central perspective was totally unexpected, apparently, to judge by the criteria governing the seventy Schemes to be discussed in the Council, but in reality, in its most profound consciousness, the whole Church was looking for it and asking for it. The voice of her Head, as the theology of infallibility requires, brought to the light of day her unconscious intuitions, and turned the inarticulate depths of her aspirations into an explicit idea. And in this way there began to take shape, in the most fitting place and manner, a new era of Christianity, which we might call the ecumenical era.

3. THE ECUMENICAL ERA

For centuries the Church has adopted a historical attitude which may be described as polemical: not only has she continued to fight, with mystical arms, against the powers of evil, but she has taken also to opposing the mentality, the research methods, the political ideals and the scientific hypotheses of this world. Having to struggle against the heresies which had torn her asunder and set themselves against her in Christ's name, and being obliged to defend herself against the principles of radical secularism, which not only rejected her teachings but in many ways even attacked her visible organism, the Church has quite legitimately assumed an attitude of self-defence. She has elaborated her theological systems, her disciplinary institutions, even her liturgical teaching, so as to render more difficult, and less dangerous, the contact between her faithful and the world, and to prevent the doctrines of "negation" from filtering into the Catholic mentality. The polemical era of the Church, looked at as a whole, is a great era: anyone who is unprejudiced by certain learned mythologies willingly acknowledges this.

On the other hand, it is for the Church to recognize, at the right moment in history, the *kairos*, the will of God, which is the universal and unchangeable desire for men's salvation, but which in the course of history finds expression in particular forms, all diverse, although directed towards the same end. There is the way of condemnation, and the way of mercy. When is it lawful to pass from one to the other? While leaving to the Church the responsibility of its historic choices, it is nevertheless not hard to find objective reasons for this change of method.

Heresy and apostasy, that is the partial or total rejection of the Christian truth, are morally reprehensible when they contain in themselves the formal element of stubbornness, which means the obstinacy of pride. Already in 1140 the famous Bolognese jurist Gratian, in editing his *Decretum*, the most important Patristic texts (and it is still on Gratian that the *Diritto Canonico* of 1918 is based), describes in the following terms, with the support of St Augustine, the difference between heretics and non-heretics:

Those are heretics who, in the Church of Christ, having been warned, in the hope that they would rectify them, that their opinions are false and unsound, resist with great obstinacy and refuse to correct their pestilential and fatal doctrines. But one cannot in any way number among the heretics those whose opinions may be false and mistaken, but who do not defend them with stubbornness and pride, and above all, those who are not themselves the authors of these but have received them from their parents, who were in their turn deceived.

Operating within a Christianity which had once enjoyed a state of total unanimity, the Church has gradually come to find herself surrounded and threatened by heretics and apostates. We may believe that many of these were not formally such, but it is equally probable that the phenomenon of rebellion brought with it, at least in its initial stages, a large dose of stubbornness and aggressive violence. Thus began an era of especial gravity for the Catholic Church which, in obedience to her own organic laws, began to use all her instruments of defence. The modern world was meanwhile organizing itself in accordance with new values, which the Church judged more in their powers of divergence from the faith than in their capacity for eventual convergence. Theology busied itself above all in tracing, with admirable precision, the line of demarcation between the Catholic truth and modern errors. In this effort to define in clear terms what separates Catholic truth from the modern world, there arose a certain style of formulation, which corresponded perfectly to the polemical purpose dominating the Church but which, at the same time, made it more and more difficult for secularized man to enjoy the inheritance of Catholic teaching. Not all Catholics succeeded in overcoming the difficulties of a formulation which became the private preserve of specialists. For the most part they were content to live their faith according to the psychological capacity of their understanding and will: as for the intelligence, once it had paid the homage of assent it rejected the discipline of the patient assimilation of formulae, and preferred to turn to the sphere of worldly values.

The grave consequences which Pope John, with his courageous intuition, set out to correct through the work of an Ecumenical Council, are, on the one hand, the spiritual deafness of Catholics themselves to ecclesiastical preaching (which now interests them very little, because of the abyss that separates their own natural idiom from the ancient formulae still used by the clergy) and, on the other hand, the vast and well established indifference of the modern world to the appeals of the Church. Has the time perhaps come when it is no longer necessary for the Church to preserve her polemical attitude to the world of today? Certainly not. But the work of the Church cannot be taken up entirely with polemics, nor can her theology satisfy itself with the list, drawn up centuries ago, of all man's errors. Today the old errors persist, but they have lost a great deal of their former stubbornness and, above all, most of them have abandoned the presumptuous attempt to offer themselves as alternatives to the truth of Christ, as if, in their turgid ideology, they were new religions, destined to bestow on men what men formerly sought in the teaching of Christ.

I do not mean that there are no longer false doctrines, and opinions, and dangerous concepts which we must try to guard against and disperse: but they are so evidently in conflict with the right rules of honesty, and have given such fatal results, that men today seem disposed of their own accord to condemn them, especially ways of living in defiance of God and his laws, and excessive confidence in technical progress, and a notion of welfare based exclusively on the comforts of life. Men are more and more convinced of the supreme value of the human person and his welfare, and of the effort required to bring this about. What counts most is that they have learnt from experience that violence inflicted on others, and armed power and political tyranny can make no contribution to a successful solution of the grave problems which harass them.

This appraisal of the factual conditions of the modern intelligence is not, naturally, incontrovertible, based as it is on a process of induction, inspired by the preference felt for certain aspects of the world of today, rather than for others. This preference is, when all is said and done, a moral choice rather than an inconfutable logical deduction: it is an intuition of love. Now that the whole Church, in her major organs, has made this intuition her own, we may say that upon the inspired decision of Pope John will in great part depend the history of the Christianity of the future. Meanwhile it is certain that, in the space of a few months, from the speech of 11 October to the promulgation of *Pacem in terris*, the world has been shaken, the Church has solemnly reformed its judgment on the values of the modern world and has started the process of a cautious and fertile assimilation of these same values. The Council itself, because of Pope John's explicit and insistently reiterated desire, will be obliged to restate Catholic truth within a formulation more suitable to the modern mind.

Our duty is not only, as if we were concerned solely with antiquity, to guard this precious treasure; it is to dedicate ourselves willingly, eagerly and fearlessly to the work required by our own era, thus proceeding on the way the Church has followed for twenty centuries.

The salient reason for this Council is not therefore the discussion of this or that theme in the fundamental doctrine of the Church, in a more widely diffused repetition of the teaching of the Fathers and of theologians of ancient and modern times, for we must suppose this teaching to be ever present and familiar to our minds.

This alone would not have necessitated a Council. But from renewed, serene and tranquil obedience to the whole teaching of the Church, in its integrity and truth, as it still shines in the decisions of the Councils from that of Trent to Vatican I, the Christian, Catholic and apostolic spirit of the whole world expects a forward leap towards an interpretation of doctrine and a training of consciences, in a more perfect and harmonious loyalty to the authentic doctrine, this also to be studied and expounded in accordance with the forms of enquiry and literary formulation natural to modern thought. The substance of the ancient doctrine of the "deposit of faith" is one thing, and the manner of expounding it is another: and it is this latter which must, with patience if necessary, be considered as of the greatest importance, and be in conformity with the needs and requirements of instruction of a prevalently pastoral character.

This work is the responsibility of theologians, but God alone knows all the benefit that may accrue from it for the instruction of Catholics, until now so ill furnished with theological aids, and so exasperated by prolonged irritation against the modern world; but alongside it there will have to be a new alignment of Catholics on the practical plane, in order to assist mankind's effort to build a more just and peaceful world. This spirit of collaboration with regard to movements of different ideological inspiration is based upon an intuition entirely analogous to that we have already spoken of: the intuition of the real difference between a historical movement and an ideology.

It must also be borne in mind that, for the same reason, we cannot identify false philosophical doctrines about nature and the origin and destiny of the universe and of man with historical movements for economic, social, cultural and political ends, even if these movements originated in these doctrines and have drawn and still draw their inspiration from them. Doctrines, once elaborated and defined, always remain the same; but the above-mentioned movements, operating within historical situations which are perpetually evolving, cannot avoid being influenced by these, and therefore must be subject to changes which may even be profound. Moreover, no one can deny that those movements, to the extent to which they are in harmony with the requirements of right reason, and have made themselves interpreters of the just aspirations of the human person, contain positive elements worthy of our approval.

For this reason, it may happen that a *rapprochement* or a meeting on the practical plane, yesterday considered to be inopportune or useless, may today be advisable, or may become advisable tomorrow (*Pacem in terris*).

4. EXAMINATION AND ACCEPTANCE OF THE MODERN WORLD

How much the Church had needed the historical intuition of Pope John was shown by the Council from the very start of its labours.

One of the first Conciliar acts was a "Message to the Modern World", an entirely new event in the history of the Councils, and one which well expressed the religious intuition of Pope John. According to that intuition, the Church will have to get used to looking for herself outside herself; she must act as she did during the first period of her Mediterranean activity, that is, graft the eternal truth entrusted to her on to the authentic growth of human life today, which must be examined and measured, not by comparison with the mind of past ages, but according to its correspondence to the nature of man, which continually creates for itself its own ways of expression and the organs of its growth.

Moreover, as soon as one looks at the modern world with the serene gaze with which Pope John has accustomed us to regard it, it is easy to see maturing within it realities that are quite reconcilable with the Catholic truth, which indeed might find in them the opportunity and the historical material for a wider expression of herself. Which are, according to Pope John, these "elements" of modernism which, rightly understood, far from setting themselves against the Church, offer her a historical setting capable of affording her a new incarnation? What are, in short, the "signs of the times", in which may be traced the noble countenance of the world of today?

On many occasions Pope John set out to interpret these signs, above all in his *Pacem in terris*; it would be possible, therefore, for us to trace, with the help of his own words, a chart of the modern world which is encouraging and consoling. Many features of the life of today would find their place there, elements which were introduced, at least at the beginning, with anti-Christian intentions, such as, for example, the juridical guarantees of the rights of man, proclaimed by the French constituent assembly, or the distinction, ever more profoundly emphasized from the institutional point of view, between Church and State.

Pope John's image of the Catholic of today is very different from that which was, for example, widely dominant in the era of his childhood, when the Catholic seemed to be more or less aware of being besieged within a "Christian world", which was to be opposed and defended against a "modern world". Pope John's Catholic is distinguished from modern men by the virtues of faith, hope and charity, cultivated and lived within a visible community, the Church. As regards the modern world, Pope John's Catholic does not feel himself alien to it; all that is good in it is his too. He desires and does what he can to promote the rise of the working classes, not only towards better social conditions but also towards full and direct political responsibility: he opposes colonialism in all its forms, including those in which capitalism seeks to perpetuate it, in disguise; he prefers the democratic system to any other political system, and this not simply as a makeshift, that is, as a means of setting up other social systems, but because it best corresponds to the dignity of the human person; he distrusts armaments, and considers the use of atomic weapons to be criminal in itself; he champions the cause of international organizations, as the only ones capable of giving juridical guarantees to the new historic forms assumed by the pursuit of the common good; he does not condemn the process of socialization brought about by improved techniques, but sees also its positive contributions, once it has been adequately incorporated and directed towards forms beneficial to the community as a whole;

he does not reject the collaboration of other men who do not share his ideas, but seeks to work with them, within the limits permitted by real and proven good will. In short, Pope John's Catholic is perfectly at home in the modern world, and if he opposes it, he does so, not because he is a Catholic, but because the modern world is in many of its aspects inhuman, smitten asunder by the onslaught of evil; he opposes it because he is a man like his fellows, a man among men. In fact, he knows that his faith makes him, on the one hand, less perturbed by the evil in the world, because of the victory already won by Christ, and on the other hand gives him a sense of his own greater responsibility to appear and to be, among men, more just, more active, more sincere, in short to excel by virtue of a more integrated humanity, and by a more enlightened collaboration in the process of the unification of mankind, which has shown an almost miraculous progress in recent years.

Already in the Bull summoning the Council, dated 25 December 1961, Pope John, in opposition to the confirmed pessimists, had presented a serenely objective picture of the world of today. But hardly anyone took enough notice of this. To understand to what an extent he trusted in his own intuition we had to wait for his speech of 11 October 1962, which is already a prelude to *Pacem in terris*. In that first Conciliar document he certainly does not deny the grave and deep wounds of the modern world; in fact he enumerates them all, and speaks with profound sorrow of militant atheism.

The painful knowledge of these facts remind us of our duty to be watchful, and to keep alive our sense of responsibility. Disconsolate souls see nothing but shadows darkening the face of the earth. We, instead, wish to reaffirm all our trust in our Saviour, who has not forsaken the world which he redeemed. Indeed, following the advice given by Jesus himself, to study the "signs of the times" (Matthew 16. 4), we think we perceive, in the midst of so much darkness, several indications that give us grounds for hope in the destiny of the Church and mankind. The bloody wars which have followed one another in our own times, the spiritual havoc wrought by many ideologies and the fruits of so many bitter experiences, have taught some useful lessons. Scientific progress itself, which has enabled man to create catastrophic instruments for his own destruction, has produced some anguished heart-searchings; it has obliged human beings to think, to be more aware of their proper limitations, more anxious for peace, and more conscious of the importance of spiritual values; and it has accelerated that process of closer collaboration and mutual integration among individuals, classes and nations, towards which, in the midst of innumerable uncertainties, the human family seems directed.

If such is the world of our times, is it presumption or daring courage to believe, as Pope John said on 11 September 1962, that the hour in which we live is one of the "historic hours" of the Church, and "ready for a new thrust upwards towards loftier peaks"?

Pope John recognized the hour when it came, and gave the Church the upward thrust which can no longer be arrested.

"Now that the hurricane has blown over let us relight our torches"

The problem of the liberty of the Church in the service of Catholic life and the apostolate, and in the service of the rights of the religious conscience, is still a problem of today. After so much blood poured out for the cause of political and national liberty, while our ears still ring with the heart-rending cries of millions of suffering victims whose sole consolation was the thought that they would be contributing to remake a better world, how is it that, in the midst of words of peace, threats of violence can still be heard? The great teaching of the Gospel: "So whatever you wish that men would do to you, do so to them" is still a dead letter for many who are ignorant or forgetful of the great charter of the Christian social order, the Sermon on the Mount.

You understand me well, over and above my words, you people of Lyons, who are the heirs of a glorious tradition of liberty, faith and apostleship, who are set for the edification of the whole of France. You know that in the domestic economy, as well as in questions of the moral and religious order, the revenues and reserves of the past which were stored in the granary, are no longer sufficient to sustain life: it is necessary to work, produce and fight. Let me then urge you to work and fight. Ah! the battle to which I summon you has nothing fierce or violent about it, according to worldly standards. It consists, above all, in respect for the freedom of others. An Apostolic Nuncio can be the bearer only of messages of respect, charity and peace. On this sacred earth, *"Princeps Gallorum"*, where have flourished and still flourish works which make its name famous and admired throughout the world, any reference to effort or conflict can only be rendered in resolutions of an intense and peaceable activity, confident and joyful. But one must be on one's guard. One must do honour to the right and duty to fight *pro Fide et Libertate*, for faith and freedom.

The historian of the Council of Lyons, Matthew Paris, makes us tremble when he tells us of the final scene of that great assembly, and describes how Pope Innocent, after having pronounced from his throne of stone the terrible condemnation: "The Lord Frederick, ex-Emperor, unworthy of the Empire and of the royal sovereignty, is dispossessed by God of all power to rule and reign," threw down on the ground the smoking taper he held in his trembling hand and trampled on it. All those present then threw their tapers to the ground, in imitation of the papal gesture. Upon which the defender of Frederick, Thaddaeus of Suessa, terrified, cried out in terror: "Oh, fatal day, day of wrath! of calamity and misery!"

My brothers of Lyons, the days of wrath, calamity and universal misery have passed over our own heads. But God has abased the proud who wanted to conquer the world. He has struck down those who were responsible, and their formidable armies. The Head of Christendom has not needed to repeat the words of Pope Innocent. Now new horizons are opening before us, and new opportunities are presenting themselves for the improvement and progress of the social order.

Let us gather up all the blessed tapers which the terrible hurricane extinguished. Let us light them again with a new flame, and, gathered joyfully around our father, the august Pontiff Pius XII, like the soldier pilgrims of old, re-form the procession of the Church and march forward, to the music of our hymns.

The Feast of St John the Baptist, the forerunner of our Saviour, to whom this great cathedral church is consecrated, offers us the lyrical inspiration and the melodious notes of the canticle of Zechariah: "... we, being delivered from the hand of our enemies, may serve him without fear, in holiness and righteousness before him all the days of our life."

The centuries pass, my beloved brothers of Lyons, but the Church, like truth, is one and eternal. God's light shines on us from on high. Let us work here below, nobly and indefatigably, for the triumph of true liberty, in all senses of the word. Let us share in works of edification and the apostolate. Let us direct our steps in the paths of truth, so that Christ may be exalted, to his glory and our joy. Let us work for the glory, the prosperity and the blessing of France and all peoples in all ages. Amen. (Allocution delivered at Lyons on 24 June 1945 on the occasion of the 7th centenary of the 1st Council of Lyons. In *Souvenirs d'un Nonce*, pp. 64 *et seq.*)

The prophets who foretold evil

In this modern age the face of the world has changed profoundly, and it is surviving with difficulty amid the fascinations and dangers of the almost exclusive search for material goods, in the forgetfulness and decay of the principles of the spiritual and supernatural order, which characterized the growth and extension throughout the centuries of the Christian civilization. In this modern age, therefore, it is more important, not so much to dwell on one point or another of doctrine or discipline, which must be renewed at the pure sources of Revelation and tradition, but to restore to its significance and splendour the substance of human and Christian life and thought, of which the Church has been the heir and mistress through the centuries.

It is right to deplore most gravely the errors of the human mind, tempted and urged towards the mere enjoyment of the goods of this earth, which modern scientific research has set within easy reach of the children of our generation. God forbid, however, that we should exaggerate the proportions of this, going so far as to persuade ourselves that God's heavens have been finally closed above our heads, and that darkness has fallen upon the whole earth, so that nothing now remains for us to do but to water with tears our wearisome path.

The celebration of a Council of the Catholic Church involves the examination of a whole complex system of relationships, not only regarding individuals and families, but regarding all the nations, upon which turn the hinges of human existence.

In fact, from the Ten Commandments of Moses to the four Gospels, everything draws its strength from the same source: Christ and his Church with, at the centre, our blessed Jesus who says to us: "I am the light of the world. I am the way, the truth and the life" (John 8. 12; 14. 16). And these words and their meaning are divinely sealed by the last words of St Matthew's Gospel: "Lo, I am with you always, to the close of the age" (Matthew 28. 20).

Beloved children! During these recent months while we have been re-reading many extracts from the copious literature about the last Ecumenical Council, Vatican I, convened by our predecessor of revered memory, Pius IX, in 1869–70, we chanced to find a pamphlet, printed for the general public, written by one of the most restless and applauded spirits of that age of accentuated anti-Roman fanaticism. It was dedicated, with an irony which seems in poor taste, to the bishops who would be attending the Vatican Council from all over the world, whom he compared with the old bishops of the Eastern Church who had come to Nicaea in 325, to the first Council.

"You have come today to the new, and last, Council in Rome. The first, that of Nicaea, was a solemn, venerable consecration of triumph and ordered unity in the religion which the times required. This last Council, yours, will inevitably, whatever your own intentions are, testify to the significant fact of a religion that is dying, and therefore, inevitably, to the approaching rise of another."

These are the actual words of the challenge and the prophecy.

A hundred years later we can take note of their foolishness, and of what these prophets of Baal deserve—and some of them still survive—who "have seen false and deceptive visions" (cf. Lamentations 2.14). Let us then, as an exercise of watchfulness and patience, so that we may see the promise fulfilled, say: We remain faithful to the words of Christ, the words with which Matthew concludes his Gospel: these are our assurance of the victory of the Church of Jesus, of our Church, until the end of the world.

Do you not seem to hear a voice from long ago, which speaks in our ears and in our hearts? "Arise and shine, Jerusalem, for your light has come, and the glory of the Lord has risen upon you" (Isaiah 60. 1). The old prophet Isaiah offers us our first song of triumph, which gathers to itself the echoes of fervent melodies arising in every tongue, and from every tribe and people.

We are in truth, as we love to repeat, expecting great things from this Council, which will result in a strengthening of faith, doctrine, ecclesiastical discipline, religious and spiritual life, and also a great contribution towards the reassertion of those Christian principles which inspire and support also the progress of civil, economic, political and social life. The law of the Gospel must be felt everywhere and prevail in all things, even those which come to us from "the dew of heaven and the fatness of the earth" (Genesis 27. 28). But, if it is to prevail, there must be a conscious, enlightened, sincere collaboration between all the members of the social order, priesthood and laity, constituted authority, intellectual work, and all other work, the whole social order wholly absorbed in striving for perfect harmony of relations between heaven and earth, between the life of today, so uncertain and beset with dangers, and the life of the future which will be everlasting and full of perfect joy in proportion to our efforts as men and Christians to correspond to the gifts of grace and the mercy of the Lord. (*Discorsi Pg.*, vol. III, 14 Nov. 1960, pp. 22–24.)

The Angelus for the astronaut

The *Angelus* consecrates for all time the union of heaven and earth, the divine with the human. In this hour today we wish to associate with the intentions of our prayer the young pilot in space.

Beloved children, belonging to all races, you have come together like good brothers, while the pilot is proving, in an almost decisive and certainly a most scientific manner, the intellectual, moral and physical powers of man, and continues that exploration of the created world which we are encouraged to make in the first pages of Sacred Scripture, when the Lord told man he was to multiply and fill the earth.

The nations, and especially the young generations, follow with enthusiasm the developments of the wonderful flights and navigations in space. Oh, how ardently we wish that these enterprises could assume the significance of homage rendered to God, the Creator and supreme Lawgiver!

May these historical events which will be recorded in the annals of the scientific exploration of the world become expressions of true and peaceful progress, the firm foundation of human brotherhood.

The apostle Peter encouraged the Romans to study, love and imitate Christ, whose word is "a lamp shining in a dark place, until the day dawns and the morning star rises in your hearts" (cf. II Peter 1. 19). (*Discorsi Pg.*, vol. IV, 12 Aug. 1962, pp. 470–1.)

The rule of the spirit

On the eve of the Second Vatican Council here is the humble successor of Peter adding his own poor homage to that of so many who have come here before him. Today's Papal pilgrimage to this ancient and venerated shrine is like a solemn seal set on the prayers which, in all the churches of the world, from East to West, and in the sacred seclusion of suffering and penitence, have risen to God for the successful outcome of the great ecumenical congress. It also symbolizes the Church's upward climb towards the conquest of that rule of the spirit, established in the name of Christ, who is the "light for revelation to the Gentiles" (cf. Luke 2. 32): a rule which is brotherly service and love, and the yearning for peace, and ordered and world-wide progress.

The act of veneration to Our Lady of Loreto which we perform today takes our mind back to sixty years ago, when we came here for the first time, on our way back from Rome, where we had obtained the Jubilee Indulgences bestowed by Pope Leo. It was 20 September 1900. At two o'clock in the afternoon, after receiving Holy Communion, we could pour out our soul in long and fervent prayer.

What is there more enjoyable for a young seminarist than lingering in conversation with his dear heavenly Mother? But alas! the painful circumstances of those years, which had spread abroad in the air a subtle spirit of mockery of all that represents spiritual values, religion and Holy Church, turned that pilgrimage to bitterness as soon as we chanced to hear the chatter of the populace. We still remember what we said that day as we left for the homeward journey: "O Lady of Loreto, I love you so much, and I promise to keep faithful to you, and be a good seminarist. But you will never see me here again."

Instead we returned there several times in the years that followed, at long intervals, and here we are now, with the family of our closest collaborators; here we are welcomed ceremoniously by a splendid group of illustrious people: the President of the Italian Republic, the noble representatives of the Italian government, and others, enough to convince us that even here, in these exceptional circumstances, the characteristic note of our Church which arouses admiration is her catholicity and universality. (*Discorsi Pg.*, vol. IV, 4 Oct. 1962, pp. 557-8.)

Scientific progress

We share in the joy which greets with such enthusiasm the successes of the technicians and scientists, whose skill subjugates nature in a way that only yesterday seemed to challenge the most fertile imagination.

We have said recently: "Oh, how ardently we wish that these enterprises could assume the significance of homage rendered to

God, the Creator and Supreme Lawgiver! May these historical events which will be recorded in the annals of the scientific exploration of the world become expressions of true and peaceful progress, the firm foundation of human brotherhood." (*Scritti e Discorsi*, 1962, vol. III, p. 139.)

Thanks be to God, we have now entered an epoch in which, we hope, the conflicts between the conquests of thought and the requirements of faith will be less frequent. The First Vatican Council brilliantly affirmed, in 1869–70, the relation between reason and faith. The magnificent discoveries and realizations of the twentieth century, far from casting new doubt upon these, on the contrary aid our minds better to understand their value. The progress of science, which enables us to have a wider knowledge of the extraordinary wealth of the created world, enriches in an exceptional way the praise which the creature raises as thanksgiving to his Creator, who is also the Redeemer of our souls. Our heart and minds are eager to reach out to the absolute and to give themselves to what is supreme.

And how could we forget, Gentlemen, on the eve of the now imminent opening of this great assembly, the Ecumenical Council, the promises which, with the aid of the prayers of Catholics, it will fulfil, and the expectation of the whole world? This is a brotherly, peaceful and spiritual vision: a meeting which shall be all for the glory of God and the service of man, in his noble aspirations to know the truth and to seek, find and embrace the object of his love. (5 Oct. 1962, at the *Accademia delle Scienze*.)

CHAPTER ELEVEN

Peace on Earth

I. THE END OF THE "UNDUE INTERFERENCE"

THE autonomy of the temporal order in relation to the supernatural order, the former being entrusted to the rule of reason, and the latter to the rule of faith and the protection of ecclesiastical authority, is not a convenient invention of modern Catholicism; it is a truth which the Church has laboriously safeguarded, since the first centuries, from the depressing confusions of mystical pessimism.

The theocratic idea, which seemed to prevail in certain moments of the medieval era, was in fact in line with the trends of Augustinian pessimism, and particularly with the extreme theory of "radically corrupt nature", upon which could be based neither the autonomy of philosophical reason nor the autonomy of the political order. In the modern era, the theocratic tendency has survived more because of its practical opportunity than because it arouses any real theological conviction.

Pope John recognized that the practical usefulness of the theocratic tendency had come to an end, and that the temporal order had now sufficient authority for assuming its proper role.

As the Council has shown, the old questions of jurisdiction which, in old Europe, so much embittered the relations between State and Church, are destined to end. The progressive institutional objectivization of natural law will enable the Church to enjoy more and more of the freedom she needs. This optimistic intuition does not presuppose that complete identification has been reached between the natural law and international good order; it is merely the realistic recognition of the dynamic which now guides the community of peoples towards the consolidation of world organisms capable of guaranteeing to individuals and to institutions the peaceful exercise of their liberty.

This enables the Church to put her trust in her own pastoral laws, without, in the name of painful necessity, modifying them to political requirements, and without making them depend, for greater security, on subsidies from State organs. The total emancipation of the Church from the manoeuvres of the political blocs, and so from the power of parties: this is the programme which inspired the action of Pope John, and which he bequeathed to the Council.

That this was a programme which presented certain risks he understood from the start: indeed, with the most careful timing, he devoted to it many initiatives of his pontificate, the most important documents expressing his teaching authority, and finally the Ecumenical Council itself.

Once the social and political safeguards of peace have been entrusted to all men of good will, once it has been recognized, on the political plane, that there exist bodies capable of maintaining peace in the world, what prevents the Church from placing herself above the opposing parties and approaching men of every nation and of every ideology, not as the exponent of a definite political order in opposition to those already existing, but as the bearer of a message of eternal salvation?

The prejudices of the Communist bloc against the Catholic Church, which they believe to be, by natural inclination, the ally of the capitalist nations, are not worth while confuting. Nevertheless, they have made good use of the tendency of not a few Western circles to utilize the prestige of the Church in order to further their own political ends. Respect or scorn for the Catholic Church may be the result of moral and religious choice, in which case its significance is unequivocal; but it may also be the result of a purely political or economic choice, and then it foments, among foes and friends alike, passions and presumptions which end by making the real countenance of the Church almost invisible. It was enough for Pope John to free his own action from the grasp of political conflicts for the erroneous character of certain judgments to be shown in a clear light, and for "the thoughts of many hearts to be revealed".

We cannot believe that there will arrive on this earth an era of perfect tranquillity, nor that the enemy of truth has only one face. We must not trust too much in the assistance and understanding of earthly institutions of any kind, because, whether they behave well or ill, they are primarily interested and occupied with purely material and economic progress.

We must say this with some sadness, but without fear or dismay. The kingdom of this world often smothers the noblest aspirations of man, and hinders the progress of his preparation for the eternal life. And we, we must repeat, are here for the cause of the kingdom of God, and we must ourselves give the example of this service, which we render to man and to the whole human family.[1]

The service which the Church renders to man and to the human family is not, primarily, of a temporal order, because it concerns the directing of the whole of creation towards the Kingdom of God, which is not of this world. The Christian message is indeed, of its nature, one of peace, but in an eschatological sense, in so much as it foretells and prefigures the final setting up of the peaceful sovereignty of Christ, the Prince of Peace. Every pope, in as much as he speaks and acts as pope, is a messenger of peace, the prophetic witness to the peace of Christ. It is wrong to deny this peaceable nature of the Church with the excuse that, for more than a thousand years, she has tolerated the use of war, and even sometimes blessed it! Without debating the actual historic responsibilities of the Church it is enough for us to assert that the more the Church is faithful to herself the more willing she is to favour peace, to keep herself remote from any complicity with wars, or at least to restrict the outbreak within its just bounds.

Earthly society is ruled by the laws of natural justice, the realization of which necessitates the use of force, and in certain cases, at least in the past, the use of war. The distinction between a just and unjust war belongs to the historic development of natural justice: there is nothing surprising in the Church's recognition of the validity of this. At one time the conflicts between institutions did not become, as today they become, conflicts so

[1] Speech to the Central Commission for the Council, 12 May 1962.

extended as to involve in the same complicity all citizens alike, even those who belong canonically to the supernatural hierarchy of the Catholic Church. The Church could in those days remain apart from wars, and leave the responsibility for them to rulers or military bodies: until the Napoleonic age, there was no compulsory mobilization, no citizen was obliged to go to war against his conscience. On the other hand, as the people's rights were not codified or guarded with effective sanctions, the struggles between the rulers always used the last fatal resource, that of force. Being herself an institution, the Church in this way found herself obliged to protect, with all morally legitimate means, her own independence. The liberty of action in accordance with the laws of one's own nature is, even for the Church, a supreme good which has never, historically, been adequately guaranteed. What else could she do but try to select, in her various vicissitudes, the political system most likely to protect that liberty? Alas! the choice of a protector was also, virtually, like signing a contract of partial subservience, producing in the Church, if not precisely the obligation, at least the disposition to overlook the warlike methods used by her protector and indeed to do what she could to promote his victory over the enemy. From Pepin the Short to Napoleon III, and even to the Atlantic Pact, the Church has not concealed her political preferences, among the reasons for which have always figured prominently, at least in her intentions, her search for firm guarantees of her liberty. We should be mistaken if we maintained that most of the Church's intentions have been fulfilled, or if we denied that, in her tacit or explicit collusion with the rulers, she has more than once compromised that same liberty which she meant to secure.

In fact, it is enough even to glance through the pages of ecclesiastical history to see very clearly that the Ecumenical Councils themselves, whose deeds were a series of glorious achievements for the Catholic Church, were often held amid the gravest difficulties and sorrows, because of the undue interference of the civil authorities. Indeed, these authorities no doubt intended quite sincerely to protect the Church: but more often than not this situation resulted in spiritual loss and danger, because they acted in accordance with the calculations of a selfish and dangerous political scheme.[2]

In the years preceding the pontificate of Pope John there was a widespread conviction that the Church must entrust the protection of her liberty to the Western political world. There was no official treaty, no concordat between the Western political bloc and the Holy See to give firm support to this conviction. But circumstances left no doubt about it: the so-called popular democracies had cruelly persecuted the Church, to the point of robbing her faithful even of that modicum of liberty which belongs to the order of natural law. On the contrary, the Western democracies, sometimes going counter to old secular traditions, had shown in various degrees their gratitude for the moral support the Church had given to the cause of freedom. The gates of the Vatican were open to the men of the Atlantic bloc and tightly closed to the men from behind the iron curtain. In the difficult equilibrium maintained between the two blocs it seemed natural for the Church to give her support to one of the two, with the result that the autonomous attitude of some Churches behind the iron curtain, especially that of the Polish Church, was either understood as a prudent compromise imposed by necessity, or was openly condemned as cowardly surrender to the pressures of tyranny.[3]

The originality of Pope John lies precisely in the fact that he understood by intuition the extraordinary novelty of the historical situation in which the Church has found herself, and the resultant possibility of modifying her attitude with regard to the

[2] Speech for the opening of the Council, 11 Oct. 1962.

[3] The Polish Primate has given proof, on occasion, of the most determined intransigeance, but he has never wished to identify the destiny of his Church with that of a particular political ideal. Without ever dissimulating his rejection of Marxist ideology, he had already noted, before *Pacem in terris*, that political movements cannot be identified with the ideologies which inspire them, and that the Church, in depriving herself where the need arises of many rights which belong to her as a society perfect in her own order, loses nothing of what is essential to her, and in fact becomes—as he declared in one of his speeches at the Council—through an inevitable process, the symbol and refuge of human values, gaining in spiritual prestige what she renounces in the sphere of power and juridical security. It is well known that Pope John was very fond of Cardinal Wyszynski and showed his affection immediately after his election to the pontificate (see Speech of 30 Nov. 1958).

political forms which alternately establish and disturb the equilibrium of peace on earth.

2. THE NEW HISTORICAL SITUATION

If Pope John's work for peace differs in some respects from that of his pontifical predecessors, this difference is due to the historical situation which providentially coincided with his pontificate, and which he was quick to realize.

In Pope John's view of history a decisive part was played, as we have seen, by the consolidation of the organization of the United Nations. A world community is now no longer a Utopian idea; it is a juridical body equipped with its own institutes, sanctions and executive organs. When the Church lived in the midst of European powers at war with one another, the people's rights were still an *ens rationis* which could offer no guarantee for the restoration of the rights of the offended party and the safeguarding of these rights once restored. It is enough to refer to Napoleon's schemes, which did not spare the unarmed dignity of the popes of Rome. The "new order of human relationships" praised by Pope John in his inaugural speech before the Council has given a positive structure to the rights of peoples, and has brought the natural law down from the sphere of abstractions to the concrete form of institutions. Political mediation in conflicts between nations now belongs, of right and in fact, to international organizations, whose increasing vitality is moreover ensured by the fact that the present economic and technical development of mankind necessitates, with all the force of actual events, that international power which until now the defenceless idealism of men's consciences had dreamed of in vain. The armed power of the individual nation is, although this is its only justification, no longer sufficient to provide for its own welfare. The welfare of the individual nation coincides more and more, objectively, with the welfare of all peoples.

Pope John's optimism had this historical foundation also, which became particularly evident during the years of his pontificate.

During the Stalin era, it was the general conviction that the international aims of the United Nations were little more than formal statements: the Marxist bloc had never disowned, either with words or deeds, the ideological principle of the overthrow of world capitalism by means of violence, that is, by means of war. It is only during recent years, through the realism of some great statesmen, that the idea that war cannot be considered as an instrument of justice has become general. This has been rendered more obvious by the entrance into the United Nations of the new nations of the Third World, which since the conference of Bandoeng in 1955 have, with their obstinate neutrality, blunted the edge of the antagonism between the two blocs.

3. CONSCIENCE AND INSTITUTIONS

The sum total of these circumstances has given an objective foundation to the activity and teaching of Pope John regarding world peace. It is impossible to understand his doctrine, especially that of *Pacem in terris*, without emphasizing its appropriateness to its own temporal setting, and the events of today.

Some have said that Pope John's teaching about peace contains nothing new, and this is true in the sense that the principles upon which it is founded belong to the tradition of the Church and have been fully dealt with by the popes of this century, especially by Pius XII. Nevertheless the impression of extraordinary novelty which it has given is not without its due cause.

The novelty lies precisely in his cordial acceptance of the novelty of the age, an acceptance so profound and habitual as to give the impression that his theoretical premises were merely the result of an objective examination of the "signs of the times".

Meanwhile, and this is a detail of great importance, Pope John never alludes to the doctrine of the just war. His conviction that it is no longer possible to believe that in the future a war could be considered just, induces him to ignore completely a subject which might seem to belong of rights to a complete treatise on peace, such as his *Pacem in terris* sets out to be. For him peace is morally unavoidable, because its only alternative is the destruction of the human race. This strict limitation, which excludes even the consideration of the possibility of war, obliges his discourse on peace to turn in on itself, so to speak, and to consider the web of moral, institutional and psychological conditions which make peace integral and indivisible.

The national authorities, which could once deduce from abstract principles of justice the necessity of an armed defence, must now, in the name of those principles, accept a twofold control. First of all, they must subordinate their individual sovereignty to the sovereignty of the world community, the final criterion which cannot be rejected without *ipso facto* rejecting the sovereignty of natural law. This subordination, we must repeat, is imposed by the ever wider links which bind the welfare of the individual to the welfare of all, as all subjects are now well aware. In fact, and this is the second control, institutions must now settle their accounts with the consciences of individuals, accepting their criticism and ensuring their liberty.

The dynamic function of the conscience assumes, in the teaching of Pope John, an unusual prominence. As is well known, traditional moralists considered the judgments of institutions as the final criteria in decisions of conscience, especially with regard to those which concerned the lawfulness or unlawfulness of a war. This resulted in widespread abdication on the part of the best consciences which, in the name of obedience to these institutions, accepted without revolt the most terrifying contrasts between ruling principles and natural rights.

The rapid transformations of social life now offer the natural law an ever richer content; the discovery of this increase does not directly concern the State; it concerns consciences, which will therefore have to stimulate institutions to a constant striving for improvement, in accordance with the changing requirements of the social order. The relations between conscience and the institution, which in the past were completely to the advantage of the latter, must now, because of the historical dynamism which is transforming social relations, be modified to the advantage of the conscience.

For the first time, at least to such a marked extent, the doctrinal discourse of a pope hinges on the historical development of man, with the result that the witness to principles is strengthened by the support of facts, and ecclesiastical teaching, without denying its divine source, enters of its own right the wide areas of modern rationalism, reintegrating, in its own humanistic synthesis, the scattered and contradictory principles of secular teachings.[4]

It is not enough to have a sublime notion of the human person as the free cause of events, in order to be able to influence the course of history. Too many people, even among Christians, are convinced that for the construction of a right social order it is enough to concentrate on the human person as the central principle of moral order. Undoubtedly the idea of a human person is the standard for measuring every historical fact and project. But the person has, within him, a temporal constitution: in his actual existence he has a number of needs which are continually changing in accordance with the changing forms in which he is incarnate, and in which he evolves. Too much concentration on the human person, especially when this concentration takes a delight in its own abstractions, easily becomes rhetorical and conservative because, clinging to its own rigid schemes, it leaves the flow of constantly changing activity to find its own level. Below the arches of rhetorical moralism history flows as immoral as ever!

Against pure metaphysics materialistic realism has enjoyed a great advantage. Fascinated by the mechanics of historical development, it has recognized therein the prime sources of every value, including the human person, considered no longer as the cause but as the result of changes of growth. But the materialists have already during the course of history used up what little reason they ever had, and now bear the burden of a truth they had

---

[4] Pope John himself, in the speech he made after signing his *Pacem in terris*, 9 April 1962, emphasized, so to speak, the "lay character" of this document, with these words: "The Encyclical bears on its brow the shining imprint of divine revelation, which provides the living substance of the thought. But the doctrinal framework depends on the intimate needs of human nature, and for the most part belong to the realm of natural law. This explains an innovation peculiar to this document, which is addressed not only to the episcopate of the universal Church, and to the faithful of the whole world, but also to all men of good will. Universal peace is a blessing for all, without distinction; we have shared our thoughts with all."

forgotten: that it is the human person that is the causal principle of history.

Precisely in relation to this contradiction between spiritual and material values, upon which modern culture seems to rest, the teaching of the Encyclical *Pacem in terris* comes as a novelty; in fact the Encyclical seemed to some dangerously progressive, and to others still weighed down by old prejudices. Instead, the great "historical plan" of the Encyclical grasps, in what they still possess of truth, the terms of the antithesis which tears the world asunder, and offers to modern man an intellectual pacification, to precede a pacification of the heart. It gives full credit to the changed economic and technical structures, recognizing in them the historic development of the human person which, in its turn, is not idolized as an abstraction, but set in the living flow of change, without thereby impairing its metaphysical integrity. Indeed, it is precisely in the tension between the human person as the source and standard of the moral order and the social structures, as they have taken shape today, that we can detect those human rights which have not yet been respected.

The juridical provisions obtaining today do not satisfy that tension, and therefore conflict with the natural rights of the person. It is from this fundamental intuitive knowledge that the Encyclical derives the progressive force that has aroused so much surprise and even some dismay[5]:

"It is necessary that the organs in which authority is embodied, becomes active and pursues its purpose, should be constructed and should act in such a way as to be able to translate into reality the new programme for the common welfare, required by the historical development of society."

Authority, when it does not make up its mind to study the new historical data, and therefore the new rights which they render necessary in the relationship between men and the State,

[5] In his Christmas message for 1963 Paul VI refers at length to the "great Encyclical", and praises its moving vision of peace: "This Encyclical has taught us, if we may say so, the new problems connected with peace and the driving force which must create the conditions from which it will derive: the classical Augustinian definition 'tranquillity in order' seems to us today to proceed rather from the ordered movement of factors which promote tranquillity and the assurance of peace, than from a static immobility: we must have *equilibrium in movement*."

ends by losing all legitimacy.[6] The protest of free consciences, in this case, is not a threat of revolt, but the necessary stimulus for the reform of these organisms, and therefore for the restoration of the legitimacy of authority. The theoretical abstractions of those who praise the human person, the family, the fatherland, without ever considering whether in the meantime those august values have not perhaps changed their content and therefore require, more than rhetorical praise, a bold operation which may save them from suffocation, are misleading. This sort of abstract theorizing indeed fosters a result which is the contrary of that which is so piously desired. Juridical positivism also, which sets the source of law in an authority that has been empirically conceived and scorns the authority of the natural law, ought to recognize that between legalistic formalism, which smothers progress, and instinctive rebellion, there is no other way to reform society than that directed by a rightly understood concern for the human person.

4. ACTIVE NEUTRALITY

The risk run by the Catholic is that he may judge the reality of history either with the measuring rod of canonical sanctions against heretics and unbelievers, or with that of the unchangeable theological system, and that consequently he may perceive in the movement of history more its remoteness from Christian ideals than its positive victories for good, more the ideological conflicts than the ontological development fostered by "good will".

[6] It is very interesting, in this connection, to read a message presented by the French delegation to the recent fourth International Congress of the *Secrétariat International des Juristes* of *Pax Romana* on the theme: Law and Social Peace. "It is perhaps useful at this point to remember that Catholic theological tradition recognizes the historical and material variety of natural law, and that therefore it would be mistaken to attempt to base a certain conservative conception of social peace on a certain theology of natural law. Catholic theological tradition is energetically opposed to any *metaphysical* and *formal* variability of natural law. This may be supported by numerous passages in St Thomas or St Bonaventure. 'Justice and goodness', says St Thomas, 'are formally and everywhere the same, because the principles of law which spring from natural reason do not change . . . but on the other hand, considered from the material point of view, they are not everywhere or among all men the same, because of the mutability of human nature and the diverse conditions of men and things in differing places and times . . .' (St Thomas: *Quaestiones disputatae de malo*, 2, a. 4, *ad* 13)." The text should be studied in its original language in *Justitia*, no. 4, 1962, pp. 429–37.

Pope John's way of looking at all this was just the opposite: the Christian synthesis is not assumed as a standard to be used for the radical discrimination of evil and good in their actual forms, but as the ideal goal, never entirely reached, of every evolution which aims at the fullness of Christianity. The standard by which historical movements are to be judged is "good will", measured not according to the principles divinely revealed to us, but according to the dictates of right reason.

And this good will exists and is productive of good even where the ideologies are erroneous and irreconcilable with Christianity. The Church renounces judgments which deny or impair the primacy of good will, which means that the human person is now recognized as the free and creative maker of history. The disappointment felt by some people at Pope John's "politics" was caused by the Church being more and more clearly set apart from the various political trends, and her neutrality so clearly defined that in no way could her spiritual prestige be used to the advantage of this or that political bloc.

It was not that Pope John refused to recognize the gravity of the persecutions inflicted by certain States on the Catholic Church, or the unjust conditions which stifle her activity.[7] It was simply that he felt that the Church need not react against oppression in the same manner as earthly societies. Because of her nature the Church is not in a position to act in the political sphere, in the strict sense of the word: her diplomacy is a branch of her pastoral activity. When she reacts to a persecution she does so in such a way as not to fall short of her missionary vocation, even when she would legitimately be entitled to react differently. Those who persecute religion trample on the rights of man: strong in the conviction of this identity of interests the Church makes her appeal, tacit or explicit, to international law, just as Paul, imprisoned and threatened with death, appealed to Caesar as a Roman citizen. By making use of this human means the Church

---

[7] On several occasions Pope John condemned the régimes which persecute the Church. But in recent months, particularly with the Council in mind and in consideration of evident acts of good will on the part of the Soviets, he had for the most part refrained from mentioning the "painful Calvary of the Church of silence". (These are the words used, for example, in his Christmas broadcast, 1959.)

safeguards her transcendent character, and is able to appeal, in a friendly way, even to those who are her enemies, thus pursuing without discrimination her own universal mission. In this way she is, more than any other institution, able to work for the cause of peace among men.

The words spoken by Pope John when he received in private Audience the Balzan Prize committee, on 7 March 1963, defined with the utmost clarity the Church's mission of peace, identifying it with "active neutrality".

> You are paying your homage to the constant action of the Church and the Papacy in favour of peace: an activity which has been made ever more strikingly apparent in the circumstances of our own days. This is because, without yielding any essential element of the free and complete sovereignty of the Roman Pontiff, these events have shown in a clearer light the perfect supernatural neutrality of the Church and her visible Head in the sphere of international disagreements, whether these are armed conflicts or merely wars of words. This neutrality must not be understood in a purely passive sense, as if the Pope's role were limited to observing events and keeping silent. On the contrary, it is a neutrality that preserves all its vigorous power of testimony. In her desire to teach the principles of true peace the Church does not cease to encourage the use of a language and the fostering of habits and institutions which guarantee its stability. We have said on frequent occasions: the Church's action is not purely negative, it does not consist solely in urging governments to avoid recourse to the use of arms; it is an action that aims at forming men of peace, men who will have peaceful thoughts, hearts and hands. The peacemakers proclaimed as blessed in the Gospel are not inactive: they are those who build peace. (Matthew 5.9.)

We do not mean that the Church, once she has reaffirmed her own active neutrality with regard to political institutions, will enter an age of tranquillity and become the object of universal affection. Such an idyllic vision contrasts with the very nature of the Church and with the perverse tendencies of the human spirit, which so often prevail over its right tendencies. As we have seen,

Pope John's optimism in no way excluded the causes for pessimism of a biblical sort, which moreover so exactly coincide with our own daily experience.

Just one year after the award of the Balzan Prize, which saw the Soviets willing to recognize Pope John's work for peace,[8] the publication of the Ilicev report clearly proves that State atheism remains in the Soviet world, not only in direct contrast with the message of the Catholic Church but, because of being a doctrine fostered by political organisms, producing within the human society oppressive discriminations and, when these are pushed to extremes, ideological war.

Peace is indeed an indivisible good: the cultural and political men and movements which aim at achieving and ensuring it in this world have daily opportunities to testify to it and to construct it: to the habit of mere ideological contest they must oppose the habit of dialogue, to the methodical inhibition of the liberty of religion and thought the effective respect for the conscience of others, and the disposition to use all means, including political means, to favour the peaceful discussion of ideas upon a plane of institutional equality.

Pope John clearly chose this method, certain that the frank and sincere comparison of doctrines will never be a cause of loss to the Church, and that all positive elements of progress may and will be perfectly reconcilable with revealed truth. According to Pope John the Church, without renouncing her theological pessimism, may have confidence in the resources of the moral liberty of man as long as this liberty is safeguarded from external influences, whether economic or political. If she rejects passive neutrality she does so in the name of peace, as well as in the name of the rights of truth.

[8] Indeed, Khrushchev showed openly and repeatedly his admiration for Pope John. For example, in the interview granted to the American journalist Drew Pearson (published in the *Mittag* of Düsseldorf on 29 Aug. 1963), the morning after the signature of the nuclear agreement, he said: "The late Pope John was a man of whom it might be said that he *'felt the pulse of the age'*. He understood the times in which we live." In fact Khrushchev's admiration was so obvious that it became a motive of the Russo-Chinese ideological controversy. The *Ching-Po* of Pekin, in a sarcastic comment on the message of condolence sent by the Soviet premier, regretted that Khrushchev had not had time to visit John XXIII. It suggested that, in view of his "progressive reconciliation" with God, he should have the Russian people baptized. It is very probable that there is more than one link between the Chinese and the group of which Ilicev is the mouthpiece.

Peace necessitates the fervent and active recognition of all that truly makes for brotherliness among men and nations. A sceptical tolerance, which is at the base of passive neutrality, is in reality, even while it seems to be guaranteeing peace, slowly preparing its downfall, because of its indifference in the face of the inhuman forces which, with the slow action of water that eats away the bridges, corrode, within men's consciences and in the organization of social life, the moral resources which promote communion and understanding among men and nations.

Pope John's doctrine is very far from being confuted by the appearance of the new wave of atheism in the Soviet world. Indeed, the universal distrust which the champions of this revival are arousing, even in circles in which their words were once applauded with cowardly subservience, is becoming ever more evident. A Christian who is, according to Pope John's ideal and example, a man of peace will never assert that the atheist is, because of his atheism alone, a second-class citizen; still less will he demand the forfeiture of his civil rights. He will consider him with respect, sure that he has something to learn from him. An atheist citizen who condemns as stupid, outdated and dangerous the men who believe in Jesus Christ, in vain invokes peace and bears its banners aloft: he will already have destroyed it around himself, and will have sown, in human society, the seeds of war.

God alone knows how much spiritual strength has been rejected or sterilized, in the past, by the confessional States, that is by the States who have associated with their notion of a true and perfect citizen the confession of a particular ideology. Did this happen also in the so-called Catholic States? We have no intention of defending them. Certainly, Catholics who have recognized their own peaceful vocation in the doctrine of *Pacem in terris* will always be very careful not to use their own convictions as motives for social discrimination. They will not oppose to State atheism a State Catholicism, even if such a possibility presented itself. Following the example of the Church they too, as Christians, will try to diffuse "language", "habits" and "institutions" which may safeguard the stability of peace.

State atheists introduce a terrible class distinction, much more dangerous and unjust than that based on economics: on the one hand the wielders of power, who are the best and most intelligent citizens and therefore atheists; on the other hand the minority, dull, slaves of ancient prejudices and morbid complexes, and therefore believers. Faced with such an obvious contradiction, the peacemakers have no other course left open but that of open denunciation, in the name of the very principles which State atheism so emphatically proclaims.

In this peaceable denunciation lies the strength of the Church. The earth will be inherited by the peacemakers, because now the warmakers have no other alternative: either they must pursue their method to its extreme consequences and so be faced with the unthinkable choice of an armed conflict, or they must continually suffer the shame of a hypocrisy now unmasked. What is important is that the men of peace should never give in.

At one time the Church tried to keep the nations in order, ensuring by means of canonical sanctions the correct behaviour of rulers, and blessing that sword which seemed most reliable in the service of justice and peace. Today, in conformity with the political situation, she has chosen another way, that of "forming men of peace, men who have peaceful thoughts, hearts and hands".[9] When she is able to do so, as Pope John did on several occasions, she will invoke peace with a loud voice, from her loftiest pulpit; but, as a general rule, her peacemaking efforts must be expressed in the daily and active presence of peacemakers trained in her school.

The peacemakers know that, in the long run, the conflict between free consciences and oppressive institutions is resolved in favour of liberty and peace.

[9] On 10 May 1963, on the occasion of the award of the Balzan Prize for peace a few weeks before his death, Pope John reasserted this educative mission of the Church, also to the unbelievers: "These four principles which sustain the whole edifice belong to natural law, and are engraved on the hearts of all. That is why we have addressed our appeal to all mankind. We are in fact convinced that in the years to come, in the light of past experiences and in the objective and serene re-examination of the language of the Church, the doctrine she offers to the world will be accepted because of its clarity. When it is presented to the men of today freed from any particular deformation, it must of necessity increase in the world the numbers of those who will have the merit and glory of being called the builders and makers of peace."

"The mourning of the nations"

The mourning of the nations. This cry reaches my ears from every part of Europe and beyond. The murderous war which is being waged on the ground, on the seas and in the air is truly a vindication of divine justice because the sacred laws governing human society have been transgressed and violated. It has been asserted, and is still being asserted, that God is bound to preserve this or that country, or grant it invulnerability and final victory, because of the righteous people who live there, or because of the good that they do. We forget that although in a certain sense God has made the nations, he has left the constitutions of States to the free decisions of men. To all he has made clear the rules which govern human society: they are all to be found in the Gospel. But he has not given any guarantee of special and privileged assistance, except to the race of believers, that is, to Holy Church as such. And even his assistance to his Church, although it preserves her from final defeat, does not guarantee her immunity from trials and persecutions.

The law of life, alike for the souls of men and for nations, lays down principles of justice and universal harmony and the limits to be set to the use of wealth, enjoyments and worldly power. When this law is violated, terrible and merciless sanctions come automatically into action. No State can escape. To each its hour. War is one of the most tremendous sanctions. It is willed not by God but by men, nations and States, through their representatives. Earthquakes, floods, famines and pestilences are applications of the blind laws of nature, blind because nature herself has neither intelligence nor freedom. War instead is desired by men, deliberately, in defiance of the most sacred laws. That is what makes it so evil. He who instigates war and foments it is always the "Prince of this world", who has nothing to do with Christ, the "Prince of peace".

And while the war rages, the peoples can only turn to the *Miserere* and beg for the Lord's mercy, that it may outweigh his justice and with a great outpouring of grace bring the powerful men of this world to their senses and persuade them to make peace. (*Journal*, 1940, pp. 238–9.)

The dignity of the episcopal ministry

The law of the apostolate and the priesthood is above the law of flesh and blood. Therefore I must love my own kith and kin, and go to their assistance when their poverty makes this necessary, because this is an obvious duty for one who does so much to help strangers, but all must be done discreetly, in a purely priestly spirit, in an orderly and impartial manner. My closest relations, brothers, sisters, nephews and nieces, with very few exceptions, are exemplary Christians and give me great joy. But it would never do for me to get mixed up in their affairs and concerns, so as to be diverted from my duties as a servant of the Holy See, and a bishop!

Patriotism, which is right and may be holy, but may also degenerate into nationalism, which in my case would be most detrimental to the dignity of my episcopal ministry, must be kept above all nationalistic disputes. The world is poisoned with morbid nationalism, built up on the basis of race and blood, in contradiction to the Gospel. In this matter especially, which is of burning topical interest, "deliver me from men of blood, O God". Here fits in most aptly the invocation: "God of my salvation": Jesus our Saviour died for all nations, without distinction of race or blood, and became the first brother of the new human family, built on him and his Gospel.

With what enthusiasm and liberty the tongue of the priest and bishop, thus loosed from earthly ties, will be able to preach to all the Lord's commands, and to praise his justice, mercy and peace, in the name of the Father who is God of all virtues, the Son who is God of salvation, and the Holy Spirit who is God of peace! In the enjoyment of this holy liberty how much more joy is felt in the sacred ministry of souls! "Thy statutes have been my songs in the place of my pilgrimage" (Psalm 118 [119]. 54). "Come let us praise the Lord with joy; let us joyfully sing to God our Saviour" (Psalm 94 [95]. 1). (*Journal*, 1940, pp. 251–2.)

Nationalism

The two great evils which are poisoning the world today are secularism and nationalism. The former is characteristic of the men in power and of lay folk in general. The latter is found even among ecclesiastics. I am convinced that the Italian priests, especially the secular clergy, are less contaminated by this than others. But I must be very watchful, both as bishop and as representative of the Holy See. It is one thing to love Italy, as I most fervently do, and quite another to display this affection in public. The Holy Church which I represent is the mother of nations, all nations. Everyone with whom I come into contact must admire in the Pope's representative that respect for the nationality of others, expressed with graciousness and mild judgments, which inspires universal trust. Great caution then, respectful silence, and courtesy on all occasions. It will be wise for me to insist on this line of conduct being followed by all my entourage, at home and outside. We are all more or less tainted with nationalism. The Apostolic Delegate must be, and must be seen to be, free from this contagion. May God help me. (*Journal*, 1940, p. 260.)

Peace is indivisible

Peace is an incomparable gift of God. But it is also man's supreme aspiration. It is *indivisible*. Not one of the elements which make up its true character may be overlooked or excluded.

Even the men of our own time have not entirely satisfied the requirements of peace, with the consequence that God's ways for peace have not been the same as man's. Hence the abnormal international situation of this post-war period, which has created two opposing blocs, with all the disadvantages that follow. It is not a state of war, but neither is it peace, true peace, that which all peoples long for so ardently.

Recent events have created a more relaxed atmosphere, which has caused hope to flower once more in many minds, that have lived for so long in a state of fictitious peace, in a most unstable situation which more than once has threatened to break down.

All this shows that the longing for peace is rooted in the minds of all peoples.

In order that this general desire may soon be fulfilled, the Church prays with confidence to One who rules the destinies of nations and may convert to good the hearts of rulers. Although not a daughter of this world she lives and works in it and remembers that since the dawn of Christianity she has, as St Paul wrote to Timothy, raised "supplications, prayers, intercessions, and thanksgivings, for all men, for kings and all who are in high positions, that we may lead a quiet and peaceable life, godly and respectful in every way" (I Tim. 2. 1–2). So today too she supports with her prayers all that in international relations fosters serenity of intercourse, the peaceful settlement of disputes, the reconciliation of peoples and mutual collaboration.

Besides her prayer the Church places her motherly services also at men's disposal, pointing to the incomparable treasures of her doctrine, and urging her children to collaborate actively in the cause of peace, remembering the famous warning of St Augustine: "It is a greater joy to destroy wars with words than to destroy men with arms; and it is a true glory to achieve peace with peaceful means" (*Epist.* 229.2; PL 1019).

This is the proper task and office of the Church, to work for peace, and she knows that she has neglected nothing in her power in order to ensure it for nations and individuals. The Church looks favourably on every sincere initiative which may serve to spare humanity further mourning, new slaughter, and new and incalculable destructions.

Alas! all the causes which have disturbed, and still disturb, the international order have not yet been removed. Therefore we must try to dry up the springs of evil; otherwise the dangers for peace will always threaten us. (Broadcast for Christmas 1959.)

A double appeal for Algeria

This year on this festive anniversary, we must call your attention, not to a motive for serene joy, alas! not to tranquillity or peace, but to the suffering peoples whose groans reach us from various parts of the world—Europe, Asia, Africa, the Americas— where the instability of social conditions has brought about the overthrow and ruin of civic order.

The fatal and dangerous points of this menacing disorder are known to you in association with names of places which have in recent months been the scene of tragic and fatal events.

Let us refer openly to one country, which we visited in 1950 and which left us with beautiful and unforgettable impressions: Algeria. Every day, every night, the gravest deeds of violence multiply their victims. Such sad events, happening in various parts of the world, some of which have become so much worse during the last few weeks as to provoke incidents of open disorder and crime, make us feel profoundly sad and anxious. We frequently hear of new attacks on the life and property of numerous citizens. Alas! experience proves that violence begets violence: "He who takes up the sword perishes by the sword." It is not in this way that we must defend the good things sacred to man: his liberty, civic order, true progress, civilization, peace.

We are grieved by violent episodes of all kinds: as much by reckless revolts as by arbitrary repressions, which continue to stain the world with blood. These disorders have even cost the lives of some missionaries, who were but obeying Christ's command to spread the light of the Christian revelation, thus promoting also spiritual and social progress.

In order to achieve in every land the longed-for peaceful collaboration between communities of different races it is first of all necessary that, having set aside all enmity, they should cherish "thoughts of peace and not of affliction" (cf. Jeremiah 29. 11). (*Discorsi Cn.*, 2 Feb. 1962, pp. 54-5.)

Today we wish to open our heart to you, to reveal what most grieves and torments us, so that you may join in the prayer we raise to the all-powerful God, the Lord of all our wills, begging him to turn them to absolute respect for his holy law, which is universal; a prayer which, with our hand on our conscience, looking to the rulers who can decide and the collaborators who may bring some influence to bear, we wish to hear echoing from the four corners of the world.

We are deeply distressed at the sight of the blood that stains the earth, wherever this may occur, according to or against the rules of armed conflicts. But what can we say when the human victims are sacrificed in spite of agreements initiated or sought, sacrificed recklessly, because of a mistaken assertion of rights?

The divine command rings out in firm and solemn tones: Thou shalt not kill. It is a definite command, given by the Author of life. It is affirmed for the protection and defence of a law that is equal for all, and which, if ignored, causes fatal consequences and harmful repercussions in international relations.

Oh! Mediterranean shores of Africa, which we visited twelve

years ago, in the whole vast region from Tunis to Morocco, lands which work and peace could have enriched, can still enrich, for the benefit of the peoples and the triumph of justice, may the day soon rise when there shall be peace, that peace which means brotherhood desired and proclaimed in unity, peace which is prosperity for all families.

As before we renew this appeal which comes from our heart: let no one take upon himself the right to cut short a human life. Let all instead see in every man the image of God the Creator, the heavenly Father of us all, and let all clasp their brothers' hands in the name of Christ the Redeemer.

Do not kill! Neither with the sword nor with the word, and not with the printed word; neither by acquiescence nor because of nationalistic bitterness.

The earth is the Lord's and the fullness thereof: God is the Owner, we are the inhabitants of the earth. On this earth it is our duty to promote that peaceable evolution of peoples which recognizes the rights of others, even when this implies personal restrictions or renunciations.

So we pray that men of diverse origin, treating each other with respect, may offer the world a spectacle of loyal collaboration, of the mutual integration of their various energies and interests: all of one accord working for the common good and the betterment of the peoples.

May God grant our prayers and our requests; and you, beloved sons and daughters, hold up the arms of your Father as he prays, and echo his words.

Let all men hear the strong though trembling voice which rises from this glorious tomb of the apostle Peter.

So, having set aside all obstinacy and violence, may the rule of law prevail in mutual love, and may God bless the authors and builders of peace in the blood-stained land of Africa. (Speech of 3 June 1962.)

"It is time that peace made some decisive steps forward"

Living among men who do not wish to recognize any other relations but those depending on physical force, the Church's duty is to reveal all the importance and efficacy of the moral strength of Christianity, which is a message of integral truth, justice and love.

These are the foundations upon which the Pope must work to establish a true peace, destined to educate the peoples in respect for the human person and to procure a just freedom of worship and religion; a peace that fosters agreement between States even when, and this goes without saying, it demands some sacrifice from them.

The natural consequences will be mutual love, brotherhood and the end of the struggle between men of diverse origin and differing mentalities. In this way we shall facilitate the so urgently needed assistance we must give to the developing peoples and we shall further their true welfare, to the "exclusion of every aim at domination" (*Mater et Magistra*). This is the great peace which all men await, for which they have suffered so much: it is time that peace made some decisive steps forward!

The Church has pledged herself to work for this peace: with prayer, with her profound respect for the poor, the sick, the old, and the spreading of her doctrine which is one of brotherly love, because men are brothers and—we are moved as we say it—all children of the same Father. The Council will undoubtedly help to prepare this new atmosphere and to dispel all possibility of conflict, especially of war, this scourge of the nations, which today would mean the destruction of all mankind.

Your Highnesses, Excellencies and Gentlemen, before us in this Sistine Chapel glows Michelangelo's masterpiece, the Last Judgment, the solemnity of which makes us think and ponder deeply. Yes, we must render an account to God, we and all those who bear the responsibility of the destiny of nations. All must understand that one day they will have to give an account of their actions to God the Creator, who will also be the Supreme Judge. May their consciences be aroused as they listen to the cry of anguish which, from every part of the earth, from innocent children and the old, from individuals and whole communities rises to God: peace, peace! May the thought of the Last Judgment ensure that no one gives up the effort to attain this good, which is, on earth, superior to all else.

Let men continue to meet, to debate together and arrive at loyal agreements, generous and just. Let them be ready, moreover, for the sacrifices necessary to save the peace of the world.

Then all the peoples will be able to work in a climate of tranquillity; the discoveries of science will serve progress and contribute to make ever more peaceful our sojourn on this earth, which is already overshadowed by so many other and unavoidable sufferings. (Speech to the Representatives of the Nations, 12 Oct. 1962.)

Appeal during the Cuba crisis

"O Lord, let thy ear be attentive to the prayer of thy servant, and to the prayer of thy servants who delight to fear thy name" (Nehemiah 1. 11).

This ancient biblical prayer rises today to our trembling lips, from the depths of our anxious and sorrowful heart.

The Second Vatican Ecumenical Council has hardly begun, amidst the joy and hope of all men of good will, and threatening clouds have already come once more to darken the international horizon, spreading dismay in millions of families.

The Church—as we said when we received the Extraordinary Missions present at the opening of the Council—the Church holds nothing dearer than peace and true brotherhood among men. Therefore she works indefatigably to consolidate these. In this connection we spoke of the grave duties of those who have the responsibility of power. And we added: With their hands on their hearts let them listen to the cry of anguish which, from every part of the world, from innocent children and old people, from individuals and communities, rises to Heaven: peace, peace!

Let us today renew our solemn appeal, and let us implore all governments not to remain insensible to this cry of suffering humanity. May they do all that is in their power to save peace: by so doing they will spare the world the horrors of a war, the frightful consequences of which no one can foretell.

Let them then persevere in negotiation, because this frank and open disposition has a great value as witness for the individual conscience and before history. To promote, to favour, to accept negotiations, at every level and at all times, is a rule of wisdom and prudence, which brings down blessings from Heaven and deserves the blessings of men.

All our children, all who bear the mark of baptism and are nurtured in the Christian hope, all those in fact who are linked with us in the bond of faith in God, must unite their prayer with ours to obtain from the Lord the gift of peace: a peace that will never be real and lasting unless it is founded upon justice and equity.

Upon all the makers of this peace, and all those who sincerely work for the real good of mankind, may the great blessing descend, which we now lovingly invoke upon them in the name of One who wishes to be called the "Prince of Peace" (Isaiah 9. 6). (*Discorsi Pg.*, vol. IV, 25 Oct. 1962, pp. 514–615.)

"By being faithful to herself the Church serves peace"

The Church, as we have often said, does not pursue merely temporal ends; she does not aspire to any temporal domination. The golden rule which her Divine Founder left her is the Our Father, the sublime prayer which establishes the order of values: first the name, the kingdom, the will of God; then our food and other necessities of our daily life.

This is a wonderful thing, which has struck the imagination of many thinkers and historians through the centuries: the more the Church endeavours, in the midst of human vicissitudes, to be faithful to this ideal programme, the more effectively she works for the happiness of mankind and first of all for the great cause of peace.

The cause of peace! It is your cause, Gentlemen. Are you not, by profession, the negotiators, the enemies of hasty and violent solutions of disputes between States? But better still, it is the cause of the whole human race, especially today. Is there anyone in the world who does not desire peace, who does not fear to lose it? What horror everyone feels when it appears to be in danger!

The year that is coming to its end, as you remember, gave us reasons for fear and trembling about this. But is it not a very encouraging sign for the new year that the danger was rapidly averted, that wisdom and prudence happily triumphed, restoring confidence and courage to suffering humanity? It is obviously essential for the maintenance and consolidation of peace that international law, founded as it is upon the natural law, should be respected at all times and by everyone. Whoever works for the affirmation of law in discussions among States works for the good of men, and performs an action blessed by God.

It is a characteristic of the world of today that it has set up on a world-wide scale institutions which aim at teaching respect for law, to prevent the outbreak of violence. It is the duty of all, we have no hesitation in saying this, to maintain and support these institutions and do everything possible to ensure the success of the tasks which face them. Those who work in this way and go on working intensely and with unshakeable confidence in the service of peace, these people will be blessed by future generations. History will write their names in indelible characters.

Thanks to these men who cherish thoughts of peace, "thoughts of peace and not of affliction" (cf. Jeremiah 29. 11. Douai), men can devote themselves in noble rivalry, not only to the great and urgent problems of economics and the social order, but also to the continued exploration of the cosmos and the most daring achievements of modern technical skill. All these efforts, the investigations of scientists, the application of the technicians, and the boldness of the experimentalists, are equally applauded by the Church, who praises man's growing domination over the forces of nature. She rejoices at this progress, present and future, which enables man to form an idea of the infinite greatness of his Creator and to pay him, with increased admiration and humility, the due homage of adoration and gratitude. (To the Diplomatic Corps, 23 Dec. 1962; *Discorsi Cn.*, pp. 191–2.)

CHAPTER TWELVE

Christian Unity

I. A NEW DRIVING FORCE

POPE JOHN kept his gravest thoughts to himself, as Mary kept the words of her Son, which she did not understand. He kept them to himself, probably not even confiding them to his diary. He gave open expression to cheerful thoughts, in order to maintain his own optimism and that of others; and even when grave thoughts found a way of expressing themselves, they had the air of improvised reflections, lightened with hope.

Occasions for "grave thoughts" had not been lacking. His long sojourn in Eastern Europe, as we have seen, had kept him in contact with the few surviving remnants of the ancient Christian community, and had convinced him that, in order to remedy this state of total decay, there was needed, more than an attempt at Catholic reconquest, a return to the Gospel, a return so humble and loving as to allow the Roman Church to turn once more to her alienated children with the certainty of touching their hearts.

He was Patriarch of Venice when he wrote:

"I think with sadness of the scanty results of the pro-union movement in the East. And yet this is our duty: to continue to persevere, even against all hope. We are all to blame for this; and we Latins, I mean the Latins in the East, have had and still have our share of the responsibility. If we do not make an effort to shake ourselves out of our ease and look further afield, our decadence will be like that of the orientals, Greeks, Slavs and Arabs."

His realistic way of observing human affairs had ripened his convictions that all the necessities of the common welfare, and first of all peace and justice, would not have found their fullness and stability without the decisive contribution of the Christians, and that the Christians, in their turn, would not have a determining influence in history unless they first rediscovered their own unity. And this unity—at least this seems to have been his secret thought—was broken only because of the prevalence, within the Christian family, of nationalistic pride and theological abstractions, in short through infidelity to the simple Gospel truth.

If we wonder what was his real opinion of scholastic theology or the so-called "new theology", or the theological trends now prevailing among our separated brothers, we are asking ourselves questions that can probably never be answered. It is likely that he never attributed much importance to the theological reasons for the division, which must have seemed to him little more than pretexts, and that he believed that all had come about through men's failure to observe the primacy of charity above all other values, even those of doctrine and discipline. When he spoke of the conditions of the Christian Churches today he avoided any description that might contain in itself a theological judgment. His ecumenical language was drawn largely from the Gospel, from which he developed, through a rich use of analogies, the fundamental conception of the unity desired by Christ, a unity of love, and he was, as far as possible, careful not to make use of notions and schemes of systematic theology or canon law. In this he anticipated the method which Cardinal Bea suggested to the Council as the most suitable to follow for the furthering of unity among Christians, that is the return to the language which the Church had used before the tragedy of separations.

But this return to the language of unity was not, in him, merely tactical: it illustrated his conviction that, during the era of separation, the different theologies have developed by accentuating the lines of divergence and imposing upon concepts, language and behaviour a polemical character, which has ended by freezing itself into the doctrinal systems to such a point that in order to perceive the truth it is necessary to use the flame of charity. But Pope John's mind was too realistic to believe that charity alone was enough to dissolve age-old misunderstandings, now materialized in doctrines and institutions. In order that the intuition of love, which after all has never been lacking in the Catholic

Church, may demand to be translated and put forward in definite formulae of action and thought, favourable objective conditions must first have been realized. According to Pope John, these favourable conditions are now here.

The world's desire for unity is not today, as it once was, a mere spiritual idealism, destined to continue to feed upon itself, in spite of historical disavowals. It has now, as we have seen, obtained objective results and objective guarantees. The separate Churches still have also a role of individual political loyalty—witness the Anglican Church—which stifles their residual longing for the unity desired by Christ. But today the dynamic of world unity proceeds of itself, according to political ideals and by means of political organs. The Christian Churches have thus found themselves stripped of nationalistic support: once freed from this individualism they have rediscovered their former obedience to the voice of the Spirit. It is now easy to see that, in a world that is rapidly unifying itself, a separated Church loses that remnant of spiritual power which might still have its significance in the age of political individualism.

One of Pope John's most fertile intuitions is that a world community will not achieve complete success without the unity of Christians and that, in its turn, the unity of Christians will draw advantages from the progressive building up of the world community. This is why, among the purposes of the Council, he has constantly remembered peace on earth; if the Council furthers peace among Christians it will also further and guarantee peace among all men. In his first Christmas broadcast he said:

Oh, why should this unity of the Catholic Church, directed by her divine vocation towards spiritual interests, not be engaged also in the reconciliation of the various races and nations who are all equally intent on aiming at social welfare, in accordance with the laws of justice and brotherhood?

This is taught by the principle, familiar to believers, that good service for God and for his justice is also to the advantage of the secular communities of peoples and nations.

We still vividly remember how, some decades ago, some representatives of the Orthodox Churches, as they are called, of the Near East, with the practical co-operation of certain governments, tried to bring about a union among civilized peoples, initiating this with a reconciliation among various Christian Churches of different rites and histories.

Unfortunately, the intervention of more obtrusive material interests and nationalistic anxieties nullified these intentions, which were in themselves good and worthy of respect. And there still remains the painful problem of the broken unity of the heritage of Christ, to disturb and prejudice all efforts to solve it, along a road beset with grave difficulties and uncertainties.

2. ONE CHRISTIAN FAMILY

The other circumstance, which offered a God-given opportunity to Pope John's charity, is the ecumenical movement already in existence for more than half a century among our separated brothers.

Before him the Catholic Church had not failed to show her satisfaction with the ever more successful efforts of the Protestant confessions towards establishing unity. But she had declined any formal adherence to the movement even after the representatives of the Orthodox communities had joined the World Council of Churches. To prevent her from taking part in this common effort there was, and still is, her conviction that, for her own part, she already possesses the desired unity, both as regards the distinguishing marks Christ demanded for his Church, and the uninterrupted continuity of the apostolic tradition. She is, moreover, divided from the Protestant communities by the concept of unity itself, which for her is visible as well as invisible, and for most Protestants merely invisible, even when it aims at a visible external form, to be fully achieved only at the end of time. Through these ecumenical meetings, the Protestant communities in recent years seemed to have grown willing to accept a different conception of unity and tradition: they may be said to be obeying a Catholic principle of growth, perhaps fostered by the presence of the Orthodox, who have introduced into the ecumenical dialogue the Catholic demands.[1] As the polemical attitude towards Catholics has become less rigid, the Holy See also has in recent years modified its regulations about contacts between Catholics and the separated brothers.

Pope John recognized the work of the Holy Spirit in the new directions taken by the movement for unity, and he saw also the conditions which justified a new attitude on the part of the Catholic Church, an attitude which would not have been at all justifiable, or even predictable, for example, in the age when the Encyclical *Mortalium Animos* of Pius XI appeared.

> We find joy and hope in the spectacle of the generous and increasing efforts made on all sides to restore that visible unity of all Christians, which worthily corresponds to the intentions, commands and hopes of our divine Saviour. Knowing that unity, which is the breath of the Holy Spirit in so many well-intentioned souls, can never be fully and firmly realized until, in accordance with the prophecy of Jesus Christ himself, "there will be one fold and one shepherd", we beg our Mediator and Advocate with the Father, that he may bestow on all Christians the grace to recognize the marks of his true Church, so that they may become her devoted children.[2]

It is unnecessary to say that in Pope John's words there is never a hint of theological compromise or of a practical pan-Christianity: the zeal of charity, which longs to hasten the process of union, never led him to hide his belief that the Catholic Church has all the characteristics (the "marks" as theologians say) of the Church established by Christ:

[1] "Some of the Reformation theologians had opposed the idea of the visible unity, whereas now, as the result of the studies of the different confessions, the following text has been proposed to the general Assembly of the World Council of (non-Catholic) Churches at New Delhi: The unity of the Church 'is made visible when all those who are baptized in Jesus Christ and confess him as Lord and Saviour are led by the Holy Spirit to form a whole community, confess the same apostolic faith, preach the same Gospel, share the same Bread, join in common prayer . . . and find themselves in communion with the whole Christian community in all places and all times'. Although this description of unity is not entirely identical with the Catholic conception it proves what results may be obtained by a more profound study of Scripture and Christian tradition." (Cardinal Auguste Bea, in his speech to Catholic intellectuals, Paris, 23 Jan. 1962.)

[2] *Aeterna Dei Sapientia*, 11 Nov. 1916.

"Has not the Lord told us that the Father always hears him? We may then believe that the Church, for whom he prayed and sacrificed himself on the Cross, and to whom he has promised his everlasting presence, has always been, and remains, the one, holy, catholic and apostolic Church, as she was instituted."

But the fact that only in the Catholic Church is preserved the fullness of truth does not mean that the separated brothers are totally cut off from the unity of the Christian family: the visible rift does not mean a total rupture of spiritual and sacramental bonds, such as faith, baptism and Scripture. What is needed for the strengthening of the surviving bonds? Once the action of the Holy Spirit is recognized in all the scattered limbs of Christianity, what can be done to make its revivifying breath felt once more?

Here also Pope John's method was simple; he applied, to this difficult problem, the principle which has inspired all aspects of his magnificent pontifical activity: we must insist on what unites believers in Christ rather than on what divides them; we must rejoice in the unity which still survives and grows, rather than keep our gaze fixed on the fact and extent of our diversity. Charity becomes, this time too, not only a theological virtue but a principle to be followed in the service of truth. What are the rules of this method inspired by charity?

3. THE PRIMACY OF CHARITY

The first rule is that it is for the Catholics first to give visible testimony to the conformity of their Church to the words of Christ. This is what the Council aims at: to restore the countenance of the Catholic Church according to all the requirements of her vital principle, so that the separated brothers, by virtue of the faith they still preserve, may recognize her once more:

"When we have realized this enormous task, eliminating what might from a human point of view be an obstacle on a path we seek to make more easy, we shall present the Church in all her splendour, without spot or wrinkle, and we shall say to all the others who are separated from us, Orthodox, Protestants, etc.:

See, brothers, here is the Church of Christ, we have done our best to be true to her . . ."[3]

In this plan two acknowledgments are implicit: that the Catholic Church has, in her structures, language and customs, more than one feature which supports the contention of those who are doubtful of her fidelity to Christ, and that the good will of the separated brothers is such that, to recall them to full union with Peter, in all probability it would be enough to show them the objective signs of Catholic holiness.

The Fathers of the Council, particularly the members of the Secretariat for Christian Unity, have already in the first session and specifically in the second developed more widely the principles of the ecumenical method. Pope John restricted himself to very broad generalizations, leaving to others the *munus theologicum* (theological task) of definitions, and reserving to himself the testimony, proclaimed and living, of the primacy of charity in its relations with truth.

His insistence on the pastoral character of the Council in a subordinate way also served this ecumenical intention, which certainly cannot triumph without some modification of the theological presentation within the Catholic Church. The pastoral orientation is not, as some think, a pragmatic intention which must remain subordinate to the doctrinal control guaranteed by the theologians. "The bishops", Bernhard Häring writes,[4] "are in the Church to be the model for theologians, who must always be at the same time shepherds of souls": otherwise they risk becoming unaware that the Christian truth, in its essential nature, is intended for the salvation of souls, and not for external practical convenience.

The hypertrophy of the theological systems has been evident just in those periods that have been marked by a scarcity of pastoral sense and has raised between various Christian Churches more or less artificial barriers, which would easily be knocked

---

[3] *O.R.*, 10–11 Aug. 1959.
[4] In *Il Vaticano II nel segno dell'unità*, Edizioni Paoline, 1963, p. 34. Häring's small book is particularly useful for the thorough understanding, in the spirit of Pope John, of the relation between charity and truth, both in the actual distortions to which it has given rise, and in its positive strength for making new efforts.

down once the disciples of Christ had recovered the lively consciousness of the essentially missionary purpose of their faith.

Pope John's example did nothing to warrant that spirit of
reform which delights in criticizing the Church and produces
subtle complexes of guilt. He was content to place the emphasis,
discreetly but fearlessly, on her "mission" as the primary need of
the Church and, by means of a Council, to ensure the reorientation
of the whole ecclesiastical structure from theology to canon law,
around this requirement.

In fact, as soon as he had been able to discover with certainty,
in the course of the first session, that the majority of the Council,
in obedience to his guidance, were unwilling to accept the far
from pastoral project which the theological commission had taken
three years to prepare, he exercised his primacy with a memorable
gesture, by sending the schema back to a new mixed commission
and reminding the Council explicitly of what he had said in his
opening speech: that the "deposit of faith" ought to have a
theological form more in keeping with the pastoral character of
the Church. In this way he rendered a great service to the ecu-
mical cause also; in fact he sent back to the workshop a theology
that had been elaborated and directed according to the polemical
inspiration of recent centuries. The separated brothers had to
acknowledge, this time at least, that the authority of Peter is a
providential and indispensable instrument of love for the benefit
of Christian unity.

In the same way in which, within the Catholic Church, Pope
John tried to diffuse, not the harshness of polemics or the anxieties
of a guilt complex, but the enjoyment of truth, so, in his relations
with the separated brothers, he was always careful to show them
his joy at being able to consider them brothers in Christ.

It is useless to conceal that, on the part of the Orthodox and
Protestant world also, the prejudices and resentments were, and
in part remain, profound and consolidated in mental forms or
psychological complexes. To overcome the hard barrier that had
grown with the centuries a confrontation between the theologians, however diligent and courteous, would not have sufficed:
so it was necessary to put forward Christian charity as the reason

and modality of the meeting: a charity unfeigned, not blinded by secondary ends, but shining and frank, like that of Pope John.

Now we know that his charity, far from being a sudden acquisition, either in essence or in its practical style, had been ripened through a long apprenticeship. With what tact, I might say with what brilliance of intuition, Pope John, in the Audience he granted to the Observers of the separated Churches on 13 October 1962, avoided the temptation to deliver a lofty speech, steeped in theology! Who else but the Pope would have had the idea, and I would add the right, on that very day when, for the first time for centuries, the separated Churches were gathered around him, of avoiding the mention, even the charitable mention, of the faults of the past and the distance which separated them in the present? He merely spoke in a friendly way of what the Lord ("it is God who has brought us here!") had taught him, during his long experience as a churchman, about the mystery of Christian unity. In recalling the ecumenical contacts he had made during his Nunciature in Paris he came out with these humble but significant expressions:

"We did not debate, we spoke; we did not discuss, but we became fond of each other!"

Later, when he spoke about the day of the inauguration of the Council, he confided to them, in memorable words:

"In that providential and historic hour, I was above all careful to do my immediate duty, which was to remain recollected, to pray, and to thank the Lord. But every now and then my glance turned towards all my sons and brothers. And when it lingered on your group, on each one of you, I found that your presence gave me joy."

Never had the Spirit of the Lord seemed to us so extraordinarily delicate in its way of entering the history of the world as in these years: and, because it was delicate, it was effective. He came among us as silently as a dove: only the most watchful hearts were aware of him. The supernatural value of this simplicity, to which the greatest theologians of the future will perforce be grateful, was well emphasized by the man who first experienced it as a "separated brother", that is, by the Anglican Primate

Geoffrey Fisher. That was the first of the series of ecumenical meetings, and it soon had great repercussions.

In a few short years the Pope led the way in bringing about this astonishing change of spiritual climate in Christendom by wise and friendly acts. Friendship may appear to cost nothing and to change nothing. In truth it changes everything and in the end is the costliest thing there is. It is indeed a miracle that in a short time the Pope should have accomplished so much—and yet no miracle. For he did only, in the large and public scene to which he was called, what can be done by any man altogether dedicated to the service of Christ. His dedication did not separate him from his fellow Christians but brought him closer to them—which is to say that he was a devoted person who believed in all persons and loved them all with the robust and simple faith of Christian dedication. We are all his friends and all his debtors; and praise God for our every remembrance of him. . . . That great movement goes forward, though there are ferocious lions still in the way: none can see where it will lead to. But all of us know by faith, as the Pope knew by faith, that the Holy Spirit is leading us away from the darkness of the past and towards the light.[5]

4. TO INSIST ON WHAT UNITES MEN

The second rule of the ecumenism of Pope John has a more direct theological significance, and may also be expressed in his own words: "We always prefer to insist on what unites men, and to go along with them as far as we can, without prejudice to the requirements of justice and the rights of the truth."[6]

Meanwhile, as we have said, he never denied the existence of a Christian family, larger than the Catholic family, certainly not yet fully united, but not completely divested of real unity and, precisely because of this, in a position to prepare for the visible fulfilment of the mystery of unity, which may come about through a natural development of its own nature.

Unfortunately the whole Christian family [he said in his speech of 11 October 1962] has not yet fully reached this

[5] B.B.C. European Service, 2 June 1963.   [6] Speech of the 26 June 1961.

visible unity in the truth. Meanwhile the Catholic Church considers it to be her duty to do all she can for the fulfilment of the great mystery of that unity for which Jesus Christ prayed so ardently to his heavenly Father, just before his sacrifice. She rejoices in her peace, knowing well that she is intimately united with that prayer: and her joy is greater when she sees that this prayer is answered, with saving grace, even among those who are no longer nursed at her breast.

The conceptual definition of that unity, as we see, remains always opportunely vague. What is important is that it should already, in some sort, exist even now, and that it should show by reflection the adorable beauty of God. The manner in which it will be joined by ever wider visible links will be a matter for the Council to establish, as far as the Catholic Church is concerned, but without a doubt these links will be suggested by the charity diffused by the Holy Spirit in the hearts of all the faithful as time goes by, according to ways and times that it is well to leave in the hands of Providence.

The Protestant theologian Cullmann said that the separated Churches have something in common with the Catholic Church; in fact, he said that the Catholic Church has all that these have, with "something more", which is entirely her own, and which she alone believes to be of divine origin. The ecumenical problem for the separated Churches consists in enquiring whether their will for reform has now missed some Gospel truths which are instead preserved in the Catholic Church: in her turn, the Catholic Church must ask herself whether her "something more", may perhaps have come from men, rather than from God.[7]

---

[7] The passage from Oscar Cullmann deserves to be quoted entire: "What separates us, apart from the different conception of unity, is not in the positive elements of our faith, but precisely in what Catholicism has *more* than we have, in our opinion, what she has *extra*, and *vice versa*, in what we have *less* than they have, in the opinion of Catholics, what we *lack*. To my mind the talks between us will make some progress only when our Catholic brothers no longer consider as purely negative what they find we 'lack', when they look at this therefore, not as a deficiency or arbitrary restriction, but as a conscious concentration, inspired by the Holy Spirit, upon what we believe must remain the sole centre of our faith in Christ. Precisely for this reason we welcome with joy in the Council every proposal for reform in liturgical activity and in theological studies, and any proposal directed towards such a concentration, and we are disappointed by any further development of that 'extra' which we mentioned above." Häring, who refers to this passage (*op. cit.*, pp. 117–18), quotes some precise examples of that "extra" which does not come from Christ, and which should therefore be sacrificed to the ideal of unity (pp. 118–24).

It is easy to admit that in the "Catholic share" there are some elements of a human origin. Possibly, in giving up these elements, the Catholic Church may be able to show her motherly love. But there is, in her share, a nucleus that comes from Christ, and that the Church can never set aside without denying her very foundation. Without any precise indications, Pope John has given us to understand that for the joy of refound unity the Catholic Church will be willing to take any legitimate step forward.

Every time that, in his speeches, he revealed his hopes for Christian unity, his language was full of prophetic joy; he did not attempt to hide the difficulties, but he testified that the Holy Spirit was at work in this. When the Spirit blows there rises, from the depths of the Christian family, a common eagerness of love and hope. Without trying to hasten the process we must whenever possible offer the Spirit the necessary means and the necessary docility: the results then surpass all human prevision. With this confidence he said on 11 September 1962:

> The precious links of the golden chain which, even from the first centuries of the Christian era, the grace of God had spread over various European countries and the then known world, for the perfection of Catholic unity, and which through various circumstances seemed in later ages to be slackened, and afterwards broken asunder, now once more arrest the attention of all who are not insensible to the breath of new life which the project of the Council arouses here and there, in the anxious desire for brotherly reunion in the arms of the ancient mother of all, the holy and universal Mother Church. This gives us tranquil joy, and already outshines the first ray of light which presided over the preparation of this world congress. Oh, the beauty of the liturgical prayer: that God may be pleased to grant peace and unity to all Christian peoples. Oh, how all hearts rejoice when they read in chapter 17 of St John's Gospel: "That all may be one." One in thoughts, words and deeds.

5. SIGNS OF THE THAW

It is easy to prove that, in the space of a few years, the Holy Spirit has rewarded Pope John's confidence. On Saturday,

13 October 1962, Cardinal Bea, who has been himself another unforeseen instrument of the Holy Spirit, coming out of a special Audience granted to the Observers, exclaimed with emotion: "It has been a miracle, it has been a miracle!"[8]

Without presupposing a long maturing process, anterior and extraneous to any gestures of diplomatic courtesy, it would be impossible to explain the presence of the Observers of the separated Churches at the meetings of the Council, especially as their presence soon became an organic, if discreet, participation in the Conciliar debate, through the Secretariat for Christian Unity, in which it exercised considerable influence.

On 30 August 1959, during an Audience, Pope John put forward the idea that, if the separated brothers came to the Council, they would be welcomed, because "the Church is still their home". The next year, on 16 November 1960, he referred directly to the participation of the separated Churches. It was only in the Bull summoning the Council—25 December 1961—that the question appeared to be solved: the separated brothers "are today glad to be able to send to the Council, in the name of their communities, some representatives who will enable them better to follow its deliberations". During the first months of 1962 that indefatigable pilgrim for unity Mgr Jan Willebrands had already made sure of the presence of the delegates of the chief Evangelical Churches. His mission of persuasion to the Orthodox seemed more difficult and less successful, because of their doctrine about the nature of the Ecumenical Council. For the Orthodox bishops, who rightly consider themselves to be successors to the apostles, a Council that has been summoned and in fact assembles, without their participation, cannot truly be called ecumenical. This was the decision of the Pan-Orthodox Conference of Rhodes, in the autumn of 1961. We are already in a position to say that Pope John had planned to overcome this difficulty, certainly of great

[8] Cardinal Bea's impression was largely shared by the Observers. Oscar Cullmann, for example, declared to the Press on 23 Nov. 1962: "Every morning when we take possession of our places, as if they were seats of honour, in front of the Cardinals, and when every morning the Secretary of the Council pronounces his *'exeant omnes'*, while we are allowed to stay in our places, I marvel anew at the way and manner in which we are welcomed in this assembly. . . . Externally we are passive onlookers, but internally we share in this activity with our Catholic brothers."

theological delicacy, with a journey to the Holy Land. The extra-ordinary pilgrimage of Paul VI has initiated, as we have already seen, a programme which Pope John had already suggested, in general terms, to Athenagoras, the Patriarch of Constantinople. It was the Patriarch of Moscow who, quite unexpectedly, broke the abstentionist front agreed upon by the Orthodox among themselves. On various previous occasions he had not failed to show a spirit of distrust, almost of hostility, towards the Second Vatican Council. All the reasons adduced by the Patriarch for his original refusal had a political character: it is difficult to estimate how far they were sincere. In any case the deciding factor was Pope John's behaviour towards the Soviet government. For one thing, he gave the government and the Patriarch explicit guaran-tees that in the Council, the political spirit, however legitimate, would find no expression. The news of the arrival of two repre-sentatives of the Russian Church spread as soon as the Council opened, and was disconcerting. It not only created an understand-able dismay in the autonomous Greek Churches, but it roused, in the Western and even the Catholic world, a chorus of tendentious interpretations which could, however, in no way impair the joy of Pope John and the Council.

He had said, on 30 April 1960, to the students of the *Russicum*: "We must prepare all things well, with very great charity and thorough knowledge of peoples, and we must know how to hold in consideration also the children of a most ancient tradition, who at this moment need to be understood and attracted by proofs of brotherliness, sweetness and peace. There is no doubt that the Lord will intervene with his grace, and will give us great joys, even if it will be for others, in the future, to enjoy the abundant results."

Here also the evangelical realism of Pope John was more successful than the retrospective gloom of the "wiseacres". But a realism like his, inclined as much to daring gestures as to long and silent preparations, cannot be imitated, as if it were a technique to be learnt. Pope John's ecumenism was Pope John himself. His personality, especially from the opening of the Council onwards, acquired in the eyes of all, even of the "heretics", a halo of convincing fatherliness. When he died the Protestants for the first time mourned the death of a Pope. And that mourning also signifies and promises unity. But, above all, for the first time the Protestants, on more than one occasion, have had to admit that, if unity is to come among Christians, to keep it firm and to be its symbol, we shall need a man just like Pope John.

It is for the purpose of enabling the Church better to carry out this supreme task in our own times that we have proposed to summon the Second Ecumenical Vatican Council, in the confidence that this imposing conference of the whole Catholic hierarchy will not only strengthen the bonds of unity in the central See, in worship and in discipline, which are the prerogative of the true Church, but will also draw the gaze of innumerable believers in Christ, and invite them to gather around the "great Shepherd of the flock", who entrusts its perpetual guardianship to Peter and his successors. Our warm appeal for unity is then an echo of the appeal launched several times by St Leo in the fifth century, reminding his hearers of the earlier appeal addressed to all the faithful of all the Churches by St Irenaeus, whom divine Providence had called from Asia to rule over the See of Lyons and glorify it with his martyrdom. In fact, after he had acknowledged the uninterrupted succession of the bishops of Rome, heirs of the authority possessed by the two Princes of the Apostles, he concluded with this exhortation: "And because of its pre-eminent superiority it is with this Church that every other Church must be in agreement, that is, all the faithful throughout the world; and it is through communion with her that all these faithful have preserved the apostolic tradition."

But we wish our appeal for unity to be above all the echo of the prayer of our Saviour to his divine Father at the Last Supper: "that they may all be one, even as thou, Father, art in me, and I in thee, ... that they may be one. ..." There is no doubt about the answer to this prayer, as there is no doubt that this prayer will be fulfilled, as the dreadful sacrifice on Golgotha was fulfilled. Has the Lord not told us that his Father always hears him? Therefore we believe that the Church, for which he prayed and sacrificed himself upon the Cross, and to which he has promised his continual presence, has always been and remains one, holy, Catholic and apostolic, just as when it was founded.

Alas! as in the past, so also in the present must we sorrowfully observe that the unity of the Church does not in fact yet consist of the communion of all believers in one single profession of faith and in one single practice of worship and obedience. Nevertheless we find joy and hope in the spectacle of the generous and increasing efforts made on all sides to restore that visible unity of all Christians, which worthily corresponds to the intentions, commands and hopes of the divine Saviour. Knowing that unity, which is the breath of the Holy Spirit in so many well-intentioned souls, can never be fully and firmly realized until, in accordance with the prophecy of Jesus Christ himself, "there will be one fold and one shepherd", we therefore beg our Mediator and Advocate with the Father that he may bestow on all Christians the grace to recognize the marks of his true Church, so that they may become her devoted children. Oh, may the Lord be pleased to bring about the dawn of that blessed day of universal reconciliation, when an immense chorus of joy and love will rise from the one great family of the redeemed, when, exalting the divine mercy, they will sing with the Psalmist: "Behold, how good and pleasant it is when brothers dwell in unity!" (Encyclical *Aeterna Dei*, 11 Nov. 1961.)

The ecumenical Age

The Church has always opposed these errors, and frequently condemned them, even with severity and firmness. But now the Bride of Christ is more anxious to offer the medicine of mercy than to wield the weapon of severity; not with condemnations but with a more ample bestowal of her valid doctrine does she seek to satisfy the needs of today. This does not mean that there are no longer errors, or dangerous concepts that must be distrusted and dispelled; but these are teachings so openly conflicting with the right principles of honesty, and have given rise to such fatal consequences that today men themselves begin to condemn them. In particular they condemn those conceptions of human life which leave no room for God and his laws, excessive trust in technical progress, and an idea of social welfare founded merely on the comforts of life.

Men are more and more convinced that the dignity of the human person and his proper development are matters of extreme importance which cannot so easily be set aside. And, which is even more important, they have learnt from experience the absolute insufficiency of brute force, of weapons, and of political oppression as a successful solution of the grave problems which harass them. Above this agitated scene the Church holds aloft the torch of religious truth: she wishes to be an affectionate, kind and patient mother; she is moved by compassion and goodness towards her alienated children. To mankind that suffers from so many ills she says, as Peter said to the poor beggar: "I have no silver and gold, but I give you what I have: in the name of Jesus Christ of Nazareth rise and walk" (Acts 3. 6). The Church offers the men of today no fading riches, no mirage of a happiness to be enjoyed only on this earth: she pours out a wealth of supernatural grace which, raising men to the dignity of children of God, offers them a firm protection and assistance for human life: she reveals the sources of her fertile doctrine which sets men in the light of Christ, making them conscious in their hearts of their true worth, of their supreme dignity, and of the end assigned to them; finally she sends her sons to extend the sphere of Christian charity, a charity which with singular vigour plucks out the seeds of discord and wonderfully promotes agreement, just peace and the brotherly unity of all. (Speech at the opening of the Council, 11 Oct. 1962.)

"We did not discuss, but we became fond of each other"

Dear Gentlemen, our meeting today, so welcome to all, has a family air, a note of confidence: it is to be marked by respect and simplicity.

The first thought that rises from my heart is a prayer; it is a useful lesson to all, taken from the 67th Psalm: "Blessed is the Lord who daily bears us up; God is our salvation" (Psalm 67 [68]. 19).

In 1952 Pope Pius XII, with an unforeseen and surprising gesture, asked me to become Patriarch of Venice. I told him that I did not need much time for reflection before accepting. In fact my own will did not enter into this proposal at all; there was in my mind no desire to be directed to this rather than to any other ministry or office.

My episcopal motto was a sufficient answer: Obedience and Peace!

When then, after thirty years of service under the direct orders of the Holy See, I prepared to start an almost new kind of life and meet the people of Venice, whom I was to lead for six years as their Pastor, I thought over and meditated these words of the

Psalm: "God bears us up." He bears us up as we are, and with what we have: with the wealth he gives us and the poverty we create for ourselves.

This same thought was with me when four years ago I accepted the succession to St Peter, and has been with me in all that has been done since then, day by day, until the announcement and the beginning of the Council.

As far as my humble person is concerned I do not like to speak of special inspirations. I hold to sound doctrine: it teaches me that everything comes from God. In this perspective I have been able to consider as a heavenly inspiration also the idea of the Council which was opened on the 11th October.

I can assure you that I was full of emotion on that day. In that God-given and historic hour I was above all careful to do my immediate duty, which was to remain collected, to pray, and to thank the Lord. But every now and then my eyes turned to all my sons and brothers. And when my glance fell on your group, on each one of you, I found that your presence gave me joy.

Without wishing to anticipate the results, let us be content today to state the facts. Blessed be God for each day as it comes.

As far as you yourselves are concerned, look into my heart: you will perhaps find there much more than my words can tell you.

How can I forget the ten years I passed at Sofia? And the ten more years passed at Istanbul and Athens? They were twenty happy and well spent years, during which I made the acquaintance of venerable personalities as well as of many generous young people. I observed them with affectionate respect, even if my mission as representative of the Holy See in the Near East did not directly concern them.

Then in Paris, which is one of the most typically cosmopolitan centres, and this was particularly true immediately after the last war, I was able to meet innumerable Christians belonging to various denominations.

There was never between us, as far as I know, any confusion of principles or conflict in the sphere of charity, in our common labour, necessitated by the circumstances, of assisting all who suffered.

We did not debate, we talked; we did not discuss, but we became fond of each other!

One day long ago I handed to a venerable old man, the prelate of an Eastern Church not in communion with Rome, a medal of the pontificate of Pius XI. The gesture was intended as, and was indeed, a simple act of affectionate courtesy. Some time afterwards the old man, about to close his eyes to the light of this world, desired that when he died this medal should be placed on his heart. I saw this with my own eyes, and the memory still moves me.

I have alluded to this episode on purpose. In its touching simplicity it is like a wild flower: as the new season returns, it can once more be plucked, and offered. (Speech to the Observers, 13 Oct. 1962.)

From the depths of the centuries, a longing desire

God has heard and granted the prayers of consecrated souls, of children, of the sick and suffering. He has heard the prayers also of those who wish to pray and do not know how to do so, of those who long to rediscover in their consciences the harmony between eternal laws and the requirements of a personal vocation.

A characteristic fruit of this Ecumenical Council is the spontaneous appearance, almost unexpected by most people, of the sense of unity, or better, of the attraction, felt, recognized and welcomed, towards Christian brotherhood, expressed in the Apostles' Creed, as the convincing affirmation of the Church, one, holy, catholic and apostolic. The Church aims, not at ruling but at serving the peoples, for whom the kingdom of Christ is an aspiration sincerely desired, even if not always understood in its forms and developments.

Over the vast, complicated and still most agitated horizon of the created world, described in the first lines of Genesis, the Spirit of God is moving over the face of the waters. Apart from more detailed analyses and applications it is certain that, in what survives of the spiritual inheritance of Holy Church, even where this is no longer there in its fullness, there has seldom during the twenty centuries of the Christian era been felt such a heart-felt longing for the unity desired by the Lord. We have been able to notice that this first presentation, through the Ecumenical Council, of the problem of religion to our contemporaries has aroused a response which seems to wish to concentrate attention on the image of the "one shepherd and one fold". It is a timid approach to unity and not always free of prejudice, which we can imagine and which we wish also to understand, so that by divine grace it may be overcome.

The appeal, "one fold and one shepherd", referred to again in moving accents in the prayer on the night of the Last Supper, "that they may be one" (John 17. 21), echoes imperiously from the depths of twenty centuries of Christianity, and knocks at everyone's door. (Christmas broadcast, 1962.)

Miraculous results

We wish to add a few words about what from various quarters reaches our ears concerning the growth of trustful expectation on the part of public opinion, with regard to the problems of peace and Christian hopes, which the great movement of the Council has been arousing, not with a subdued murmur but with the effectiveness of persuasive speech and the sureness of firm assertion.

To tell the truth, the idea of an Ecumenical Council did not at its first announcement seem to have much interest for the secular opinion of the world. But three years from the beginning of its preparation and especially after the first example of Conciliar activity, that is, from 11 October last to 8 December, it has everywhere, even among people belonging to different religious, ideological or political trends, met with an attitude so respectful and reverent in every part of the world, that we are bound to ask ourselves if the light of heavenly grace has not already descended into the hearts of men, gradually urging them towards Jesus Christ and his holy and blessed Church.

To mention only one aspect, we have seen with pleasure that the communication and invitation sent to our separated brothers, who still glory in the name of Christians, suggesting that they should despatch their delegates as Observers and witnesses of the Ecumenical Vatican Council, have met with most successful, important and promising results.

For our own part, these invitations and the singular respect with which they were received, a rare event in the history of the Church and her Councils, makes us wonder whether this is not the sign of an approach of many souls to the profound meaning of the prayer of Jesus to his heavenly Father, a prayer which he uttered on the mysterious eve of the supreme sacrifice: "Father, the hour has come; glorify thy Son that the Son may glorify thee. . . . I am praying for those whom thou hast given me, for they are thine. . . . Holy Father, keep them in thy name, which thou hast given me, that they may be one, even as we are one" (John 17. 1, 9, 11).

We can already see that this prayer is, to some degree, being realized. The Council summoned by us is directly concerned with those who belong to our own Church, one holy, catholic and apostolic. This is the principal aim we have set ourselves. But if we were to occupy ourselves only with Catholics and our action were restricted to our own Church, such a manner of acting, we consider, would not sufficiently correspond to the word of the Divine Redeemer, of whom the beloved disciple wrote: "He (Jesus) is the expiation for our sins: and not for ours only, but also for the sins of the whole world" (I John 2. 2).

Is it not true that the same evangelist affirms of the Divine Saviour, the light of men: "the true light, that enlightens every man, was coming into the world" (John 1. 9)?

And was the evangelist St Luke not inspired by the Holy Spirit when he wrote: "All flesh shall see the salvation of God" (Luke 3. 6)?

Moreover, St Paul—oh, how rightly he is counted among the apostles and prophets!—sternly warns the Romans: "but glory and honour and peace for everyone who does good, the Jew first and also the Greek. For God shows no partiality" (Romans 2. 10–11).

How joyfully does Paul himself, writing to Titus, emphasize the nature and the strength of the mystery of salvation! "For the grace of God has appeared for the salvation of all men" (Titus 2. 2).

To close these quotations we wish to refer to a maxim of the authoritative and eloquent interpreter of St Paul, St John Chrysostom, a maxim which has made a great impression on us ever since our boyhood: "Remember, O my brothers, that you have to render an account not only of your lives, but of the whole world" (Homily XV on St Matthew).

It is certainly a great joy to note the welcome accorded to our Council by numerous brothers separated from this Apostolic See. But what a far greater and richer hope, and more full of heavenly graces, we might cherish if the widespread longing of our sincere love could be felt by all those who are called to rejoice with us in the same faith and salvation in Jesus Christ, to be fulfilled in the one fold!

This is hidden in the secret design of the Lord: and in this we seem already to see the first dawn of that longed-for day whose future coming Jesus Christ hailed with these loving wishes and trustful words: "I have other sheep, that are not of this fold; I must bring them also, . . . so there shall be one flock, one shepherd" (John 10. 16). (Letter to the Bishops, 6 Jan. 1963.)

CHAPTER THIRTEEN

Catholic Diversity

I. THE WHOLE AND THE PART

As Cardinal Cajetan shrewdly observes, the unity of the Church is threatened every time a part of her organism claims to act as if it were the whole; *agere ut pars*: this is the law in which liberty and obedience are reconciled. The pope alone, because he is pope, must act and speak as the whole, preserving in all charity his supremacy above all other organs of the Church and all the movements of ideas and actions which stir our human life and promote its expansion in the world.

The ecclesiastical monarchy is not to be compared with absolute monarchies, in spite of certain exterior resemblances. Whereas these, by their very nature, tend to concentrate all power in the Head and to transform the autonomous social bodies into mechanical processes, the ecclesiastical "monarchy" is founded upon the sacramental sharing of every member in Christ, the Head and Body of the Church, source of all spiritual power, the first supernatural Cause which directly communicates its efficacy, although in differing degrees, to all the organism. This causality is expressed in acts of the governing and teaching magisterium, under a hierarchy which has at its summit the successor of St Peter, but this does not mean that the individual Christian's right to liberty comes to him by a benevolent concession of the Head: it has its origin, primarily, in all the faithful in the sacramental sign immanent in all: external authority is at the service of this increase of personal and common liberty.

The visible Head of the Church is the Pope. But he has the distinguishing and significant title of "Servant of the Servants of the Lord". This title goes far back in the centuries. The first to sign himself in this style was St Gregory I, in the sixth century; but this does not mean that it was not used before. All can understand the lofty meaning of this expression and therefore the character of that loving and devoted co-operation which the Sacred College, the Bishops and other dignitaries, the priests, and the lay folk dedicated to the apostolate, give him.

The Church indeed, because she has this fundamental divine spirituality, cannot be confused with the systems and organisms of men which, although worthy of respect, have purposes which are much more restricted and of an earthly nature. The Church, instead, is constantly inspired by God; she seeks the perfection of man, the masterpiece of God's creation, and promotes his welfare in the hope of the joy which will be eternal and is within the reach of all.[1]

Pope John never directly tackled, on the doctrinal plane, the most serious of the theological problems discussed in the second session of the Council, that is, the problem of the collegiate authority of the bishops in relation to the primacy of the pope. But, with word and example, he has set in the clearest light the bond which, in the Church, sustains and sanctifies all other bonds: charity. The image of the Church which he has caused to shine before our eyes, and to which the Council seeks to give juridical confirmation, is that of an organism *sui generis*, in which Peter is at the service of the apostles, the apostles at the service of the priests, the priests at the service of Christian people and the Christian people at the service of peace and the salvation of the world.

Once this "service" has become, not an occasional gesture, or an article of faith, barely perceived through the patina of authoritarianism which might conceal it, but a visible style of government, many problems which are still awaiting a solution on the doctrinal plane will be already almost solved. Among these, as we have already mentioned, is that of collegiality, and the other that of the rights of the lay people in relation to the clergy, or indeed the problem of the unity of all Christians. The more evident it becomes to all, through objective and empirical testimony, that the vital principle of the Church is charity, the more

[1] Account in *O.R.* of the general Audience of 12 Dec. 1962.

swiftly will pass into the background aspects and traditions which at present cast shadows and furrows of division within Christianity.

Among the inspired words in which Pope Paul VI praised Pope John, at the opening of the second session, was his account of how his "dear and venerable" predecessor had "revived in the consciousness of the ecclesiastical authority the conviction that the Christian doctrine is not only truth, to be explored with the reason enlightened by faith, but also a message engendering life and activity, and that the authority of the Church is not to be used merely to condemn errors which offend her, but must be extended to proclaim the positive and vital doctrines with which she is so richly endowed." The teaching authority of the Church, not merely theoretical or negative, must in this Council more and more reveal the life-giving virtue of the message of Christ, who said: "The words that I have spoken to you are spirit and life."

This vital service is indispensable to the unity of the Church which, proceeding from God through one sole Mediator, cannot be in herself divided and discordant without failing in her mission to reveal to the world the mystery from which she springs.

If I had to express in a single sentence the manifold gifts which the Catholic Church has received from Pope John, I would say that, as a consequence of his example, Catholic unity has rediscovered, in the realm of feeling and of objective guarantees, sufficient freedom for her spontaneous and tranquil expansion. The very fact that, before and during the Council, the various tendencies which sometimes showed themselves in a very lively manner have been able and obliged to confront each other without being allowed to invoke, each in his own support, the verdict of the supreme authority, is a perfect revelation of the pontifical genius of Pope John. In the most dramatic moment of the Conciliar discussion—the question of the relation between revelation and tradition—he said, in an Audience granted to the French bishops: "It is right for them to debate, it is necessary: they must debate like brothers and all will go well. As for myself, I am an optimist." And he applied to himself the words Scripture uses for Jacob, who listens to the disputes among his sons and keeps his own counsel.

Only when the real opinion of the majority of the Council ran the risk of being set aside because of some formal ruling, did he, on 21 November 1962, take the historic decision to send the schema on the sources of revelation back to a new commission. His action had an extraordinary repercussion and, in fact, broke the last dykes which had prevented the manifestation of full agreement between the Council and the directives given by him on 11 October 1962, in his memorable speech.

Never as in that moment had the primacy of Peter been revealed as an indispensable service for the unity of the Church. And, when it was known that the new commission would be presided over by the two chief exponents of the two tendencies, we seemed to see once more the cheerful fatherly spirit of Pope John. Beyond all the differing opinions, he was sure that his children were at one in love; in the name of the love they shared they would know how to overcome all divergence.

2. THE INTERNAL DIALOGUE

Our brotherhood was then lovingly safeguarded: within this affectionate protection the liberty of our thoughts began to circulate like blood which had for a time remained stagnant.[2] The extraordinary sense of renewed youth which had taken hold of the Church by the end of the first session was due to this dialogue within the Catholic Church having begun again, as if we had recovered the visible exercise of the holy liberty of the sons of God. It was Pope John who, at the end of the first session, expressed the general feeling perfectly:

> It was necessary that the brothers who had come from afar and who were all reunited around the same hearth should

[2] "The Catholic world", wrote Cardinal Montini in his pastoral letter on the Council (Lent 1962), "listened willingly to Rome, but often had the impression that there was no opportunity for a dialogue or invitation to a collaboration, and that the unity of the Church was to be testified rather in passive obedience than in joyful brotherhood, inspired by the principle of this unity. There was felt in so many sectors of its world-wide activity a wealth of experience and a desire to communicate and to report and ask questions in a more lively way, and not only with Rome but also among the diverse sectors." And he added that Pope John, announcing the Council, had divined the "secret longing of the whole Catholic world," the longing "for the great dialogue within the inner unity of the Church".

make contact with each other for greater mutual knowledge: it was necessary that our eyes should meet, to feel the throb of our brotherly hearts: it was necessary to relate the individual experiences, for a thoughtful and most useful exchange of pastoral contributions, expressions of the most diverse climates and circumstances of the apostolate.

In such a vast framework it is also understandable that some days were needed to arrive at an agreement about what was, *salva caritate*, a reason for natural and anxious divergences; this also has its own providential reason for the sake of bringing the truth to light, and demonstrates to the world the holy liberty of the sons of God, as found in the Church.

Without this liberty unity would have been compromised. The danger in fact had been this, that the "part" might claim to be the "whole". That is, that a particular, and in itself admirable, theological trend might be proposed as the doctrine of the Church, *sic et simpliciter*, relegating every other opinion to beyond the pale of orthodoxy. Catholic unity is not a uniformity of theological trends, or rational elaborations of the faith: it is built, not upon the work of man, but upon the work of God, and therefore upon a divinely established foundation.

"The Church of Christ", said Paul VI when he opened the second session, "is one and therefore must be unique", and "this mysterious and visible unity can only be obtained in identity of faith, in sharing the same sacraments and in the organic harmony of a single ecclesiastical control, but with respectful consideration for a wide variety of linguistic expressions, ritualistic forms, historical traditions, local privileges, spiritual trends, legitimate institutions and popular activities."

There is then, at least by rights, a "pluralism" in the development of unity. This pluralism may be found, not in revealed truth, which may not be tampered with, but in the changeable and manifold situations of the human spirit, which may give rise to a variety of Catholic traditions even at the theological level. Is this not one of the most profound causes of that rift between the Church and history which the Council should try to mend?

A theological tradition is always a synthesis between particular cultural values and the deposit of faith, which does not belong to any one culture because it belongs of rights to all. If it were ever to occur that any one synthesis, because of the special prestige attached to it, should wish to impose itself upon the whole Church as definitive, then, just because cultures are so numerous and changeable, there would be less possibility of a universal diffusion of revealed truth, which would remain blocked in an imposing but particular form. If the dialogue comes to an end, the process of the vital incarnation of Christianity ends also: the Church remains the prisoner of a culture she has herself inspired and created.

Already in his Encyclical *Princeps Pastorum* Pope John had written a passage full of significance about this, also because he quoted Cardinal Newman, the great "prophet" of the Second Vatican Council, whom theologians have entirely forgotten.

> There are nevertheless certain points which the Catholic Church leaves the theologians at liberty to debate, in so far as these things are not quite certain, and also because, as the famous English writer Cardinal John Henry Newman said, these disputes do not break the unity of the Church. They encourage, instead, a deeper and better understanding of the dogmas, because they prepare and confirm the way of arriving at this knowledge. In fact, new light always springs from contrasting opinions. It is always best at all times to bear in mind that fine familiar axiom attributed in various forms to various authors: where necessary, unity; in doubt, liberty; at all times, charity.

> But it was above all in the summoning of the Council that he showed the need to distinguish between the truth of God and human elaborations of language and conception, and to safeguard the truth by modifying its presentation in human terms. In this principle, which was solemnly repeated at the end of the first session, is found the Christian's right to freedom of cultural and theological formulae.

> In fact, there already exists in the Church a twofold theological tradition—besides those of the law and the liturgy—the Latin of the West and the Greek of the East. It is clear therefore that unity

of faith, sacraments and government does not exclude the variety of Catholic cultures, or even of theological traditions. And the Council has set in a clear light this truth which had previously seemed doomed to disappear from the Catholic conscience.

As Father Häring writes:

> In the past it frequently happened that a bitter struggle between the various schools distracted men's attention from the pastoral necessity of preaching, and hampered a true advancement in theological science. The lack of love had damaging consequences for theology. Only the dialogue of the many, endowed by God with such different gifts of grace, originating in the most diverse cultures which, in their various languages, testify eloquently to the one spirit—only this dialogue of love in a true sharing of unity and multiplicity will serve for the union of Christians as well as for the conversion of non-Christians, and for a more enlightened understanding of the revealed truth.[3]

In effect, no testimony is today more likely to touch the hearts of those outside the Church than freedom of dialogue—and it is hardly necessary to say that it must be a freedom in love. Not only the non-Catholics but the Catholics themselves were so convinced that true unity, within the Church, is difficult to reconcile with divergences of opinion in theological matters, that, as soon as the Council showed a noticeable diversity of opinion, there was an outcry from those zealots who feared a scandal, and if they did not cry more loudly it was lest the scandal should become even greater.

In a public Audience of 6 February 1963 Pope John dwelt at some length on this unjustifiable stupor, and was inspired by this to deal, delicately, with the necessity of dialogue within the Council:

> Some superficial observers, hearing inexact rumours about this or that difference of words, have at once made rash judgments: Just look, they said, they cannot agree. On the contrary, there was perfect agreement, which could not have been greater, because the same ardour burns and inspires them all;

[3] *Op. cit.*, p. 34.

it is simply a question of choosing the most adequate means to diffuse more and more widely this immeasurable grace from the Lord.

The enterprise may be difficult: but it is blessed by God. In the world conflicts are considerable and profound; we have only to think of what happens in human assemblies, for disputes are certainly more likely to arise when the problems concern material situations and enterprises. In the Council, instead, all those who have spoken have expressed their own opinions, but with heartfelt respect for the integrity of the doctrine and character of their brothers. Sometimes what one has said has been explained more clearly by another: but the differing points of view have always been expressed with a profound reciprocal deference.

One more great satisfaction has come, to many people's surprise, from the Council. Many of those who, though Christians, are still separated from the Church, imagined that we should discuss everything among ourselves in order later on to present our conclusions in so harsh a manner that they could hardly be accepted. It is not so. There is the truth of God, and it is the same for ever: but truth is always accompanied by peace, gentleness and love.

3. THE RIGHT TO BE DIFFERENT

We might say that the Council aims at nothing other than restoring within the Church the conditions, more spiritual than canonical, for the reopening of a dialogue intended to foster the development of diversity in the heart of unity. In order to bring this about, it suffices to place at the centre of the legislative and doctrinal work of the Church the idea, which has never been lost sight of, that Christian unity rests on fundamental principles on a plane which is neither the plane of politics nor that of law, nor even that of philosophy, but the plane of revealed Truth. And just because they are above the natural order, their acceptance does not in any way imply the choice of this or that culture rather than any other, or of this philosophical trend rather than of that other. Once the diversities that have arisen and grown in the course of history enter the circle of light that descends from on high, they suffer from no inhibition or discrimination. In so far as they obey the natural requirements of men, they may produce diverse incarnations of Christianity. Only by enlarging the area of the Church's internal manoeuvres will it be possible to engage in dialogue with the modern world.

Vatican II is the first Council which can be called ecumenical in the geographical sense: in comparison, the First Vatican Council was hardly even Mediterranean. Pope John's eyes shone with joy when he gazed at the Assembly, precisely because, in the variety of colour, robes and language, he saw the start of a new historical process. When he spoke of the first "Council", that of Jerusalem, he recalled the great question put by St Paul: Is it necessary for a Gentile who becomes a Christian to accept circumcision? This was as good as saying: Is Christian unity founded on membership of the Jewish race? In some ways the question before the Second Vatican Council is the same. Must the theological, liturgical and juridical unity proper to the Latin Church be assumed to be universally valid, or should it be understood as one of the particular forms in which is expressed that mystical unity of Christianity which is nevertheless always able to express itself in a thousand other forms? Can "Latinity" be identified with "Catholicity"?

It is true that theoretically this identification is admitted by no one. But in practice it seems to have been accepted in numberless ways as valid, and to be, to some extent, at the root of many difficulties in which the Church now finds herself. More or less consciously, this placing of Latinity and Catholicity on the same plane of practical validity carries with it the instinctive use of means of diffusion and defence which are not worthy of the message of Christ. The choice of these means—for example, the political order, the Greco-Latin philosophy, the forms of language —as if they were in themselves the most suitable for the supernatural purpose of the Church, means that every diversity of judgment or preference is treated as the beginning of schism or heresy. And so the dialogue ends and suspicion and sanctions take over, having at their source, not the defence of what is true, but the defence of what one or the other considers it is opportune to defend. The criterion of this opportunity is no longer theological but historical, and it is absurd to demand the uniform assent of Catholics to the judgments of history. Hence the great dilemma, to which the Council will have to find a solution.

> A Church which tried to use the powerful weapons of this world to preserve its sacred unity and the integrity of its faith—the Inquisition, temporal power, or privileges which are essentially not a service but a request for service—would be weak. She would dim the glory of her mission, her own true power of appeal. The Church of the Second Vatican Council is firmly decided to set aside all those outer forms and juridical customs which no longer seem suitable for the presentation of her message to the world of today.[4]

To become poor—and much was said of the "Church of the poor" in the Council, echoing Pope John's speech on 11 September 1962—means that the Church must first of all strip her essential form of all the apparatus which makes her unlike her first Cause and Example: Christ. As soon as the idea of power (at least that idea of power which Rosmini, attributing it to the Germanic tribes, called the "barbaric idea") enters the context of Church values, not only are many bonds of charity disturbed and cut, but the very conditions for dialogue are smothered under the briars of legalism.

Pope John restored to us an ideal of Catholic life to be measured by the pure standard of the Gospel: with him we have better understood that we Catholics, to respect one another, do not always need to have the same ideas; it is enough to have the same love. Even the world beyond our confines has understood that the Catholic Church is not a barracks of God's Grenadiers but a warm-hearted family, which rejoices more over one who comes in from outside than over one who has always stayed at home.[5]

[4] Bernard Häring, *op. cit.*, pp. 23–4.
[5] In this way, although he introduced into the Church fewer reforms than did Pius X or Pius XII, Pope John has enabled the Church to pass, according to an expression of Cardinal Doepfner, from a static condition to one of dynamic movement, simply by changing her spirit, leaving free to act some innovating forces which were already acting in the shade. Pope John's revolution is a revolution *par ressourcement*, brought about by a return to the sources, allowing the more recent traditions to die off not in the name of the rights of the future, but in the name of the most ancient traditions of the past. Cf. the shrewd and practical observations of Roger Aubert, *loc. cit.*, pp. 20–33.

Who knows how many unbelievers, during Pope John's last hours of life, felt the desire to give a gentle push to the door that had been left ajar and, on tip-toe, to enter and sit down at our table, so as to take the first opportunity of joining in the general conversation, asking and answering, without any shyness, as if they had never left our threshold to set out for those "far regions" where one day they set up their home.

Cardinal Montini said very rightly of Pope John:

> He has taught us the elementary lesson, which is yet so difficult and so rarely learnt: to proclaim the truth with love. He has made us see that truth, and especially religious truth, is not intended to divide men and to arouse disputes and conflicts among them, but to draw them into a unity of thought, to serve them with pastoral affection, to fill souls with the joy of finding brotherhood and a more human life. We knew this already, but he has enabled us to enjoy the experience of life, he has given us a new hope for it and has promised us its fullness.

By the side of the bishops' pulpits others had been set up here and there, and anyone, however slight his authority, seemed to think himself entitled to use these to throw stones at anyone else, sometimes without any respect even for persons who occupied important posts in the hierarchy. This was done with the specious excuse of opposing and uprooting in this way the last shoots of modernism already so energetically and wisely condemned by His Holiness Pius X. Mgr Radini, who had in his turn also taken part in enthusiastic and vigorous argument in defence of the Pope's ideas and cause, and whose soul still glowed with the old fire, certainly no less ardent than that of these last comers, did not feel he could share the government of his diocese with those whose methods were destructive of the principle of discipline and of that charity and peace, the lack of which always compromises the victory of truth.

The sturdy and fearless conscience of the bishop, who worked for what was good, and all that was good, considered that by using these methods one hand took away what the other hand was building up, thus greatly impairing the dignity and prestige of the Pope's person, instead of adding to this and making him still more beloved. He believed that through these excesses the very difficulties which he had hoped might be cleared away would be created once more.

In his judgment on things and persons, because of his long experience and his delicate sense of spiritual fatherhood, which had become more and more sensitive with the passing of the years, Monsignor felt more and more drawn, as he himself said, to dip his pen into the inkwell of St Francis de Sales, rather than in that of St Jerome.

In a diocese, as in the whole Church, he thought the bishops are bishops by divine appointment, that is, they are the real and authentic teachers, judges and pastors in union with the Vicar of Christ; and they owe nothing of their dignity or authority to newspapers or men, however respectable and full of good will and sincere zeal these may be. Therefore he thought it right to hold his own position, and he knew how to make his authority clearly felt, although never in public or in a sensational way. He used the most direct and effective ways every time he noticed some undue and unjust attack on his diocese or on one of his clergy, and he made everyone understand that it would not be easy to find fault with him. Nor was he willing to hand over to anyone his task as teacher and judge, in that sphere where the responsibilities of government were his alone. (*Mons. G. M. Radini Tedeschi*, ed. cit., pp. 150–51.)

"The truth with thunders and lightnings"

Father M. showed himself to be, as I had expected, a most cultured man and a powerful debater, an expert well versed in the errors of the Modernists. One can understand why he fought them ruthlessly without granting any respite, either to them or to the currents of thought which tended towards them. But what at once surprised me and disappointed my expectations from his first lectures onwards, not lessening as he went on but rather gathering in intensity, was his impulsiveness and the liveliness, not to use a harder expression, of the learned Father's attacks. With a facility which from the first surprised me and which I could not reconcile with the calm and serene atmosphere of the school, he made personal attacks on one after another, mingling certain obvious accusations with others which seemed to me unsound exaggerations. Certainly Father M. was right to tell many hard and painful truths during his lectures, and especially with regard to anyone who was guilty in any way of indulging in modernistic ideas: but was there anyone like this in the *Scuola Sociale*? It was certainly not the seminarists whom the good Father had in view, for they are educated with the most affectionate and scrupulous care—I speak for my colleagues on the teaching staff and for my own humble self—in the pure, exact and integral doctrines of Rome. Nor can he have been thinking of the other students and listeners, all good and peaceable folk, so far as I know. Even if it was necessary to tell the truth and the whole truth, I could not understand why it had to be accompanied by the thunders and lightnings of Sinai rather than by the calm and serenity of Jesus by the lakeside and on the mount. For myself, I can add this, that I tried several times while I was listening to him to find Father M.'s method good and satisfying, but I must confess I never succeeded: there was too great a contrast between that way of behaving and my own character. For this reason I was afraid I was mistaken and I suffered inwardly. But I soon perceived that this impression was not only my own but a general one, shared by all who attended those lectures and afterwards talked with me about them.

This fiery zeal of Father M. which every now and then in some passage seemed even inspired by a personal grudge—which certainly was not there—had a harmful effect on the order and clarity of the lectures, dragging the teacher into numberless parentheses and digressions. Sometimes these digressions were of another kind: passages of philosophical or theological speculation which demonstrated the profundity of his own studies in these subjects, and the shrewdness and versatility of his intelligence, but which seemed to me to wander too far from the principal argument and were unsuitable for the school.

I confess that several times I was tempted to say to myself, basing my conviction also on what I had learnt from my five brief years of teaching experience, that Father M. had come to this school with little special preparation, contenting himself perhaps with some general notions, and for the rest trusting to the resources of his learning and culture, and also that he had taken the school too much for granted, and this was in striking contrast with the courtesy and precision of concepts and forms admired in the other professors. In fact, once I begged Father M. to be so good as to summarize the substance of his whole speech at the end of each lesson, for the convenience of the seminarist students. He promised me he would do this, and certainly had no lack of good intentions, but very seldom, according to what those who attended all his lectures told me, managed to keep his promise.

In his feverish enthusiasm to judge and refute, he was sometimes driven to put forward concepts and verdicts which, although containing the truth, presented it in too absolute and unilateral a manner, so rendering it difficult for the immature minds of the young men to reconcile the true principles he expounded with other principles which were equally true and of the greatest importance in Catholic doctrine. (*Mons. G. M. Radini Tedeschi*, ed. cit., pp. 247 *et seq.*)

"Thus Christian liberty was saved"

The so-called Council of Jerusalem was in the year A.D. 50. Think of the personages who took part in it. They were the most authoritative and illustrious men of those first years of apostolic effort and Christian conquest. Peter the Head, Peter himself, the foundation stone of the Church, and James the Less, the first Bishop of Jerusalem; and Paul and Barnabas who had worked so hard to set up the first Church at Antioch, and who from there and from the other young churches bore witness to the great fervour of those early days: "reporting the conversion of the Gentiles" and giving "great joy to all the brethren" (Acts 15. 3).

A grave problem had brought about that first meeting of the apostles with the elders. The doors of the Church were open to all: Hebrews and Gentiles. For the Hebrews was circumcision still necessary, and the other Mosaic rules? Were Gentiles also obliged to submit to the same ancient formalities when they became, factually and nominally, Christians, as at Antioch they were already beginning to call themselves?

How marvellous were the proceedings at that meeting! "After there had been much debate", says the author of the Acts (15. 7), for the problem was a grave one, Peter arose and proclaimed in direct assertion of his supreme mandate: "Brethren, you know that in the early days God made choice among you, that by my mouth the Gentiles should hear the word of the Gospel and believe. And God, who knows the heart, bore witness to them, giving them the Holy Spirit just as he did to us; and he made no distinction between us and them, but cleansed their hearts by faith. Now therefore why do you make trial of God by putting a yoke upon the neck of the disciples, which neither our fathers nor we have been able to bear? But we believe that we shall be saved through the grace of the Lord Jesus, just as they will" (Acts 15. 7–11). And he fell silent, and there was silence in the whole assembly, while Paul and Barnabas continued to recount the marvels, miracles and prodigies which had been multiplied through their ministry among the Gentiles.

After the pause James, the Bishop of Jerusalem, arose. Referring to what Peter had said, he led his hearers to the conclusion, now well understood by all, that those who were converted from among the Gentiles were not to be troubled, or forced to submit to circumcision or to the synagogue, and that they should content themselves with the observation of some of the regulations of the Mosaic law, avoiding, however, any doctrinal compromise that might affect the future.

Thus was resolved, clearly and peacefully, a fundamental question of faith and freedom. (Speech at opening of the first Roman Synod, 24 Jan. 1960.)

The new furrow

Concerning this conciliar activity, we wish to make two points quite clear.

First: The Ecumenical Council has its own structure and organization, which may not be confused with the ordinary and particular functions of the various administrative organs and Congregations which make up the Roman Curia, which proceeds during the Council also with the ordinary routine of its customary tasks in the general administration of Holy Church. There is then a clear distinction: the ordinary government of the Church, by means of the Roman Curia, is one thing, and the Council another. This, however, does not exclude, whenever necessary, a contribution of enlightened wisdom to be offered by ecclesiastics, who are especially invited because of their personal competence, well recognized and appreciated.

Second: The Ecumenical Council will consist of the presence and participation of bishops and prelates who will be the living image of the Catholic Church, spread through the whole world. The preparation of the Council will be in the hands of a gathering of learned and most competent persons, from every part of the world and of every language. This is now a principle that has entered into the spirit of everyone who belongs to the Holy Roman Church: that is, to be, and to consider oneself truly to be, by virtue of being a Catholic, a citizen of the whole world, just as Jesus is the adored Saviour of the whole world: *Salvator Mundi*. This is a good exercise of true catholicity, which every Catholic should take note of and turn into a precept for the guidance of his own mind, and as a principle for his conduct in religious and social relations.

In these months of our pontificate the Lord Jesus has granted us the grace to render good service to this principle of affirming and respecting the catholicity of the Holy Church.

We refer to the creation of several Cardinals, belonging to distant parts of the world which never before had the honour of possessing a Cardinal, the consecration by our own hands, under the roof of the Vatican Basilica, of many new bishops, almost a score within a few months, of various races and colours, and the easier and more frequent access here, not only of prelates and highly placed civil personages, but of representatives of ordinary folk, who every day wait to see and meet the Pope, content to receive his words of blessing and encouragement. Among these, many belong to communities of Christians separated from Rome, but a voice speaking in their hearts urges them lovingly to approach our humble person, as if to confide in us the intimate joy they feel at this meeting. It is like the foretaste of something sweeter and more mysterious, which Providence reserves for us for better days for the Holy Church of Jesus, Saviour of the whole world.

We must insist on this new furrow to be ploughed, which looks as if it will be further widened and lengthened, and on the cultivation of the spirit of catholicity, the joyful promise of noble and abundant fruits. (*Discorsi Pg.*, II, 5 June 1960, pp. 393-4.)

Christian unity in a new world

What shall we say of the relations between the Church and secular society? *We are faced with a new political world.* One of the fundamental rights which the Church cannot renounce is that of religious liberty, which does not mean merely liberty of worship.

The Church proclaims and teaches this liberty, and for this she continues to suffer acutely in many lands.

The Church cannot renounce this liberty, because it is of the same nature as the service she is called to perform. This service is not intended as a corrective and complement of what other institutions must do, or have appropriated to themselves, but is an essential and irreplaceable element of the Providential design to set mankind on the path of truth. Truth and liberty are the corner-stones of the building of human civilization.

The Ecumenical Council is about to meet seventeen years after the end of the Second World War. For the first time in history the Fathers of the Council will actually belong to all peoples and nations, and every one of them will bring his contribution of wisdom and experience to heal and cure the wounds of the two conflicts, which have profoundly altered the appearance of every country.

Mothers and fathers of families detest war: the Church, the Mother of all without distinction, will raise once more the prayer which was heard in the earliest ages and from Bethlehem, and later upon Calvary, pouring out a supplication for peace: peace which prevents armed conflicts, peace which in the heart of every man must find its roots and safeguard.

It is natural that the Council, in its doctrinal structure and the pastoral action which it promotes, should express the longing of the peoples to follow the path that Providence has assigned for each one, to co-operate in the triumph of peace and make this earthly existence more noble, more just and more worthwhile for all.

The bishops, shepherds of the flock of Christ, "from every nation under heaven" (Acts 2. 5), will present the concept of peace not only in its negative expression, which is the detestation of armed conflicts, but much more in its positive requirements, which demand from every man the knowledge and constant practice of his own duties: explaining the order, harmony and service of spiritual values available to all, and the possession and use of the forces of nature and technical skill exclusively as a means of raising the spiritual and economic standard of the life of all the peoples.

Fellowship, co-ordination and integration are most noble aims, which resound in international congresses, induce hope and infuse courage.

The Council, in forms even more sacred and solemn, will extol the most profoundly felt expressions of brotherhood and love, which are natural needs of men, and which the Christian must do his best to bring about, as the principle of his dealings between man and man and between one people and another.

O mystery of divine Providence, through which the imminent opening of the Second Ecumenical Vatican Council once more reveals and extols in an incomparable light its mission of service for the good of all peoples! (*Message to the world*, 11 Sept. 1962.)

Charity in truth

We are glad to assure you publicly that, during this recent time, we have been nearer to you than ever before; near in prayer, which we have confidently raised for you to God Almighty, the giver of all good things; and near in our mind, intent on following with tranquil and joyful attention the contribution everyone of you has made.

Today therefore we willingly profit by the occasion presented to us to show you all our gratitude. In fact, the pastoral anxieties which you have shown in the course of your work, or in your writings, words, or counsels, have enabled us in some way to listen to the voice of the whole Catholic world, which has now with firm hope and expectation concentrated its attention on these meetings. And we must also praise you because truly charity in truth has reigned sovereign over your gatherings—and all this urges us to express our heartfelt gratitude to the Lord.

But a word also of the joy that the spectacle of this congress of the one, holy, catholic and apostolic Church has given to the world.

Since 11 October, when the Catholic bishops walked in procession with us bearing the shining symbols of their office, until the ceremony which will take place tomorrow, it is the teaching Church which, united on a unique occasion, has begun the study and formulation of the principles for which the Council has been summoned.

And the spectacle of last Wednesday? Our glance dwelt with intense emotion on your own particular group, which stood out like a flame in St Peter's Square. It was a great and festive gathering, full of edification for the faithful who were present.

The father with his sons, and all our brothers of the Episcopate, gathered in the sight of Heaven, to pray, to hope and to rejoice together in a hymn of gratitude to the Lord and to his Mother. (Speech of 7 Dec. 1962.)

The Council novitiate

Already every element, every detail confirms that it is not human strength or energy that has brought about this great event of the Council. It is instead the work of a superior design, adequately understood and welcomed, and developed by divine wisdom. In fact, the natural and spontaneous way in which it was announced, the absence of any expectation or foreknowledge, even on the part of the world, which at times seems to have an inkling of exceptional events—all this has led us day by day, as the enterprise gradually took shape, to the conviction that it is a work of God alone.

The Lord watches over, nourishes and guides his Church. This is proved also by the events of recent weeks, which must be considered as a period of novitiate for the Second Vatican Council. We see more clearly a strengthening of the living substance, and a deepening sense of the apostolate: both are present in the initiatives already taken and the others still being discussed.

It is of course natural that, when many people are examining this or that subject, there should be many opinions and proposals about the best way of realizing and serving the fundamental principles. This is the holy liberty which the Church, especially in these circumstances, has given proof of respecting, thus arousing profound and universal admiration. (To the College of *Propaganda Fide*, 25 Nov. 1962.)

The Church, a peaceable family

The newspapers publish, together with information which is encouraging and edifying, accounts of difficulties, misfortunes and bitter disputes, due to the variety of men's judgments and of their way of considering life, concerned as they are with purely material interests. Instead, in the house of the Vicar of Christ, we see that both the pastor and the faithful who gather around him, illuminated and confirmed by divine grace, can find harmony in peaceful thoughts and proposals.

The Pope is a man of peace: his mission is to make all feel the longing for true peace, which although it might cost some sacrifice, always arouses the admiration and affection of the whole world.

When in Church we repeat *"Pax Christi"*, and *"Pax vobis"*, we are referring to a whole treasury of sublime and sacred truths. The Supreme Pontiff refers to them constantly, in every act, in every circumstance of his ministry. For example, consider the meetings which take place every now and then between the Pope and the illustrious personages who are ruling the great nations. The reason for these is simple: the Pope is speaking of peace. As regards his own work he has the Gospel always before his eyes, and in his teachings and his actions he confirms that from those pages spring perennial peace and the true and great wisdom of being contented, of considering things always in relation to the law of Christian civilization.

These are fundamental principles, and they never fail to delight our visitors. Even the non-Catholics, and the number of these is ever growing, are today more than ever before glad to come and see the Pope, the Head of the Catholic Church. They appreciate the benefits they derive from his serene and encouraging words. And so we arrive at the essence of Christianity, and every detail of everyday life is ennobled, because with great naturalness we illustrate the exercise of the noblest virtues, such as humility, gentleness and patience: these are the virtues which win the souls of all and have consequences which at times appear almost miraculous. In a word, all is said when we say that we can be perfect, if we really obey the Gospel of our Lord Jesus Christ. So, at all times, and especially in moments of stress, we can speak of peace: and when men are over-excited we are here to try to calm them, showing at the same time that we ourselves know how to maintain the same necessary control over the use of our tongue, eyes, and all our energies, directing and co-ordinating all to a noble end.

We have a shining example before us not only in the memory of the holy affection which the apostles had for each other, but also in the much admired assembly of bishops in the present Ecumenical Council, who show a friendliness and heavenly grace which surpass all expectation.

All may easily imagine what the Holy Father has felt when, from the centre of the Vatican Basilica, the altar of the Confession, he has turned his gaze to the two thousand five hundred and more bishops, all representing the same thought and feeling, united by the same fervour in their praise of God, intent on the same apostolic work: a stupendous spectacle, in which have mingled, in harmonious unity, "hearts, voices and deeds" (*corda, voces et opera*). (Account in *O.R.*, 7 Feb. 1963.)

CHAPTER FOURTEEN

The Church is Moving

I. THE ROUTE IS STILL THE SAME

IT is now not merely the personal impression of some Catholics but a certainty shared by the whole Church, that with Pope John the "barque of Peter" has raised her anchor and hoisted her sails: any Catholic who had doubts about this would have reason to doubt his own knowledge of the "mind of the Church".

As always happens in ages of transition—even in the agitated and disturbed age in which we live—it is possible to point out in the present the persistence, or even recrudescence, of survivals of the past, touched and exasperated by the presentiment of the end. But men of little faith must not delude themselves: the ship is moving forward. At least so far as the Church is concerned, there is no excuse for self-deception: the ship is moving forward, and her route remains that fixed by Pope John.[1]

Between his death and the election of the new pope it was right perhaps to be cautious about the impression I have mentioned above, for fear it might be purely subjective or, in any case, likely to meet with disavowal. But, when the new pope appeared on the balcony above St Peter's, we understood what had happened: John had left the helm in the hands of Paul, who had seated himself in his place with his eyes fixed on the same goal.

When he opened the second session, Pope Paul, without seeking to hide his emotion, recalled the speech of 11 October 1962 which "seemed to the Church and the world a voice of prophecy

[1] The traditional image of "St Peter's barque" is frequently used by Paul VI. There was an ingenious reference to this in his speech to the Sacred College on 24 Dec. 1963, when he paid homage to Pope John and declared his intention "to continue along the way he has traced for us, looking ahead in these coming years and allowing the divine Helmsman of Peter's barque to bear us all towards far shores, which we can only see with prophetic vision and with hope."

for our own times, and which still echoes in our memory and conscience, tracing the path which the Council must follow and freeing our minds from any doubt or fatigue which might seize us along the difficult way we have begun to tread." And he continued with these words which we would like to recall for the sake of all those who might be tempted to give way to doubt or fatigue: "O dear and venerable Pope John, may you be praised and thanked, for we believe it was by divine inspiration that you desired and summoned this Council, thus opening new ways for the Church and releasing, for our refreshment, new hidden springs of water, flowing from the doctrine and grace of Christ the Lord. . . ."

These new springs of fresh water, these paths that widen towards new horizons, do not belong to the rhetorical phraseology which delights in giving the illusion of long journeys and is therefore cherished by those souls who are constrained by laziness or fear to remain at home, beside the hearth. These images well express the state of mind of the Church.

The intuition which had led Pope John to decide to call a Council was, as is always the case with great intuitions, at first not entirely and thoroughly well defined: enclosed within its own light, it gave out a bright reflection, like that of a lonely lighthouse in the night. Even when the Fathers of the Council saw it, on the morning of 11 October, shining on their almost incredulous eyes, it was able, indeed, to dispel the darkness and reveal the distant haven, but all the rest, that is the exact route of the voyage, the rocks to be avoided, the discipline to be observed, the pauses and the turns of duty—all that, in short, makes it possible not so much to see the haven as to get there—was in the minds of all, guaranteed by the presence of a cheerful fatherly helmsman, who did not map the whole route at once, but day by day, with measured stages, and even left them at liberty to make mistakes—so sure was he that the ship would go where she had to go.

If the Pope had, from the beginning, pointed out the difficulties of the Council, perhaps he would have deprived them of their courage. If he had interfered, as was his right, in the work of those who were charged to prepare the doctrinal plan of the

Council, he would have aroused bad tempers. He left everyone
to do his own task, and showed confidence in all, generous in
praise where it was deserved. But, once the Council had begun,
he played his part of supreme Head from the first moment,
and spoke in such a way that everyone understood that it was
from that moment that the work of the Council had really
begun.[2]

He had not been incautious: he had applied the rule—daring,
certainly, but inspired by faith—that he had always used, that is,
to leave everyone to play his own part, never to take anyone's
place, and always to diffuse serenity and confidence. The Holy
Spirit, through the tangle of individual purposes, would achieve
the desired result: for his own part, he proclaimed, as Pope, what
the Holy Spirit had suggested to him.[3] If, when that moment
came, the band of theologians found themselves lagging somewhat behind him, it was no one's fault: everyone had given what
he could, according to his capacity, and was now obliged to admit
that what he had given was not enough.

Once he had pointed out the desired haven Pope John allowed
the Council to sail ahead with its own private discussions, re-
stricting himself to one dramatic intervention when he dislodged
it from the sandbanks on which it had stuck, and pushed it out
into the open sea again. He died, offering his life for the Council,
but without any anxiety about what might happen to it after his

[2] Roger Aubert (*loc. cit.*, p. 23), after having listed a long series of acts which appeared
self-contradictory in the sense that they disappointed at one time the expectations of the
progressives and at another those of the traditionalists, describes the state of mind of the
Church immediately before the Council and the general feeling of satisfaction of the
"integralists". To a priest who confided to him his anxieties on the eve of the opening of
the Council, a Cardinal who was soon to have a most important task assigned to him
replied: "We must trust the Holy Spirit . . . and John XXIII." "It was the extraordinary
opening speech which at once gave the Council its definitive orientation."

[3] Cardinal Montini had recognized this, as we see in his Letter from the Council
(*L'Italia*, 2 Dec. 1962), when he spoke of the Schemes which Pope John had sent back to
the Commissions: "This material was immense, excellent, but heterogeneous and unequal,
and would have needed courageous reduction and re-composition if an authority had been
there to take this in hand. This authority would not only have had to be external and
disciplinary but able to dominate the logical and organic preparation of these magnificent
volumes, and a central constructive idea would have been needed to direct and complete
this immense labour. Because of loyalty to that principle of liberty and spontaneity which
has inspired this Council, the focal point of its programme has been lacking, although
fortunately its main outlines were solemnly and wisely traced by the words of the Holy
Father in the years preceding the Council, especially in the two speeches of 11 Sept. and
11 Oct."

death, quite sure that it would continue. The ship was moving.
As for coming into port, the Holy Spirit would see to that. And
in fact the Holy Spirit has made provision. "John has left, Paul
has arrived: that is the miracle", said a "charismatic" bishop with
an eager heart some months ago.

The route has not been changed. This also is a truth that must
be acknowledged. Those who, previously, did not want the ship
to move away from the familiar shores are already convincing
themselves that the ship is now turning to look for near and safe
harbours; those who had based their lives on the axiom that the
Church is immobile are doing all they can to bolster up a declining
conviction, but it is true that the ship is moving. In recent centuries she seemed to move only as the waves struck her: few observers saw that the crew were making urgent repairs to masts and
sails, knowing that her true destiny is to move in deep waters.
Once she has left the shore, she is sure to feel the joy of obedience
to her original orders, and decide to let the dead bury their
dead.

The Church's voyage follows the route that has been foreseen
and intended: she is not sailing at random, at the mercy of the
waves. Pope John's intention has now found its interpreter: it has
been translated into clear and well-defined conceptions. In Pope
Paul's speech to the Council, and in the "three simple words" he
spoke at Bethlehem we seem to see once more, in a clear pattern,
Pope John's epoch-making intuition.[4] This was presented in a
constructive manner in the Council on the morning of 11 October
1962, when Pope John came in, on foot, his heart full of triumphant joy. For the first time in the history of the Councils, the
Church appeared, as on the day of Pentecost, formed of men from
many races and speaking many languages. Besides these, there
were the representatives of the separated Churches, attending the
solemn assembly, and not merely as spectators but as brothers
called to the same mystery; finally, the delegates of the powers of

[4] Cardinal Suenens affirmed this in his speech of 28 Oct. 1963 to the Council Fathers:
"Have we not, in this very place, received the solemn testimony of this continuity when
we heard the unforgettable speech to the second session of the Council? In every word
and between the words we felt the very breath of Pentecost. We have heard the same
appeal to be open to new initiatives and to new dialogue, the same insistence on translating
the eternal message of the Gospel into a language understood by our contemporaries."

this world were present without any intention of exploiting the moral prestige of the Church for their own political ends, and so symbolizing the new order of the nations, the post-Constantinian age.

2. TOWARDS THE SOURCE

First of all, the Church has rediscovered a language which she had never totally abandoned, but which had become, as it were, the language of intimate moments, and which died on her lips when she had to speak about herself to her prodigal sons or to unbelievers.

The Church's public language had adopted a juridical-philosophical style, elaborated during her long experience of the West. Now, in her visible assembly, she has become aware that the faces of all races are represented in her, the problems of all cultures and the wisdom of the most varied experiences. There are the civilized peoples where, for example, she still has to cope with the age-old disputes with State authorities, and there are the primitive countries, where instead she has to become poor with the poor, as in her earliest years at Thessalonica or at Corinth. So it is easier now for her to abandon a language which had vigour and meaning in the privileged area of the West in order to return to the more natural speech of earlier times, when the Christians thought more about the "Bride adorned for her husband" than of the "perfect society".

We must note the objective nature of this return to the former language: it is to satisfy, not archaeological nostalgia, but a need derived from the fact that the ways of thinking until now used by the Church are, generally speaking, linked to Western culture, and therefore no longer correspond to the world-wide character of Christianity. They must now be replaced by the more universal and more essential language which the Church has at her disposal, the language of the Bible.

As we have seen during the second session of the Council—while a less juridical and more mystical, a less Western and more biblical language was being forged—the world outlook impressed upon the Church by Pope John had not altered. At the point reached now, that is, since the speech of Paul VI at Bethlehem, we feel we can say that the visible organism of the Church is rediscovering, almost with the pains of a woman in labour, the height and depth of her own transcendental soul, and in consequence is rediscovering, not without a momentary bewilderment, the fitting terms for the double dialogue, one with her Bridegroom and the other with the world, in perfect and simple supernatural truth.

Until today it seemed to most people that the Church was an institution which, even if supernatural, once she had been divinely instituted and enriched by Christ with a truth that was perfect in every part and untouchable, had no other mission than that of speaking with men and summoning them to prepare for the kingdom of God. But she has another life than this, a life from within (*ab intra*);[5] she is in the company of her Bridegroom, in the presence of Christ, in the mystical sanctuary and, like Mary at Bethany, humble, repentant and adoring, she listens to his word. A month before the Council opened, on 11 September 1962, Pope John had said:

> Here we find a useful and happy reminder of the symbolism of the Easter candle. At a certain point of the liturgy his name rings out: *Lumen Christi*, the Light of Christ. From all corners of the earth the Church of Jesus replies: *Deo gratias, Deo gratias*, Thanks be to God, as if to cry out in assent: The Light of Christ, the Light of the Church, and the Light of the Peoples.
>
> Indeed what is an Ecumenical Council if not the return to meet face to face with the risen Jesus, the glorious and immortal king, shining in the Church, for the salvation, the joy and splendour of all races of mankind? In the light of this vision we sing the old Psalm: "Lift up the light of thy counten-

[5] Cardinal Montini, in his 1962 Pastoral Letter, after having declared the insufficiency of the juridical definitions of the Church, adds: "Yesterday it was the external history of the Church which chiefly interested us, today it is also her interior life, generated by the mysterious presence of Christ within her. . . . This means that today we find her mission more profound, more rich and more charged with evangelical duties than with historical rights, so that it comes naturally to us to think of the Church as a mystery, a mystery immense in itself, immense in history, immense in its future destinies, immense in the general framework of time and eternity, immense in its meaning for all mankind."

ance upon us, O Lord! Thou hast put joy in my heart" (Psalm 4 [5]. 5–7).

The new Ecumenical Council intends to bring true happiness to the universal Church of Christ.

This glorious encounter of the Church with Christ, "face to face", must become ever more a part of the daily life of believers. Here is the real mystery of the Church and therefore of human life; in this personal pilgrimage of all towards Christ, impelled by love—hence its joy—and by the humble wish to be saved—hence its constant spirit of repentance. Paul VI, in the first part of his speech of 29 September 1963, vigorously emphasized this supreme principle of the Church, which must also be the supreme principle of the Council: "Oh! may this Council become fully aware of this single but manifold bond which links us to our ever blessed Christ, a bond which is firm and living, mysterious and yet clear to all, a relationship which binds us to Christ and beatifies us, a bond between this holy and living Church, which we are, and Christ from whom we come, through whom we live and to whom we go. Let there be no other light shed upon this meeting but that of Christ, the light of the world, and let no other reality interest our souls." And, in his speech at Bethlehem, the first of his "simple words" was the Church's confession of love and repentance to her Lord and Bridegroom.

From now onwards we shall have to recognize the conscience of a Catholic, not by his aggressive energies nor by the delight he takes in opposing the modern world, and not even by the cold austerity of his moral virtues, but by his willingness to share in this colloquy between the Church, which is ourselves, and Jesus our Saviour. We are approaching the end of a phenomenon which has had, even in this century, paradoxical and monstrous expressions (for example, the Catholicism of the *Action française*), by which we mean the individual and collective flattery of the Catholic Church for reasons which were entirely of this world, without there being any intention of taking seriously her message of spiritual salvation, or still less her mystical converse with Christ. The Catholicism of the "temporalists" is coming to an end.

3. TOWARDS UNITY

As regards the second intention which Pope John introduced into the movement of renewal of the Church, that is the intention of Christian unity, there is no doubt that it has been productive of good results in a way that has surpassed all prevision.[6] And the method which is used to realize this intention remains that already indicated by him in the Encyclical *Ad Petri Cathedram*:

> The principal aim of the Council will be to promote the increase of the Catholic faith, the moral reformation of the Christian people, as well as the adaptation of ecclesiastical discipline to the needs and methods of our own times. It will be a wonderful spectacle of truth, unity and charity, such a spectacle, we say, that the vision of it will make all those who are separated from the Holy See feel, we hope, impelled to seek and achieve that unity which Jesus Christ in ardent prayer implored from his heavenly Father.

The central idea of Pope John's ecumenical method is the return to the sources, that is, a more perfect conformity of the Catholic Church with the positive intentions of Christ. For centuries the separated brothers, as we have seen, accused the Catholic Church of adding to Christ's explicit commands human doctrines and human institutions, and, with this process of arbitrary impositions, deforming the original Christian community founded by the apostles. The Catholic Church has never denied possessing, within her traditional inheritance, treasures which come from Christ and treasures which come from men, but she affirms that the human traditions have not impaired the divine tradition, inspired and guaranteed by the Holy Spirit. By what criterion are we to distinguish human traditions from those of divine origin, and what is the function of the former in relation to the latter, and these in relation to the Word contained in Scripture? All this still remains in the great bulk of problems which Vatican Council II must work out and which, if it cannot solve them now,

[6] On the day of his coronation Paul VI returned to the theme of Christian unity, recognizing that John XXIII "under the inspiration of the Holy Spirit aroused great hopes in this sphere, hopes which we feel it is our duty not to disappoint".

it must expound clearly for future consideration by the Church.

It is already certain, however, that as the Catholic Church is charged with the task of realizing her Lord's will, that is of gathering all his sheep into one fold, she must find in her motherly love the strength and wisdom to free the divine tradition from the accumulation, however venerable it may be, of human traditions, so that men may more clearly see her fidelity to Christ, and therefore the true road towards Christian unity. Once the principle of visible conformity with Christ has been affirmed, the criterion of the so-called reform of the Catholic Church becomes clear and unmistakable: the characteristic marks of the Church made visible must reproduce to such a degree the characteristics of the Word made flesh that men, seeing the Church, may with immediate intuition see Jesus Christ, and be as amazed by these characteristics as Christ's contemporaries were amazed before him. And, as the separated brothers have preserved the love for Christ and for his Word, the Catholic Church must trust more to sharing in this love which has survived than to doctrinal agreements.

It is certainly a great joy to note the welcome accorded to our Council by numerous brothers separated from this Apostolic See. But what a far greater and richer hope, and more full of heavenly graces, we might cherish if the widespread longing of our sincere love could be felt by all those who are called to rejoice with us in the same faith and salvation in Jesus Christ, to be fulfilled in the one fold!

This is hidden in the secret design of the Lord: and in this we seem already to see the dawn of that longed-for day whose future coming Jesus Christ hailed with these loving wishes and trustful words: "I have other sheep, that are not of this fold; I must bring them also, . . . so there shall be one flock, one shepherd" (John 10. 16).

Oh, what joy we should feel if we could read with these souls also the dear, divine words, and contemplate the delightful images, of Chapter 10 of St John's Gospel, especially where Jesus Christ tells us: "I am the door (the door, that is, by which the sheep enter); if anyone enters by me, he will be saved, and will go in and out and will find pasture" (John 10. 9).

When Pope John uttered these words on 11 September 1962, he had perhaps already foreseen that, very soon, the Pope of Rome and the Patriarch of Constantinople would be reading together, in Latin and in Greek, the Testament of Jesus according to John. It seems certain, as we have already seen, that the significant meeting between Paul and Athenagoras was the carrying out of a plan proposed by Pope John. In the meantime Paul VI had expressed, in cautious doctrinal suggestions, the ecumenical intuition of Pope John, and had given some hearers the impression that he was less confident and less eager. But on the contrary, there is in the words of Pope Paul to the Council something which Pope John had not explicitly proclaimed: the recognition on the Church's part of her own historical mistakes, and also the acknowledgment, full of reverence, "of the original and common religious inheritance preserved and in part also well developed among the separated brothers."

The diligent examination and general acknowledgment of this inheritance are not sufficient for the realization of unity: the separated brothers reject many other truths which form part of the patrimony bequeathed by Christ to his Church. "We cannot", said Paul VI at Bethlehem, "betray the integrity of this inheritance from Christ; it is not ours but his; we are but the guardians, the teachers, the interpreters.

"But we repeat once more that we are willing to consider every reasonable possibility of smoothing the way towards understanding, reverence and charity with a view to the future, and please God, early meeting with the Christian brothers still separated from us. The door of the fold is open."

The journey to Bethlehem was a sequel to the Conciliar discussion of the schema *"de Ecumenismo"*; this scheme itself, completed by the noble declaration on the Jewish religion, is the translation, into a context of doctrinal principles, of Pope John's brilliant intuition. The Church has now recognized as inspired by the Holy Spirit the whole problem of unity presented by the separated brothers, and has made this problem her own. She has her own way of proposing its solution. This method remains substantially the same as John's: to recover a greater fidelity to her own true nature, in order to cut away the ground beneath many objective reasons, of human origin, which still prevent the fulfilment of the mystery of unity desired by Christ.

4. TOWARDS THE MODERN WORLD

The loftiest and most daring point of Paul's speech at Bethlehem was, by universal admission, his appeal to the world.

There is no doubt that Pope Paul regards the modern world with thoughtful and almost disapproving eyes, which seem to disavow the sort of patriarchal joy which Pope John felt before all men of today, when he prayed for abundant blessings upon them, including those "of the dew of heaven and of the fatness of the earth" (Genesis 27. 28). But the difference between these two ways of regarding the modern world is also a providential disposition of God.

When Paul VI said: "We look at the world with immense sympathy" he was not going against his own nature, he was frankly expressing his opinion. John and Paul have shown the world the two complementary and convergent ways in which the Church has, in the etymological sense of the word, "sympathy" for the world. John was borne on the shining crest of the waves of modernity, blessing its daring achievements and recognizing in these the design of a benevolent Providence, yet without denying the dark clouds which obscure the outlook. Paul has in no way modified the judgment made by John, but he has combined it with a more sensitive feeling for the painful aspects of the world today, to which he is peculiarly alive. A Christian optimism which takes no account of the opposing and valid reasons for pessimism is thereby made more subject to corruption; in the same way Christian pessimism, which becomes incapable of sharing in the original joy with which the Creator regarded the things born of his love, is already pessimism on the way to corruption.

John and Paul, in their different charismatic gifts, present in visible form all the necessary conditions for the meeting between the Church and the modern world. Both are agreed in the method

of bringing about the meeting, openly and courageously in-
augurated by John. This method implies, first of all, the restoration of the prophetic presence of the Church in the world. The
Church must clearly tell the modern world that she is not trying
to impose upon it her own philosophies or institutions; she is not
out to oppose a world of her own to the world in which modern
man lives and struggles: instead, she wishes to offer him a message
of supernatural salvation, as Pope John solemnly declared in his
speech at the opening of the Council:

> To mankind that suffers from so many ills she says, as
> Peter said to the poor beggar: "I have no silver and gold, but
> I give you what I have: in the name of Jesus Christ of Nazareth
> rise and walk" (Acts 3. 6). The Church offers the men of today
> no fading riches, no mirage of a happiness to be enjoyed only
> on this earth: she pours out a wealth of supernatural grace
> which, raising men to the dignity of children of God, offers
> them a firm protection and assistance for human life: she re-
> veals the sources of her fertile doctrine which sets men in the
> light of Christ, making them conscious in their hearts of their
> true worth, of their supreme dignity, and of the end assigned
> to them; finally she sends her sons to extend the sphere of
> Christian charity, a charity which with singular vigour plucks
> out the seeds of discord and wonderfully promotes agreement,
> just peace and the brotherly unity of all.

Paul VI, in his speech to the Council, seems to wish to present
as a clear concept Pope John's grandiose image: "What a strange
phenomenon! The Church, seeking to restore her inner vitality in
the Holy Spirit, distinguishes and separates herself from the secular
society in which she is immersed, but at the same time shows
herself as a life-giving leaven and an instrument of salvation for
this same world, revealing and confirming her missionary vocation." How could one better express the end of the integralists'
ideas and the consequent emergence of the prophetic figure of the
Church in the world?

Certainly this will be a long process of the revelation of the
prophetic character of the Church: the announcement of the
dismissal of the Papal Court will not suffice to strip the Church

of her grasp on earthly power, which often disappoints hearts eager for spiritual salvation. "It is not for me to do everything," said Pope John to a Calvinist monk, an enthusiast for Christian unity, who asked him when he would free his Court of the last remnants of its princely pomp. Patience and moderation are organic principles which Paul, like John, will wish to respect.

The other Christian capacity which Pope John has set free from a tangle of errors and outworn customs is the pure and generous expansion of interest in the material progress of the world. Developing to an unexpected extent a process already set in motion by his predecessors, he has pushed the Church into the open sea, and reconciled her with present developments and with the temporal purposes which guide and agitate her. The Church of which he always spoke was a Church "ever living and ever young, which feels the rhythm of the age, which in every century adorns herself with new splendour, irradiates new light, realizes new conquests, while remaining always faithful to herself, to the divine image impressed on her countenance by her Bridegroom who loves and protects her, Christ Jesus".

If the Church "feels the rhythms of the age", it remains to be seen whether the age, our age, has in its turn felt the new rhythm of the Church. Now that those extraordinary and striking occasions are over in which the world seemed to be in a state of suspended animation as a sign of unusual respect, to what extent have its traditional relations with the Catholic Church also been transformed?

If we were more attentive to the phenomena of the "collective consciousness", as it is usually ambiguously described, we should be able to see and prove a great process of transformation in the mentality of men and their behaviour as regards the Catholic Church. Beginning with the pontificate of John XXIII, when the Church came out of her apparent immobility and began to undertake, in a truly miraculous manner, the revision of doctrine and institutions during a sequence of events that were obviously full of the grace of God, such as the death of Pope John and the journey of Pope Paul to the Holy Land, mankind has been forced to revise the mental attitude it had always assumed with regard to Catholicism. To what extent has this come to pass? What Paul VI said at Bethlehem remains profoundly true: "If the world feels alien to Catholicism, Christianity does not feel alien to the world, whatever may be the aspect it presents or its behaviour."

And yet the world's indifference to the Church, as being alien to it, was shaken from the moment in which one of its premises was modified, I mean the conventional notion which the world, especially the world of learning, had formed of the Catholic Church. Many learned men had succeeded, sometimes with great intellectual sincerity, in convincing themselves that for them there was no longer a religious problem. Their notion of Christianity had been drawn more from books or from vague sociological observations than from personal experience. Accustomed to see free research as the distinctive mark of true spiritual nobility, they felt a repugnance for that grandiose organization of consciences which they thought Catholicism to be: an organization which necessarily excluded the critical exercise of reason, the spirit of free enquiry, and the awareness of the ceaseless flow of new events. The loss of the faith of their childhood had come about, in most cases, simply because the most striking revelations of science, which they received with enthusiasm, were always presented as an alternative to religion. The identification of the Church with an ancient and well-defined cultural organization made it impossible to hesitate over their choice, making it a foregone conclusion, and therefore made without any struggle. Thus, after their painless apostasy, their attitude towards the Church was not even that of the anti-clerical hostility of former times; it was simply one of indifference. The only way of presenting them with this choice in such a way that they would perceive the error and the necessity of personal conviction was to set before them a Christianity that was freely and sincerely lived, that is, in its essential mystical inheritance, in its truth, which transcends all cultures.

This process of the "return to her true nature" is being carried on, through her most responsible organs, by the Church herself: we have in recent years seen in the faces of her pontiffs, first a smiling father who expresses in the tenderness of loving service the most intimate meaning of institutional authority, and then the humble awe of the pilgrim who, face to face with Christ, confesses how far he has fallen short of his divine example.

Between the privileged position of the faithful, well guarded within the domestic circle of the Church, and the tranquil indifference of the world, there was an almost impassable abyss. This abyss is being filled: the indifferent are losing their self-confidence, and the Church is rediscovering the right gestures to destroy the convenient image they had made of her, immobile and innocuous, and finding the words best suited to begin once more a dialogue which those outside the Church had thought would never be started again.

The Church is ready for a new historical adventure, without fearing to become unfaithful to herself. As Paul VI said to the College of Cardinals, the Church, "in the twofold symbol of the rock and the ship, splendidly expresses the scope of her destiny and her duty". Those outside the Church saw the rock, but they did not see the ship. They saw the immobility, but they did not see the adventure of faith, and so they thought it was right to see opposition between the rock which stands fast and history which moves on. But now they see that the Church is a ship, and that faithfulness and daring are not for her contradictory terms, but different and necessary ways of living her mystery.

It is a source of joy that this progressive alignment between the existentialist dialectic of the modern man and the essential dialectic of the Church should have begun with the cheerful blessing of Pope John. Even if we had no other proof but the serene confidence with which he blessed us for the last time, we should still be able to face the future with the certainty that with our eyes of flesh we shall rejoice to see what his soul dared to hope against hope.

The great expectation of the Ecumenical Council, just one month before its official opening, shines in the eyes and hearts of all the children of the Catholic Church, holy and blessed by God.

During these three years of preparation a band of elect spirits gathered from every part of the world and speaking every tongue, in unity of heart and purpose, have prepared such a superabundant wealth of doctrinal and pastoral material as to offer the bishops of the whole world, meeting under the roof of the Vatican Basilica, the possibility of wisely putting into practice the teaching of Christ, who has been for twenty centuries the light of mankind, redeemed by his Blood.

We are then, by the grace of God, at the right point. The prophetic words of Jesus, uttered as he contemplated the final end of time, encourage the good and generous inclinations of men, particularly in certain moments of the Church's history, which are ripe for a new effort to rise to higher peaks! "Look up and raise your heads, because your redemption is drawing near" (cf. Luke 21. 28).

Considered in its spiritual preparation, the Ecumenical Council, a few weeks before its opening, seems to be referred to in the Lord's invitation: "Look at all the trees; as soon as they come out in leaf you see for yourselves and know that the summer is already near ... so also when you see these things taking place, you know that the kingdom of God is near" (cf. Luke 21. 29, 30, 31).

This term "kingdom of God" fully and precisely describes the works of the Council. The Kingdom of God means, and really is, the Church of Christ, one, holy, catholic and apostolic, as Jesus, the Word of God made man, founded her, has preserved her for twenty centuries, and still today sustains her life by his presence and his grace. He is always renewing for her his ancient miracles which, throughout the ages, which have sometimes been harsh and difficult, have led her from peak to peak, over one pass after another, to multiply the victories of the spirit. Victories of truth over error, of good over evil, of love and peace over divisions and conflicts.

The terms of the contradiction, good and evil, remain and will always remain, because human judgment will always be free to express itself, and always capable of error: but the final and eternal victory will be for Christ and his Church in every elect soul, and in the elect souls of all peoples. (Broadcast of 11 Sept. 1962.)

Geographical Catholicity

A few steps away from here, two thousand five hundred Fathers are meeting to deal with the most important matters concerning the organization of Holy Church. Everyone may perceive the size and the grandeur of the Council, and the general approval it has met with in the whole world. And this is not mere curiosity, but a lively and profound interest.

When we re-read the list of the slender group of personalities who came to Rome on 8 December 1869, for the opening of the First Vatican Council, and compare it with the eighty-six special delegations of States and international organizations sent to Vatican Council II, we thank the Lord for the great progress made by his Church, in the midst of constant difficulties. The Council, as is known, intends to promote a strengthening of religious activity, a wider and more intense propagation of the Christian message, and hence the encouragement of those lofty ideals which support and nourish a social life worthy of the sons of God.

It is the Lord's grace which speaks, and guides us. As for the various activities, in the first days there was some uncertainty, to be sure, since for all the members of the assembly it was a new experience; but very soon the pace quickened, and although everyone has complete liberty to put forward his own opinions, we arrive at holy and profitable agreements without any sign of angry or excited disputes. It is clear therefore that the grace of the Holy Spirit is in the hearts of the bishops, the theologians and all who work for this imposing assembly. We can then affirm that we are passing through a truly blessed period in all that regards the understanding and awareness of Christian thought and spirit. (General Audience of 31 Oct. 1962; *Discorsi Cn.*, pp. 96–97.)

"It will be a new Pentecost"

God grant that these fruits may be gathered not only by the children of the Catholic Church, but also by those of our brothers who rejoice in the name of Christians, as well as by that immense host of men who, although they have not yet received the Christian light, are proud of their ancient and illustrious civilization, inherited from their ancestors. They have nothing to fear from the light of the Gospel which, on the contrary, as frequently happened in past centuries, may be able to contribute largely to the cultivation and growth of those fertile seeds of religious feeling and secular learning which are native to them. Our prophetic heart sees all this, venerable brothers, and well we know that your hearts too feel the same anxious love.

So we must extend to all fields of the life of the Church, including the social sphere, whatever is decided by the Conciliar assembly, and apply its principles with our generous assent and ready co-operation. This is no doubt a most important work which will require from our sacred ministry an effort to preach the holy doctrine and translate the laws of the Council speedily into action. There will be needed also the collaboration of the diocesan and regular clergy, of the Religious families and of the Catholic laity in all positions and responsibilities, so that the work of the Ecumenical Council may be furthered by the most willing and faithful service. It will truly be a new Pentecost which will bring to flower the rich inner life of the Church, and extend it with motherly love to all fields of human activity; it will be a new onward movement for the kingdom of Christ in the world, a re-affirmation in an ever more sublime and convincing way of the joyful news of our redemption, the shining witness of the sovereignty of God, and of human brotherhood in charity, and of the peace promised on earth to men of good will, in accordance with the will of Heaven. (Speech of 8 Dec. 1962.)

Towards a new language

The experience of the two first months of the Second Vatican Council have enabled us all, with God's help, to increase the clarity and speed of the proceedings of the great assembly.

There is hard work before us now, in this phase of the fervid and silent continuation of our labours, along the line inspired by the Lord when we summoned this Council. We are preparing a general and more enthusiastic renewal of the life of the Church, a new and energetic spreading of the Gospel throughout the world, with the Holy Spirit diffusing it, teaching it, and explaining its teachings.

This renewed pastoral effort is the constant preoccupation, indeed the aim, of the Ecumenical Council, in order that our contemporaries may be ever more aware of the maternal action of the Church in the spiritual, and also material, progress of all mankind.

Let us repeat here, for the common direction and encouragement of our preparation for the work which awaits us all, what we tried to express, simply and clearly, in our introductory speech on 11 October last, on that solemn day of the splendid inauguration of the Council. We said then, to the immense gathering of our venerable brothers of the episcopate, who were meeting for the first time in such large numbers above the tomb of Peter, that the Council is this, and that this is its chief aim: faithfulness to the recorded and irreplaceable doctrinal foundations of the sacred deposit of faith, and respect for the purest traditions of the Church's teaching. But we added at once: "Our duty is not only, as if we were concerned solely with antiquity, to guard this precious treasure; it is to dedicate ourselves willingly, eagerly and fearlessly to the work required by our own era, thus proceeding on the way the Church has followed for twenty centuries."

The salient reason—we said this in our solemn opening speech for the Council—is therefore not the discussion of this or that theme in the fundamental doctrine of the Church, in a more widely diffused repetition of the teaching of the Fathers and of theologians of ancient and modern times, for we must suppose this teaching to be ever present and familiar to our minds. This alone would not have necessitated a Council. But from renewed, serene and tranquil obedience to the whole teaching of the Church, in its integrity and truth, as it still shines in the decisions of the Councils from that of Trent to Vatican I, the Christian, Catholic and apostolic spirit of the whole world expects a great advance in the interpretation of doctrine and the training of consciences, in more perfect and harmonious loyalty to the authentic doctrine. This also is to be studied and expounded in accordance with the forms of enquiry and literary formulation natural to modern thought . . . all in conformity with the needs and requirements of instruction of a prevalently pastoral character. (23 Dec. 1962, in reply to the greetings of the Cardinals.)

"We are responsible for the world"

And do we not see today that even the forces of nature, as they are discovered and placed at the service of man, reveal most unexpected secrets and in various ways offer the opportunity for our constant endeavours to affirm the mission of the Church, the Mother and Mistress of all races? Do we not feel today, from one end of the earth to another, the gentle insistence of a voice appealing to us most urgently to do good, and everywhere to preach truth, justice and charity?

Well, it will be for us to use these instruments to acquit ourselves well before God and his Church, one, holy, catholic and apostolic, which is continually extending and affirming herself.

Here is the Council, and what a wealth of development and perfection it is showing us! In itself it testifies to the union desired by our Lord, the union of all peoples, however different in origin or race, and various in languages, rites and customs, a union which, gathered around the apostolic Chair, renders more visible to all its amazing cohesion. It is truly a historic occasion, which we perhaps at first considered with apprehension and fear, but which today fills our heart with the brightest hopes.

Among all the favourable impressions aroused by this dear assembly this is one of the most convincing, because it shows itself to be clearly a genuine outburst of faith, in the great Catholic, apostolic and Roman tradition.

There is therefore reason for a healthy and rational optimism, which irradiates precisely from this principle and endowment of universality. Considered in this vast perspective, to become and to be a priest certainly does not mean seeking one's individual comfort or good, but working fervently for the whole social body, for the complete triumph of our Lord Jesus Christ.

We must be most careful to read the Gospel well, and to apply the whole Gospel as we should. It is not enough to live our own lives according to its teaching and then take refuge in isolation, and believe that our own task is completed. That is not enough, not enough. The Lord has desired and still desires the salvation of all. And is Jesus not the "true light that enlightens every man"? And do we not read in St Luke: "All flesh shall see the salvation of God"? St Paul insisted on this: "For the grace of God has appeared for the salvation of all men", and finally St Matthew, at the close of his Gospel, records the supreme command of Jesus: "Go, therefore, and make disciples of all nations."

This is the perennial spring of Holy Church. The consideration of this sublime reality has inspired the Pope to insert, in a personal letter sent during these days to every bishop in the Catholic world, his own fatherly appeal to remember that, while it is true that everyone is obliged to do his own duty, to sanctify himself, and to guard within himself the deposit of faith and Christian tradition, all are obliged also to contribute to the diffusion of that bond of charity which makes us see others, whatever may be their origin, race or language, as so many brothers; and since human means offer us promising occasions for meetings, all must endeavour to use these entirely for the glory of our Lord Jesus Christ.

It is a fine thing to live and sacrifice oneself, to die if necessary, for such a sublime ideal, which is guaranteed by the Saviour's infallible promise: "Lo, I am with you always, to the close of the age."

St John Chrysostom sums up the precious teaching that springs from such imposing splendours, with the following comment: "Remember, my brothers, that one day you will be called to give an account, not only of your own lives but of the life of the whole world." (Speech in St Peter's, account in *O.R.*, 23 Jan. 1963.)

Bibliographical Note

To shorten the list of references the author has limited himself, in the course of this volume, to giving only the indispensable bibliographical quotations, and has made use of special abbreviations wherever necessary (see Nos. 3, 4, 5 and 6).

1. Angelo Giuseppe Card. Roncalli, *Scritti e Discorsi*, Edizioni Paoline, Rome, 4 vols.

2. Angelo Giuseppe Roncalli, *Souvenirs d'un Nonce*, Cahiers de France 1944–53, Edizioni di Storia e Letteratura, Rome, 1963.

3. Giovanni XXIII, *Discorsi, messaggi, colloqui del Santo Padre*, Tipografia poliglotta vaticana, Rome, 1960–63, 5 vols.
   Giovanni XXIII, *Encicliche e discorsi*, Edizioni Paoline, Rome, 1961–3, 5 vols.
   Giovanni XXIII, *Scritti e discorsi di S.S.*, Cantagalli, Siena, 1959–63, four volumes each year.
   Of these three editions that of the Ed. Paoline is the most easily accessible, but does not contain the *colloqui*, that is, the reported accounts of Pope John's extempore speeches, edited for the *Osservatore* by the journalist Dr. Cesidio Lolli.
   Abbreviations: *Discorsi Pg.* for the edition of the Poliglotta Vaticana; *Discorsi Pl.* for the edition of the Ed. Paoline; *Discorsi Cn.* for the Cantagalli edition; *O.R.* for the accounts in the *Osservatore Romano*.

4. John XXIII, *Journal of a Soul* (translated by Dorothy White from the *Giornale dell'anima*, ed. Mgr Loris Capovilla, Edizioni di Storia e Letteratura, Rome, 1964), Geoffrey Chapman, London, McGraw-Hill, New York, and Palm Publishers, Montreal, 1965. Abbreviation: *Journal*.

5. Leone Algisi, *John XXIII* (translated by Peter Ryde, from *Giovanni XXIII*, Marietti, Rome, 1961), Darton, Longman and Todd, 1963. Abbreviation: *Algisi*.

6. Giovanni XXIII, *Pensieri dal Diario*, La Locusta, Vicenza, 3rd edition, 1964. Abbreviation: *Diario*.

Among the extracts given after each chapter there are none from the two great social Encyclicals, *Mater et Magistra* and *Pacem in terris* because, as documents of the official teaching authority of the Church, they were not, in their final Latin version, personally written by Pope John.